creative ESSENTIALS

T0275108

Praise for *Beyond The Hero's Journey*

'Essential. Don't start writing scripts without it. And if you're writing scripts already, read it to explode every existing assumption. Modern, relevant, fresh, this book unpacks the shows and movies we're watching now. Anthony Mullins isn't just someone who inhales stories, but gets what they're doing – and nails what we can learn from them. There's so much here I wish I knew when I started screenwriting. Hell, there's so much that's helped me refine the TV show I'm writing... right now' – **Benjamin Law, creator/writer of** *The Family Law*

'*Beyond The Hero's Journey* will inspire you to rethink screenwriting. Written in a readable, conversational voice and drawing on Hollywood, independent and international scripting examples, it challenges us to focus on character arcs as the screenplay's central organising principle. It finds in arcs not only external action, but the deepest levels of internal characterisation. I cannot recommend Anthony Mullins' approach enough; he has found a powerful path to the heart of story' – **Jeff Rush, co-author of** *Alternative Scriptwriting: Beyond the Hollywood Formula*

'For decades now, screenwriting manuals have almost religiously followed the principles of "the hero's journey" and the "three-act structure". Both great frameworks... but only for a certain type of storytelling. In this "peak TV" era of long-form, ensemble storytelling, with its non-linear structures and anti-heroes, writers are crying out for new ways of analysing story. In this hugely engaging book, Anthony Mullins breaks down an extraordinary array of films, unveiling new analytical tools that are insightful, practical and, best of all, that just might inspire you to write something genuinely original' – **Michael Lucas, creator/writer of *Five Bedrooms*, *The Newsreader* and *Party Tricks***

'*Beyond the Hero's Journey* is a wonderfully fresh approach to screenwriting and story craft. Anthony Mullins is masterful at marrying large ideas about creativity with a practical, down-to-earth approach to writing. His love of screenwriting, both film and television, is clear in the way he approaches the material, resulting in an enjoyable and thought-provoking read for all experience levels' – **Warren Clarke, co-creator/writer of *The Heights***

'"The hero's journey" is a story as old as time, and the template for analysing it feels even older. Time for a revamp! Enter Anthony Mullins. His thoughtful and contemporary take on crafting and critically examining story and character is a relief to read. If our common goal as makers is to refocus attention on history's forgotten players and stories, then we have to change how we study them. Mullins provides us with new tools for excavating the psychology of characters who don't exactly know what they want and don't always change in a linear direction (or at all). It's a joy to read and a necessary evolution in critical analysis' – **Meg O'Connell, co-creator/writer of *Retrograde***

ANTHONY MULLINS

BEYOND
THE HERO'S JOURNEY
CRAFTING POWERFUL AND ORIGINAL
CHARACTER ARCS FOR THE SCREEN

creative ESSENTIALS

First published in the UK in 2022 by Kamera Books,
an imprint of Oldcastle Books,
Harpenden, UK
kamerabooks.co.uk

Series Editor: Hannah Patterson

978-0-85730-511-4 (Paperback)
978-0-85730-512-1 (Ebook)

Typeset in 11 on 14pt Adobe Garamond Pro
by Avocet Typeset, Bideford, Devon, EX39 2BP
Printed and bound in Great Britain by Clays Ltd, Elcograf S.p.A.

To Krissy

Contents

Part III: Constant Characters

Part IV: Other Characters and Arcs

Part V: Writing

I acknowledge the Traditional Custodians of the land on which this book was written – the Jagera, Turrbal and Lyluequonny (Pangherninghe) peoples – and recognise their continuing connection to land, water and community, as well as their long storytelling history. I pay respect to Elders past, present and emerging.

Introduction

There's a scene in the first season of the television series *The Sopranos* where Christopher Moltisanti, Tony Soprano's nephew, is trying to write a screenplay loosely based on his life as a wise guy. He's purchased a computer with a screenwriting programme that he thinks will do most of the work. But after weeks of labour, he only has nineteen pages and has hit a wall. He's depressed, frustrated and, according to his friend Paulie, his apartment looks like a pigsty. Paulie asks what the problem is. Surrounded by empty beer cans and pizza boxes, Christopher looks up from his saggy couch and replies, 'Where's my arc, Paulie?'

Paulie has no idea what he's talking about, so Christopher explains it to him. According to the screenwriting books he's been reading, every character has an 'arc'. In other words, they start out somewhere, something happens to them, and it changes their life. In his attempt to write about his adventures in the mob, Christopher has started to reflect on his own personal story. How does his story compare to the ones he's watched in his favourite movies? How has his life changed? What's his arc? In the end, he concludes that he doesn't have one, that nothing good is ever going to happen to him, that nothing is going to change. Christopher's problem is not simply creative. It's *existential*.

It's a classic scene from a classic television series that shows off what *The Sopranos* did so well. In a self-referential parody of the gangster genre, here is a tough wise guy driven to despair by the stories he feels he should be living out, based largely on the tough wise guys he's watched in movies as a kid. It is both insightful and melancholic – and utterly hilarious – as it digs at the fears and anxieties that drive many of the characters in *The Sopranos*, including Tony Soprano himself.

It's a scene that comments on how the stories we consume shape who we are and who we think we should be. Whether it's traditional media like television, movies, novels and news articles, or digital platforms like Instagram, Facebook, Twitter or TikTok, when we consume stories, we are always comparing and reflecting. How do I relate to this story? How does it reflect my world, my beliefs, my hopes, my fears, my desires? How is it different? What does it tell me about the world and the lives that people lead? We look into the eyes of the characters and search for ourselves. It's a deep human impulse. We need stories. Why? Because stories tell us we're not alone in this big crazy world.

When we hear a story and connect with its characters and events and ideas, when we laugh and cry and think and feel, we are connecting emotionally with other human beings. Our first connection is with the writer of the story, who looked at the world and showed us a way to make sense of it through their craft. If the story takes the form of a movie, there is also the producer, director, actors, cinematographer, designer, composer and hundreds of other people who thought deeply about the story and made their own unique contribution to it. Then there is the audience who saw what you saw and experienced the same, similar or even different feelings.

But it goes beyond that. We also connect with the real-life people, places and communities that inspired the fictional story. We may not know what it's like to actually live their life, but for a short time, while we experience their story, we have the chance to see through their eyes and empathise with their point of view, even if it's very different to our own. It makes our world a little bigger.

It's no wonder that human beings have felt compelled to seek out stories to make sense of the world around them. In Australia, where I live, the evidence of Indigenous storytelling stretches back 65,000 years, forming the oldest continuous living culture on earth. Stories are central to the survival of Aboriginal and Torres Strait Islander people. Thousands of years later, at a time when the world seems impossibly complex and unpredictable, it's no coincidence that many of us have found comfort in bingeing on an endless stream of film and television stories. When we watch these stories, apart from being dazzled and entertained, we're also thinking, 'Wow, someone out there totally gets me!'

For some of us – quite possibly you – the craving for story goes beyond watching a movie or television show or reading a book. We want to be the storyteller. Without giving away my age, my urge to tell stories started with the *Star Wars* figures I collected as a child and arranged into endless spin-off of the movies. In my version of the story, Boba Fett, the mysterious bounty hunter, was the hero of the story instead of the villain, and I teamed him up with Han Solo (my second-favourite character) to fight the evil Empire. I just liked the idea of these two outsiders taking on the bad guys, rather than that try-hard teacher's pet Luke Skywalker.

After a brief pitstop in fine arts, I swapped my paintbrush for a video camera and completed a degree in screenwriting and directing. One of my first short films, *Stop*, a comedy about a man discovering a traffic light in the middle of the outback, was selected for Official Competition at the Cannes Film Festival. The opportunities to be a full-time screenwriter/director in Australia weren't as extensive as in the US or UK, but I persevered and eventually landed a gig with *LOST* (2004–2010). At the time, this was one of the biggest television shows in the world. My job was to write and direct two spin-off web series for the show – *FIND815* and *Dharma Wants You*. The projects won numerous awards, including a Primetime Emmy Award for Best Interactive Television (2009).

From there I've built a varied screenwriting career across television, documentary, web series and interactive storytelling, and the awards – including a couple of BAFTAs and International Emmy Awards – kept coming.

Inevitably, I was asked to teach some classes on how to tell stories for the screen. 'Easy,' I thought, 'I'll just go back and teach the screenwriting books I read at the beginning of my career.' These books explored a lot of interesting ideas about how to write a screenplay, but I knew which one I thought was the most important: the Hero's Journey. Anyone who spends even a few minutes investigating how to write a screenplay will come across the Hero's Journey. It's that influential.

The concept has been around for a while, some say thousands of years, but it was popularised in screenwriting circles in 1992 with the publication of *The Writer's Journey: Mythic Structure for Storytellers and Screenwriters* by Christopher Vogler. In the book, Vogler, an industry script consultant, introduced readers to a way of understanding stories and, more specifically, movies, using a technique called the 'Hero's Journey'. It's a useful and accessible book, written with passion and intelligence. It's also a bestselling screenwriting book, so it's very popular and extremely well known. 'Perfect,' I thought, 'What could go wrong?' Before I go into what *did* go wrong, let me give you a quick overview of the Hero's Journey.

In his book, Vogler argues that the shape of most modern stories is derived from ancient myths that all display a recurring narrative pattern. Vogler presents this pattern as twelve distinct stages. I won't describe the twelve stages in detail, but in a nutshell, they go something like this:

1   A hero is called to leave their home and go on an adventure to solve a problem.
2   The hero isn't interested and refuses to go.
3   Soon after, a wise mentor persuades them to reconsider.
4   Something big happens that forces the hero to do something to solve the problem.
5   The hero enters a 'special world' where they are tested by unfamiliar forces and meet strange new allies and enemies.
6   Encouraged by their progress, the hero thinks they are ready to solve the problem.
7   Throwing caution to the wind, the hero tries to face the problem.
8   The hero fails – badly.
9   The hero reflects on this disaster and discovers a new way forward.
10 The problem is approached again.
11 Using what they learnt from their failure, the hero tackles the problem and wins!
12 After solving the problem, the hero returns home and shares the wisdom they have learnt.

Put simply, it's a story about a hero who is forced to do something unfamiliar, conquers their inner doubts and fears, and returns home a better, stronger, more resilient person. The hero is no longer the same person – they have emotionally *changed*

– and their lives are better as a result. A story like this tells you that when you step into the unknown and face your fears things can work out for you. Essentially, it's an optimistic story about emotional growth.

Sound familiar? Think of your favourite movie. If you've been raised on Hollywood films, there's a good chance it reflects this exact plot. In his book, Vogler looks at films like *Star Wars, The Wizard of Oz, Rocky, Pretty Woman, Rain Man, The Full Monty, Close Encounters of the Third Kind* and *North by Northwest* and argues that thousands of movies fit this formula.

He also adopted a well-known screenwriting technique called the 'Three-Act Structure' to strengthen his argument for the Hero's Journey. Developed by Syd Field in his 1979 book *Screenplay*, the Three-Act Structure contends that all movies are told in three parts or acts, which means that they have a beginning, a middle and an end. Field also argued that each act was a very particular size, right down to the amount of space it would take up in a script.

Drawing on studies of ancient myths, Vogler gave these acts a unique name to describe their function – Departure, Initiation and Return. In other words, the hero departs home, stuff happens to them, then they return home. There is a compelling, commonsense quality to the formula. It's simple. It's accessible. And when Vogler combined the already-popular Three-Act Structure with the Hero's Journey, it felt impossible to talk about screen stories in any other way.

For the last thirty years, almost every screenwriting book, blog, podcast or class has used terminology and techniques that either explicitly describe the Hero's Journey and/or the Three-Act Structure, or use variations of it. In his screenwriting manual *Save the Cat*, Blake Snyder shares an approach that is a stripped-down version of the Three-Act Hero's Journey. In *The Anatomy of Story*, John Truby describes a '22-Step' approach that maps out the stages a story can go through – like a souped-up Three-Act Hero's Journey. Linda Aronson uses the principles of the Three-Act Structure to explore modern non-linear storytelling in *21st-Century Screenwriting*. In *Creating Character Arcs*, KM Weiland uses a Three-Act Structure to explore character arcs in a way that has some parallels with, but also significant differences to, the approach I describe in this book.

The Three-Act Structure and the Hero's Journey, combined for the first time in Vogler's book, have shaped the minds of writers for decades. Screenwriting has never been the same. Movies have never been the same. When Chris Moltisanti from *The Sopranos* is wondering if things will change for him, if anything good will happen, if he has an arc, he is drawing heavily on the Hero's Journey. When fictional television characters start articulating an obscure industry concept like this, you know it's gone mainstream.

But the influence of the Hero's Journey goes beyond just movies. Vogler's work is an adaptation and simplification of Joseph Campbell's *Hero with a Thousand Faces*, a highly influential study of ancient myths published in 1949. Campbell claimed he'd found a recurring pattern in folktales from around the world, and they all featured a journey through unfamiliar lands where the hero discovers wisdom and wealth – again, an optimistic story about emotional growth. Campbell called it the 'monomyth', which literally means 'the one story'. According to Campbell, its influence was ancient, stretching back through movies, novels, plays and campfire tales, all the way back to our myths.

In some ways, it could be argued that the Hero's Journey is the origin story of Western Civilisation itself, a culture built around the worship of courageous individuals (invariably men) who step into the unknown (often other lands), conquer their fears (and sometimes Indigenous populations) and bring home new wisdom, riches and ideas. These heroes have included Columbus, Galileo, Isaac Newton, Benjamin Franklin, Thomas Edison, Albert Einstein, Neil Armstrong and even Jesus himself!

It's little wonder Chris Moltisanti struggled to find his arc in *The Sopranos*. He was trying to insert himself into the collective weight of thousands of years of myth-making. Everyone's story can sound lame when it's measured by that standard. It's hard to be a hero. It's hard to have an arc! This was the nub of the problem I faced with my screenwriting class.

I walked my class through Vogler's seemingly compelling theory and we looked at some classic movies to see how it all worked. If we were going to find it anywhere, it would be in the Hollywood films Vogler discussed. But while the approach worked for fairly conventional and mainstream films, there were a lot more that didn't fit at all.

For starters, a tonne of classic Hollywood movies weren't about 'heroes' in the traditional sense. Instead, these films were about tragic antiheroes – *Citizen Kane, Sunset Boulevard, Psycho, Chinatown, Apocalypse Now, Badlands, The Godfather, Taxi Driver, One Flew Over the Cuckoo's Nest, No Country for Old Men, The Ice Storm, Mystic River, There Will Be Blood* and *Mulholland Drive*. These films do not end with a triumphant return home with wealth and wisdom. They're serious downers. No matter how compelling or fascinating these characters and their stories are, it is hard to see how they are 'heroic' in the terms set out by the Hero's Journey.

Not only that, many of the so-called heroes of these stories did not seem to have an arc, or at least not the one Chris Moltisanti was looking for. They didn't psychologically transform or overcome some deep emotional flaw. Despite what the Hero's Journey argued, many of these characters stay the same all the way through. Think about it. What is Chief Brody's emotional arc in *Jaws*? Overcoming his fear of water? Surely his fear of man-eating sharks would top water any day. Maybe it's his failure to stand up to the mayor, which results in more shark attacks, but Brody spends most of the film fighting the shark, not city hall. No, Brody succeeds because he's cautious and he cares, qualities that were evident from the very first scene. Sure, he overcomes his fear of water, but it's not the character transformation that the Hero's Journey demands.

Let's look at some more examples. What's Indiana Jones' arc in *Raiders of the Lost Ark*? His fear of snakes? That sounds a bit inconsequential, like Brody's fear of water. You could argue that Indiana's doggedly scientific worldview is challenged because he witnesses the power of the Ark, but it's hardly a character transformation that shapes the whole story. Indiana succeeds because he's consistently smart and resourceful, not because he finds religion. What about Ripley in *Alien*? From the very beginning she is cool, level-headed and absolutely right about the importance of following strict quarantine procedures!

So the Hero's Journey wasn't as universal or as useful in my screenwriting class as I'd anticipated. But what about the Three-Act Structure? Surely every story has a beginning, a middle and an end. This must work. But as soon as the class started to discuss where the acts started and ended in the story, no one could agree. In retrospect, I'm not surprised.

In *Jaws*, does the first act's turning point occur when the young boy gets taken by the killer shark, or when his mother confronts Chief Brody, or when Quint the shark hunter turns up, or when

Brody sets out in the boat to catch the shark? Go online and read a few 'three-act' breakdowns of this classic film and you'll see there's little agreement. There was so much conjecture in my class that the whole exercise felt counter-productive.

It seemed that pointing out that a story has three 'acts' – a beginning, middle and end – was like pointing out that a house has a floor, walls and a roof. While this was useful information it was also kind of obvious and didn't really tell you much about exactly how the story/house was constructed (e.g., How many walls? In what configuration? What if I added a second floor? What if I wanted a shed?). Insisting on three acts in a story seemed simultaneously vague and overly prescriptive.

But there was a much bigger problem about the Three-Act Hero's Journey that was nagging me: I didn't use it in my own writing.

In fact, I didn't know any professional screenwriter who routinely applied it in their screenwriting practice. I knew a lot of beginner screenwriters who tried to use it with varying success, but when it came to writers who made a living from their craft, they had moved on from the Hero's Journey and figured out their own ways of tackling a story.

As we've seen with this small sample, the Three-Act Hero's Journey is clearly not a one-size-fits-all type of storytelling, despite what many of its followers will argue. Not every story is a tale of inner transformation and triumph. If a whole bunch of Hollywood classics don't fit this model, then what would happen if you examined films from around the world that are not influenced by Western traditions of storytelling? Would the Hero's Journey still be the universal monomyth Campbell claimed?

But there was a far more compelling reason why my colleagues and I didn't use the Three-Act Hero's Journey – we worked in television. Let me explain why this is significant. Firstly, the stories we watch on television are very long. They can span seasons, years and even decades. With this in mind, where does act one neatly transition into act two of *Breaking Bad*? Is it in the first episode? A third of the way through the first season? The end of the first season? Season 2? It's very hard to pinpoint. That's not to say screenwriters don't use the term 'acts' when plotting a television series. We most certainly do. Usually we break an episode into four, five or six acts – not three. And guess what separates the acts? Commercials. The act breaks are not determined by a mythic story structure. They're handed to us by television executives with a commercial imperative to make money.

Secondly, while television characters can be noble, transformative characters who experience an arc resembling the Hero's Journey (Peggy Olson in *Mad Men*), they're just as likely to be tragic antiheroes (Walter White in *Breaking Bad*), or characters who don't change at all (Tony Soprano in *The Sopranos*, Don Draper in *Mad Men*). In fact, because television storytelling is so long, its characters spend far more time *not* changing rather than having some sort of dramatic emotional epiphany. Indeed, traditional television sitcoms implicitly promise that you can tune into any episode of a show and see the characters make the same dumb mistakes again and again and never learn a thing ('Doh!').

The twelve stages of the Hero's Journey and the Three-Act Structure have a compelling commonsense beauty about them that, unfortunately, does not always stand up to the creative and commercial realities of screenwriting, particularly television writing. To his eternal credit, Vogler acknowledged as much in later editions of *The Writer's Journey* where he discussed reactions from around the world to his 'Hollywood' ideas. Vogler noted that in other storytelling traditions, including Asia, Germany, Eastern Europe and even my own home of Australia, hero figures were often regarded with suspicion, and the idea of change, either emotional or social, was something to be sceptical of.

As you can imagine, that first screenwriting class I taught using the Three-Act Hero's Journey didn't go as expected, but we still got to watch a lot of terrific movies, so it was pretty great anyway. Afterwards, I found myself wondering how I wrote the screenplays I was making a living off. I felt certain I wasn't leaning too heavily on the Three-Act Hero's Journey, but other than that, I wasn't sure. This is a common scenario for professional writers. There is so much internalised knowledge built up from watching and reading countless stories, not to mention writing hundreds of them, both successfully and disastrously. Professional writers know what helps them write the story they want to tell. They just don't always know how to describe that knowledge.

What was clear was that my colleagues and I had similar instincts for what made a good story in the writer's room. We all knew the 'ah-ha' moments when another writer's suggestion fitted the story, and we knew how to build on it. We seemed to have a shared understanding of dramatic principles, even if we had different names for what we were doing. One writer's 'plot point' was another's 'turning point'. Some will say 'escalation' while others talk about 'complication'. So I started to wonder what those principles were and how they allowed us to break the conventions of the Three-Act Hero's Journey and find our own voice as writers.

The result of that wondering is the book you're reading now. It is drawn from my experience in writers' rooms, sitting alone at the keyboard staring at a blank screen, writing on index cards, procrastinating, scribbling on whiteboards, drinking coffee, more procrastinating, long panicked phone calls with trusted colleagues and less panicked discussions with directors, actors, producers and investors as deadlines loomed. It's also partly born of a doctorate I wrote about screenwriting and the creative process. I'm very proud of it, but it's not required reading here. I wouldn't do that to you!

At its core, this book comes from a desire to dramatically expand the range of stories that writers, and lovers of writing, can easily identify and describe beyond the confines of the traditional Three-Act Hero's Journey. We'll do this using one of the most powerful, and yet most misunderstood, tools in a writer's toolkit – character arcs.

It's a term you might have heard before, usually at the end of a long-running television show where the fans are not happy – *'I can't believe how they finished her arc!'* Character arcs map the shape of a character's story – where do they start, what happens throughout the story, where do they end? Character arcs are widely and intuitively used by professional writers to not only give a cohesive shape to a story and its characters, but to also guide the narrative's emotional tone and hint at its bigger ideas and themes. I like to think of character arcs as the 'emotional shape' of a story.

So why are character arcs the most misunderstood tool in a writer's toolkit? Well, the Hero's Journey is why. The Hero's Journey is also a character arc (think about it – Hero=Character, Journey=Arc). But it is only *one sort of arc* – one where the hero *emotionally changes* and everything *works out well*.

Is this the only sort of story we can tell? Is this our collective 'monomyth', our 'one story'? Of course not. But for all it's talk of bravely venturing into unknown lands, the Hero's Journey is stubbornly bunkered down in a very small corner of the storytelling landscape and, because of the incredibly narrow way it is defined, is incapable of exploring what else is out there. Perhaps the Hero's Journey could do with a Hero's Journey of its own?

Unfortunately, given the influence of the Hero's Journey, many writers and writing teachers, as well as film executives and investors, have come to believe this is the only character arc there is, despite countless celebrated examples to the contrary.

This book is here to set the record straight.

We'll explore the incredible power and versatility of character arcs using a very simple technique I call 'Arc Analysis'. It pinpoints the key moments in a character's emotional arc and how they combine to shape the overall narrative. This approach is designed to be simple and jargon-free. You'll use commonsense words to describe the moving parts of the story, not mysterious terminologies.

We will look at a range of different movies to show how the character's arc shapes the story without shoe-horning it into a pre-existing formula. The range of examples will concentrate on well-known and well-regarded Hollywood films, as well as acclaimed movies from around the world. There will be a few classics to set the scene, but mostly they will be contemporary films from a range of genres, filmmakers and backgrounds, covering laugh-out-loud comedies, triumphant human dramas, gut-wrenching tragedies, nihilist horrors and everything in between.

Some of the films discussed depict sexual assault, rape and violence as well as racism, homophobia and transphobia. As a result, I've included warnings before these sections to prompt readers who may find their subject matter challenging to read. I've included these films not only because they are excellent examples of the sorts of character arcs I want to explore, but because, in most cases, they handle the issues raised with appropriate nuance and sensitivity. Where they don't, I take the time to discuss why that might be so.

There is no need to see the films beforehand, though it will help. If you're interested in films and writing, chances are you've already seen many of them.

No list of movies will ever be comprehensive. Just look at the long list of inexplicable snubs during any Golden Globes or Academy Awards season. Nevertheless, the films offered up here are a genuine but incomplete attempt to widen the conversation about the range of stories we can tell as a community.

While I'll be using a lot of movie examples, the techniques in this book can be easily applied to a television show, novel or play. Most importantly, they can be used to write your own story. Using the commonsense dramatic principles outlined in the following chapters, it is my hope that writers, both novice and professional, will *discover* what their story is, rather than be *told* by a prefabricated formula, and ultimately find their own unique storytelling voice.

When we imprison our stories in strict formulations – twelve steps, three acts, hero's journeys – we shut ourselves off from authenticity and truth in storytelling. Whenever people talk about the 'universality' of the Hero's Journey, the monomyth, the Three-Act Structure or the seven basic plots, it makes me think of Plato's allegory of the cave.

In this story, a group of prisoners are raised from birth in a cave. They're chained up in such a way that all they can see of the outside world are the shadows of people and animals cast on the cave wall. According to Plato, if this is all they can see, then the prisoners in the cave will believe that the shadows are what other people and animals actually look like. It's a powerful idea that many films have explored, most notably *The Matrix* and

The Truman Show. But this isn't just a thought experiment – it has real-life implications for how we describe our world and the people in it.

In a popular 2009 TED talk, author Chimamanda Ngozi Adichie spoke about how the children's books she read as a young child in Nigeria shaped how she saw the world. The books were all from the West, and their influence was so great that when she wrote her first stories at the age of seven, all her characters were white, had blue eyes and enjoyed doing things like playing in the snow and drinking ginger beer.

Despite living in Central Nigeria, where she and her friends were dark-skinned and the sun was always shining, Adichie's world was shaped by the stories she had read. She was imprisoned in a type of Plato's cave, watching mere shadows of the real world that was just outside her door.

Growing up in Australia, my own experience of this involved two simple yet powerful words that are central to the colonial history of this country – terra nullius. It's a legal concept that meant 'nobody's land', and it created a very specific story: that nobody owned Australia before the English arrived (despite the presence of hundreds of thousands of Indigenous people from a multitude of different clans, language groups and individual nations).

At school, terra nullius was the story we were told about Australia before colonisation. Despite being a brazen lie to justify the dispossession of Indigenous people, terra nullius remained in place until 1992, when Eddie Mabo, an Indigenous Elder, challenged the doctrine in the courts and won. It was then replaced with another popular 'story' – that Indigenous people did not resist colonisation or fight for their land. Indigenous and non-Indigenous historians are working hard to correct this myth too.

The world around us naturally sets limits on the range of our stories. Sometimes that's a natural phenomenon, like an absence of snow, but mostly it's cultural. Our culture, language and traditions help to define who we are as a community. Each is a prism through which we see and understand our world. This is vital and important. But it can also be limiting. As soon as a tradition attempts to describe who we are, it implies who we are not. It's inevitable. What isn't inevitable is assuming these traditions are fixed or universal. They are a selective interpretation of the world around us. Terra nullius was a convenient fiction for over two hundred years until it wasn't. The Three-Act Hero's Journey is not the whole story (and neither is this book!).

Using 'tradition' to set limits on the types of stories we are permitted to imagine, such as stories that only feature heroes who return home triumphant with wisdom and wealth, creates a cultural blind spot that denies most of us the chance to not only see ourselves on screen but to tell our own stories as well.

We're not all heroes. Sometimes we fail. Sometimes we screw up. Sometimes it's tragic (*The Godfather, Burning*). Other times it's comic (*Inside Llewyn Davis*). Occasionally we learn from our mistakes, but our problems linger (T*he Social Network, The Nightingale, Midsommar, Lost in Translation*). Or we stick to our guns and overcome our problems by just being who we are (*A Fantastic Woman, Erin Brockovich, Moana*). Or maybe it overwhelms us despite our best efforts to stay strong (*Sweet Country, The Father*). Sometimes, our story is about a group of people, and no one is the hero (*Shoplifters, Hidden Figures*). And other times our story is just a small one, with no big conflict, no big lessons to learn (*Paterson*).

This book is about how to look for those other types of stories. The ones that aren't always about heroes. The ones about the messier corners of life, where things are not so simple or always tied up in a bow. They can be poignant, compelling, truthful, riveting, terrifying, disturbing, authentic, inspiring, poetic, bewildering and flat-out entertaining. But best of all, they can help us see another side of ourselves too.

We live in a time when there is an expectation that everyone, for better or worse, can be the hero of their own story, curating their own Hero's Journey multiple times a day, uploading their latest victory over everything that stands in the way of their desires. And when you step back and look, it can feel like our culture, at least in the West, has been heading towards this strange moment for hundreds, maybe thousands, of years.

Like Chris Moltisanti from *The Sopranos*, we're all wondering what our arc is. And that can be hard. In a world shaped by ideas like the Hero's Journey, failure, or even a modest victory, is not an option. The stories we've been telling ourselves have played a big part in getting us to this point. But our stories can lead us somewhere else too. In fact, they can set us free.

PART I

ARC ANALYSIS

CHAPTER 1

'You know who had an arc? Noah': Understanding story using character arcs

The foundations of this book are built on the concept of character arcs, one of the most powerful tools in a writer's toolkit. Character arcs map the shape of a story and its characters, as well as guide its tone and hint at its themes. In essence, character arcs are the 'emotional shape' of the story – they map how the character feels at the beginning, in the middle sections, and the end, of a story. To help you grasp the usefulness of character arcs, I've developed an approach I call Arc Analysis. It's a technique that draws together the key dramatic principles writers use to shape their story without resorting to predetermined formulas like the Three-Act Hero's Journey.

Character: Inside and out

When writers talk about a character arc, they're talking about **change**. Does the life of the character change? How much does it change? Where do they start and where do they end? More specifically, an arc is about *emotional* **change**. Does the character change at an emotional level? How much do they change?

To understand how a character's life changes emotionally, we need to look inside them. Imagine your character in two parts

– their *external* **world** and their *internal* **world**. Their external world includes physical things around them that make up who they are: where they live, relationships, friendships, family, job, wealth, culture, nationality and even the natural environment around them. The character's internal world includes intangible things that make up the emotional life of the character: hopes, dreams, fears, desires, goals, beliefs, values, etc.

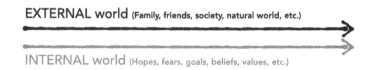

EXTERNAL world (Family, friends, society, natural world, etc.)

INTERNAL world (Hopes, fears, goals, beliefs, values, etc.)

There is a natural interplay between the external and internal worlds of the character, but at the beginning of the story, these two sides are in a type of balance. That doesn't mean things are perfect – the character might be in a crappy job, a tired relationship or even in the middle of a war zone – but their life is, by and large, **not changing**. Whatever their circumstances, the character is familiar with their life as they know it. Their external and internal worlds are running parallel, like a river flowing within its banks.

Generally, a story starts when **something changes** in the external world of the character. It can be a bad thing, like losing their job or a relationship breaking down, or even good things, like winning the lottery or falling in love. The external change creates **new or unfamiliar** circumstances for the character.

When change happens, whether it's good or bad, it creates **conflict** between the character's internal world (beliefs, dreams, fears, etc.) and their external world (family, friends, society, etc.). These two parts of the character head in different directions, like a river that has broken one of its banks, forcing them to adjust to new circumstances. The tension created by these unfamiliar circumstances creates conflict in the story. Conflict is very important. It is the river that a story floats on.

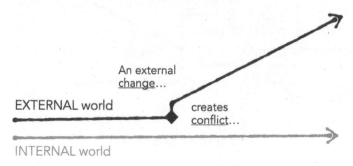

If there is no external change and the banks of the river never break, there is no conflict. If there is no conflict, there is little drama and even less story. The conflict can be extremely big (the annihilation of the universe in *Avengers: Endgame*), incredibly small (the search for poetry in everyday life in *Paterson*) or anything in between. It is the gap between the *external* world of the character and their *internal* world that creates conflict and generates story. The bigger the gap, the greater the conflict.

When an *external* **change** occurs, it creates **conflict** that puts emotional pressure on the character. How do they feel about the change? What will they do about the conflict it causes? Will they try to fix it or ignore it? No matter what happens, the character needs to make an *internal* **choice**. That choice is guided by their internal world and reveals a lot about who they are, what they care about, what they're afraid of and what they want. It goes beyond the words a character says and exposes what they choose to do under pressure. It is a tangible expression of their intangible emotional life.

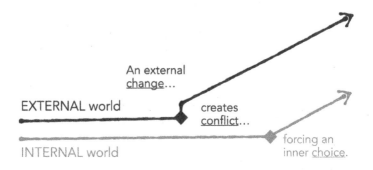

Character and choice

In Western storytelling traditions, the concept of choice goes to the very heart of both character and story. It's what writers use to bring their creations to life, as the internal thoughts, beliefs, fears and desires of their characters take shape in the form of a tangible action, a *choice* about what they will do to shape the world around them.

Generally I'll avoid quoting beardy wise old men throughout this book (e.g., 'Such-and-such said blah-blah so it must be true'). But since we're talking about Western storytelling traditions, and this guy articulated many of the ideas that shaped those traditions, it seems only right to get his thoughts. His name was Aristotle (he only had one name, like Prince) and this is what he said about characters in a story;

> *'Character is that which reveals moral purpose, showing what kind of things a man chooses or avoids. Speeches, therefore, which do not make this manifest, or in which the speaker does not choose or avoid anything whatever, are not expressive of character.' (From The Poetics)*

Let me translate. Basically he's saying *character is choice.* They are inseparable. Until a character actually makes a choice between one thing or the other, it is hard to know who they are on the inside. Do they choose to fight or back down? Do they listen to others or reject advice? Do they keep their word or betray trust? Do they tell the truth when they could lie?

An idea like this really gets to the very heart of character. This is because choice turns a character's invisible emotional life into flesh and bone actions. It makes the intangible, tangible.

If **conflict** is the river a story floats on, then **choice** is the riverbank that tries to steer the direction of the flow. For example, as the story continues, more changes will occur, forcing the character to make more choices. Often, these will be small and only impact the events in a scene; other times, these internal choices will be big enough to alter the direction of the whole story.

Each major interplay of change and choice creates a natural **act break** in the story as things reset and the character faces new challenges. They've made a new choice, but will they act on it? Being able to recognise the most significant changes and choices in a story makes it easier to comprehend the broad structure of the narrative (see diagram below).

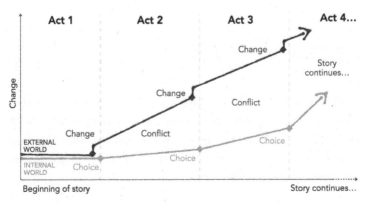

37

Types of characters

A character's choices don't just shape the story. They also tell us a lot about what sort of character this story is about. As mentioned earlier, a character's choices are a tangible expression of their intangible emotional life. Thinking of choice in this way allows us to easily identify two fundamental types of characters: **Change Characters** and **Constant Characters**. A character is a Change Character if they resort to **new or unfamiliar choices** to deal with the conflict they're facing. In other words, over the course of the story, the character's internal world will transform as they take on new beliefs, values and desires and make brave new choices. It looks like this.

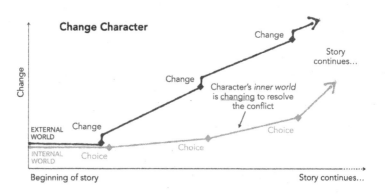

On the other hand, someone is a Constant Character if they draw on the **same old choices** they always make to deal with the conflict. That is, they approach the problem with the same internal beliefs, values and desires as usual. They do not change emotionally. It looks like this.

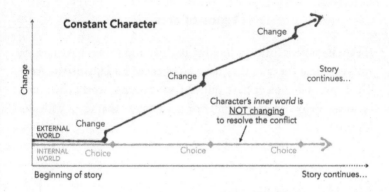

The character either emotionally **changes** or they remain emotionally **constant**. While that may sound a bit reductive, it's worth pointing out that the traditional Hero's Journey deals exclusively with Change Characters, so the palette here is significantly wider.

It is also worth noting that there are a lot of ways for a character to emotionally change or remain steadfast and constant. Depending on the story, remaining emotionally constant might be the secret superpower that will save the day, or maybe the ability to emotionally grow and change is what it's all about. If it is, when does the character start to change? How dramatic is the change? Do things work out? Maybe they do, maybe they don't, or maybe it's somewhere in between. It's all about the **shape** of the story being told and the unique qualities of the character you're dealing with.

Types of arcs

If the character's future is looking positive and things have largely worked out at the end, they have experienced an **Optimistic Arc**. Their internal choices have pulled their external world back into balance. Below is an example of a Change Character with an Optimistic Arc.

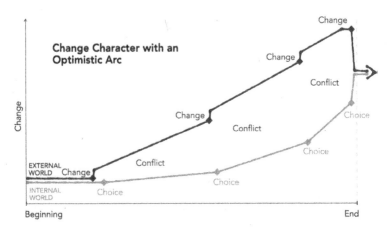

Stories that feature an Optimistic Arc include *Star Wars (A New Hope), Jurassic Park, The Farewell, Lady Bird, Call Me By Your Name, Spiderman: Into the Spiderverse, Shawshank Redemption, Black Panther, Good Will Hunting, Moonlight, Booksmart, Tootsie, Dead Poet's Society, The King's Speech, Toy Story, Gravity, Sideways, Children of Men, The Invisible Man, Jojo Rabbit, Arrival, Being There, Her, Carol* and, possibly, the entire catalogue of Pixar and Disney movies.

If, however, things are looking overwhelmingly negative for the character at the end of the story, then they have experienced a **Pessimistic Arc**. Their internal choices did not reduce the conflict and left it unresolved. Below is an example of a Constant Character with a Pessimistic Arc.

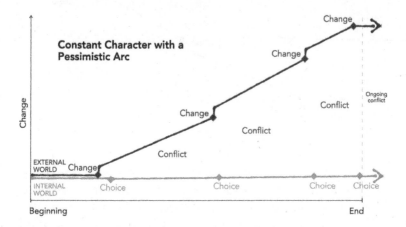

Stories that feature a Pessimistic Arc include *The Departed*, *Black Swan*, *Burning*, *Under the Skin*, *Seven*, *Mystic River*, *Uncut Gems*, *Animal Kingdom*, *Sweet Country*, *The Father*, *It Comes at Night*, *I'm Thinking of Ending Things*, *Mulholland Drive*, *Apocalypse Now*, *The Godfather*, *Kiss of the Spider Woman*, *The Talented Mr Ripley*, *Badlands*, *Hell or High Water*, *Citizen Kane*, *Macbeth* (of course) and many more.

Finally, if the character's outlook is both good and bad, then they have experienced an **Ambivalent Arc**. This is a really interesting arc where things are a bit more nuanced and complex, where internal change might be possible, but it doesn't completely resolve the conflict. Stories like this often have a bittersweet 'real-life' quality to them. Overleaf is an example of a Change Character with an Ambivalent Arc.

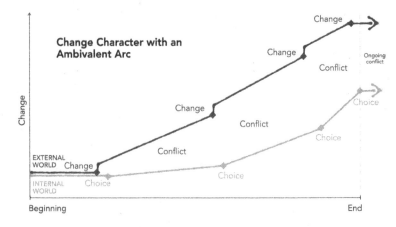

Stories that feature an Ambivalent Arc include *The Social Network, Shoplifters, Before Sunrise, The Favourite, Portrait of a Lady on Fire, Marriage Story, Thelma and Louise, Mank, The Guilty, Manchester by the Sea, Take Shelter, Los Silencios, Cold War, Babyteeth, Midsommar, The Nightingale* and many more.

In summary, you have two types of characters (Change and Constant) and three types of arcs (Optimistic, Pessimistic and Ambivalent). Combine them and you get six types of character arcs (there's actually a really interesting seventh one that's worth talking about, but we'll do that later).

As you can see in the table say overleaf, using character arcs in this way greatly expands the available storytelling landscape far beyond the limited confines of the Change Character/ Optimistic Arcs of the Hero's Journey (which occupy only the top left corner of the table). Not only are the range of character and arc possibilities expanded but each new combination creates a story with a distinctively different tone and thematic outlook. The stories "feel" different from each other because they treat the character and their arc in different ways.

		Arc		
		Optimistic	Ambivalent	Pessimistic
Character	Change	Positive, transformative, resolved *e.g., Star Wars* *NOTE: the Hero's Journey would reside here*	Bittersweet, nuanced, unresolved *e.g., Nomadland*	Powerless, dark, despairing *e.g., The Godfather*
	Constant	Resilient, courageous, inspiring *e.g., Erin Brockovich*	Tough, determined, dogged *e.g., Promising Young Woman*	Tragic, fateful, inevitable *e.g., Chinatown*

Don't assume that these are the only character arcs you can use. The character and arc combinations presented in this book can be modified, rearranged or completely discarded depending on the story. While I'm confident these character arcs will accommodate a more diverse range of stories than the traditional Three-Act Hero's Journey, I would never claim they fit them all.

The best way to think about the character/arc combinations is to imagine them as musical notes. There are seven notes in the Western musical scale, but no one would say that all songs are the same because they use the same notes. Like any musical composition, the character and arc combinations we will examine each have a tone and shape that create a different sort of story. Learning those tones and shapes will help you identify different types of stories and how they can be combined to make something unique – something all your own.

Close reading

In the following chapters, we'll take a closer look at these character/arc combinations and talk about their special storytelling qualities. To do this, we'll explore a collection of well-regarded and award-winning films that demonstrate a range of different characters and arcs. We'll perform a close reading of each film, starting at the beginning and working our way to the end, to see how the story's structure and themes are revealed by the external changes and internal choices the protagonist makes.

Close reading allows us to see the relationship between the various parts of the story in detail and how they work together to reinforce and reflect everything else. Most importantly, close reading is about seeing the story for what it is – rather than assuming a pre-existing shape or structure. After all, this is the way we generally experience a story when we watch a movie or television show or read a book.

In the beginning, we don't know if the story will feature a Change Character or a Constant Character (even if the trailer has given us a hint). We don't know if their arc will be Optimistic, Pessimistic or Ambivalent. As the story unfolds, we get clues. We gain an insight into the character's external and internal traits, such as where they live, their job, their background, their beliefs, hopes, desires and fears. They start to take shape. We're drawn into their world.

Then, just as we're getting settled, something changes. Conflict emerges. We're further drawn into the character's world. What are they going to do? Given what we know about the character, we wonder how they will cope. And the shape of the story starts to reveal itself. But we don't know how it will end. We don't assume it will work out well. In fact, when a story is well crafted, it's

44

really hard to see how things will pan out. Will the protagonist be forced to change? Will things be good, bad or somewhere in between? We're on the edge of our seats.

If this is how we usually experience a story, what happens if we approach an analysis of a story the same way, with no preconceptions or assumptions, open to surprise and possibility?

That's how I'd like you to approach the stories in this book. We'll walk through them one section at a time and see how their structure takes shape, reinforcing itself one sequence at a time. It's a very methodical approach to reading a film, but it doesn't have to be laborious. You don't have to take notes. The important questions we examine are pretty broad. Is the story about a Change Character or Constant Character? What are the big choices they make? Do they have an Optimistic, Pessimistic or Ambivalent Arc (i.e. is the future looking better, worse or a bit of both)?

The close reading of each film is accompanied by illustrative diagrams to help you visualise the concepts being discussed. I'm a fairly visual thinker, so I get a lot out of diagrams, but they're not essential. If your head doesn't work that way, just cast an eye over them and move on. Similarly, the diagrams are broad illustrations of the concepts rather than strict 'measurements'. While the approach taken in this book is rigorous, it's more a creative analysis than a scientific one (after all, stories are just things we make up out of thin air).

Close reading is a technique that can help you better understand any story you come across. The important thing is to approach the story with an open mind. Go on the journey and see where it takes you. Don't leap to conclusions; see the story for what it is. And because this approach involves a lot of storytelling, there will be, naturally, a lot of spoilers, so be ready for that!

The exercise of close reading is not confined to storytelling. Artists of all persuasions routinely dive deep into an existing work to better understand its structure and component parts. Musicians hit 'replay' again and again as they explore a new musical influence, painters pore over the work of other painters, photographers try to unravel the layered techniques used by their contemporaries, novelists and poets read and reread the same pages over and over. It's all part of being a professional. It's a common ritual in an artist's life.

If you're wondering when the 'how-to' part of the book is going to start, take comfort in the fact that you're already in the thick of it. You're going through the steps every professional writer takes to master their craft. You're exploring the possibilities and expanding your storytelling boundaries with every story you take the time to appreciate.

The more you understand and practise the techniques of Arc Analysis, the more it will become second nature, an instinct that will help you find the unique shape of the story you want to tell. And with every story you write, the closer you will get to developing your own unique voice. Because that's what this is all about. Discovering your unique voice as a writer. But to get there, you need to hear some other voices first. Let's get started.

PART II

CHANGE CHARACTERS

CHAPTER 2

'Use the Force, Luke':
Change Characters with
Optimistic Arcs

Hollywood loves a happy ending. Which is why many mainstream Hollywood films feature Change Characters with Optimistic Arcs. They're positive and uplifting stories designed to leave a smile on your face. Audiences love them (they also love a lot of other types of films, but we'll get to that later). Because of these optimistic qualities, they're also more likely to resemble the Hero's Journey style of storytelling, but not always. It's worth exploring a few here so we can understand how other types of characters and story arcs differ from the norm.

It would be easy to dismiss Change Characters and Optimistic Arcs as simplistic storytelling that avoids dealing with the 'real' stuff of life. But as you'll see in these examples, the range of stories that fits this style is quite broad.

In this chapter, we'll be looking at *Star Wars* (an entertaining space adventure), *Lady Bird* (a wry coming-of-age story) and *Moonlight* (a tender love story). These stories don't have much in common, but they all end on an optimistic note where the character overcomes a major conflict, one that *changes* them at an emotional level. Whether or not they all fit the definition of a 'hero' is another matter, but they all embrace the idea that change, particularly *emotional change*, is possible in the face of adversity.

In each example, we'll look at the big changes that happen in the character's external world, the choices they make in response, and how this creates the arc and themes of the story. Let's start in a galaxy, far, far away...

Star Wars: A New Hope (1977)

This is an obvious place to start if we want to understand a Change Character with an Optimistic Arc. George Lucas, the writer and director of *Star Wars*, has spoken often about what he learnt from Joseph Campbell and the Hero's Journey, and how he deliberately tried to emulate it in this film. The film is set, famously, in a faraway galaxy, and tells the story of Luke Skywalker, a young farmer who is called to join a rebel alliance and help defeat an evil empire.

Let's break down Luke's external and internal life at the beginning of the story. The film starts with a space battle where a powerful galactic empire is duelling with a group of rebels who have stolen some secret plans. A princess, an important leader in the rebel resistance, hides the secret plans inside a rebel robot and sends it to a nearby planet. Here we meet Luke, the protagonist of the story. In his *external* world, apart from the galactic war taking place, Luke lives quietly with his aunt and uncle and works on their farm. His parents died when he was young and most of Luke's friends have left to become star pilots.

In his *internal* life, Luke dreams of using his flying talents to join the pilot's academy and travel the galaxy, just like his friends – and his father, who was a ship's navigator (or so he's told). At the same time, he feels duty-bound to help his aunt and uncle on the farm. He's generally frustrated and unfulfilled and senses he's meant for bigger things, but he can't see a way out right now.

It's worth noting that Luke, the protagonist of the story, doesn't enter the narrative for a good fifteen minutes. Everything before this has been setting up the *external* world that Luke lives in – evil empires, secret plans, rebel alliances, etc. So Luke's life isn't ideal but it's stable. Things change when he discovers an urgent SOS message hidden inside the rebel robot. The message is from a young woman, the princess we saw earlier, and she needs the help of someone called Obi-Wan Kenobi. This is an unusual *external* change for Luke, and it raises questions for him. Who is the woman? Who is Obi-Wan Kenobi? Where would he find him? Should he help?

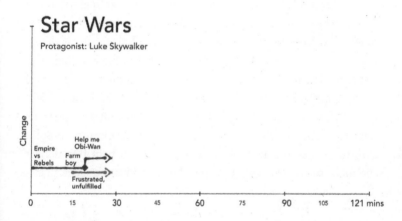

Luke's uncle discourages him from investigating and he obediently falls into line. He lets his uncle decide what to do. It's still a choice to obey his uncle, but it's not an unusual choice – it's exactly what Luke always does. It's also not a big choice. He hasn't responded to the growing conflict in a meaningful way, so his life hasn't radically changed yet.

Even after he comes across Obi-Wan Kenobi (aka Ben) and

learns the woman is Princess Leia, head of a rebel alliance fighting the Empire, Luke is still reluctant to 'get involved'. Not even the discovery that his father was a rebel too, a Jedi Knight, who was killed by an Imperial leader called Darth Vader, is enough to push Luke to do anything. Despite all the changes and the growing conflict happening around him, and despite his craving for travel and adventure, Luke's choices lead to life as usual.

But when Luke's aunt and uncle are killed by Imperial soldiers who have come looking for the robot, the loss forces his hand and he *chooses* to help Ben deliver the robot and its secret plans to the rebels and Princess Leia.

This is the first significant *internal* choice Luke makes. That's because the choice is *new or unfamiliar* and meaningfully responds to the conflict in his life. In many ways, the choice to act is thrust upon Luke, but it is still a huge decision for a simple farm boy who has never left home. He can no longer be neutral when it comes to the Empire. He has to 'get involved'. And getting involved will include learning about his Jedi Master father and a mysterious power called the Force (which forms a very important subplot through the story). It is Luke's brave choice to help Ben deliver the robot to the rebels that pushes the story into the second act.

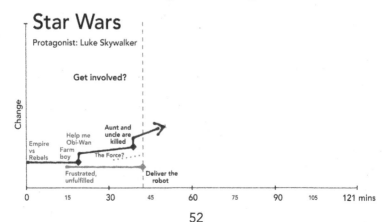

52

In the next act, Luke is trying to get the robot to the rebels. To do this, he'll need a fast spaceship that can escape the Imperial cruisers patrolling the region. So Luke goes with Ben and helps him recruit an infamous pilot called Han Solo who has the sort of ship they need. It's a close escape. As they make their way to the rebel base, Luke tries to learn more about the Force, but it's difficult. It requires the sort of concentration that Luke is usually too impatient for. Luckily, he has Ben to help him.

Everything is going to plan until Luke and the others arrive at the rebel base only to find that it's been destroyed by a planet-size battle station called the Death Star. Soon, their ship has been dragged inside. They escape the Imperial troopers but they're trapped on the Death Star. What's more, Luke and the others soon discover that Princess Leia is also being held prisoner elsewhere on the station. Luke encourages the others to rescue her while Ben finds a way to release their ship.

The *external* change of their capture forces Luke to change internally and behave in a way that's unusual to save Princess Leia. He's pushing himself and learning as he goes. He's emotionally changing from a naive farm boy into a bit of a hero. This pushes us into the next act of the story.

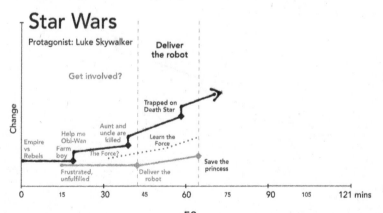

53

After fighting off Imperial troopers and almost dying in a trash compactor in the bowels of the station, Luke rescues the princess and Ben releases their ship. But to help the others escape, Ben sacrifices himself to Darth Vader, the villain who killed Luke's father.

Ouch. As far as an *external* change goes, this is pretty bad. Despite only knowing him briefly, Ben was like a father to Luke. It's a massive hit emotionally. What's the point of all this if everyone you love gets killed? This could have been the moment when Luke walked away, leaving the rebels to their cause. His old sparring partner, Han Solo, chooses to do just that and encourages Luke to go with him. But Luke chooses to fight on for two reasons. Firstly, after seeing so many loved ones die, he is now deeply committed to the destruction of the Empire. Secondly, he starts to hear Ben's voice in his head. How is this possible? Ben's dead, right? How can Ben be in his head telling him the Force will be with him? Despite the weirdness of it, Luke doesn't pay the voice too much attention – not yet, anyway.

The *external* change of Ben's death and Luke's *internal* choice to keep fighting marks the transition to the final act of the story

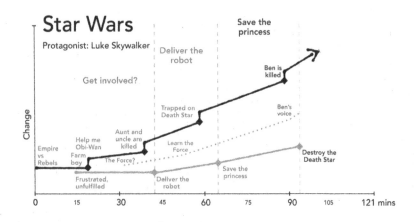

where Luke makes his most dramatic emotional choice yet. He's come a long way. But he has further to go.

In the final part of the story, Luke joins the rebels and attacks the enormous Death Star using tiny one-person ships. Many pilots die. Luke is the last one still flying. He has to fire a missile at an impossibly small target. It's a shot in a million, but it's their only hope. As he's about to take the shot, he hears Ben's voice in his head. It says, 'Use the Force, Luke.'

Luke finally understands what Ben means. To hit the target, he has to trust in the Force in a way he hasn't been able to up until this point. Luke focuses his mind, closes his eyes and fires. BOOM! He hits the target. The Death Star explodes. They win!

Luke's ability to finally trust the Force, and the dramatic *internal* change it requires, makes this final triumphant moment possible. Without it, Luke and all the rebels would have lost and their conflict would have continued.

Luke's *internal* change brings relative balance to his life again. He has conquered the Empire (for now) and understands the power of the Force. He is no longer a naive farmhand. He is a galactic pilot, a devoted student of the Force, and a hero.

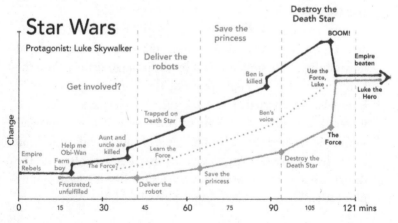

As you can see, there is a relationship between the way Luke's *external* world changes, the conflict it inflicts upon him, and the choices he makes to relieve it. Each choice pushes him further into the unknown until he is able to make a choice that he, and the audience, never thought possible at the beginning of the story – he fully gives himself over to the power of the Force. And it all ends well. All of this makes Luke a Change Character with an Optimistic Arc.

Of course, Luke made a million other little decisions along the way, but the ones outlined here are the ones that counted. They give the story its shape, its unique arc. If he had stayed on the farm, if he decided not to save the princess, if he'd gone with Han after Ben's death, if he hadn't listened to Ben's voice, Luke would never have been able to resolve the conflict.

Luke's *internal* choices also inform the story's thematic purpose. Taking a risk and 'getting involved' has opened up a new world for Luke, both physically and spiritually. The important subplot of Luke's journey with the Force maps out this process of *internal* change. It is only when Luke can trust that the spiritual power of good (i.e. the Force) will always triumph over evil that he can save the day.

Part of the thrill of stories with Change Characters and Optimistic Arcs comes from the mix of surprise and inevitability. One simple action by the protagonist (e.g. 'use the Force'), which they couldn't do at the beginning, pulls their internal and external lives back into balance. *Star Wars* is a textbook example of this sort of story, even if it is somewhat simplistic at times. For example, some of Luke's choices feel too easy – he was never going to give up after Ben's demise, and the death of his aunt and uncle has always felt like it was driven by plot rather than character (especially when Luke doesn't seem to grieve for them at all). Even his journey with the Force is not a particularly demanding one – he's a believer from the very beginning, not a sceptic like Han Solo. But there's no denying the strengths and enduring entertainment value of *Star Wars*.

Lady Bird (2017)

On the face of it, Greta Gerwig's Academy Award–nominated script for *Lady Bird* couldn't be more different to *Star Wars*. There are no evil empires, death stars or space battles in her orbit (although I suspect Lady Bird may have contemplated a Princess Leia hairstyle at one point in her life). But, like Luke Skywalker, she is a young person longing for something better than the ordinary life she sees around her. And, just like Luke, she needs to change emotionally to get what she wants.

Let's take a look at her *external* life first. It's 2002 and 'Lady Bird', or Christine McPherson, lives with her loving but financially struggling parents and adopted brother in a Sacramento suburb ('the Midwest of California' as she calls it). She is in her final year at a catholic school where, despite her obvious intelligence, she has mostly underachieved, sabotaging her hopes for a decent college admission. Lady Bird's bored contempt for her teachers and fellow students has left her on the outskirts of school life where she hangs with her nerdy best friend, Julie. She also has a combative relationship with her mother, Marion. They fight constantly over Lady Bird's lofty dreams.

When it comes to her *internal* life, Lady Bird craves a life less ordinary, far away from Sacramento. As she declares in the opening scene, she wants to 'live through something' and 'go where culture is'. Lady Bird has even given herself a new name because her real one, Christine, is too boring. Despite her poor grades and her parents' financial situation, she plans to apply to a range of prestigious New York colleges with the help of her supportive father, Larry.

So there is a lot of conflict in Lady Bird's life, but it's not on the same life-and-death scale as the evil galactic empire invading Luke Skywalker's life (although a lot of people in *Star Wars* change their names, so maybe these worlds are closer than we think).

The first *external* change that Lady Bird encounters in her life is the chance to participate in a combined school musical. It's a *new or unfamiliar* opportunity for Lady Bird to indulge her 'performative streak', as her teachers politely call it. It's also a good way to pass the time while she waits for the results of her college applications, which her dad, Larry, is secretly arranging behind Marion's back (which is an important subplot).

A school musical does not sound as dramatic as the intergalactic war that kicks off Star Wars, but the thing to focus on here is the *new or unfamiliar* change the event brings into the character's life. In this situation, the change is actually something fun and desirable, not life-threatening. But the school musical still holds substantial conflict for Lady Bird because she meets a boy during auditions, Danny. He's charming and funny and theatrical, and Lady Bird senses a kindred spirit. This is exactly the sort of guy she'll be hanging out with when she gets into an East Coast college, so she chooses to pursue him romantically.

The *external* change of meeting Danny, and Lady Bird's *internal* choice to date him, mark out a new act in the story. But before we explore the next act, let's look closely at Lady

Bird's choice. Pursuing Danny is certainly a meaningful way to handle the romantic and sexual tension he introduces into her life (the *conflict*). After all, he is exactly the sort of boyfriend she imagines hanging out with at college, so dating him makes a lot of sense. But is this a *new or unfamiliar* choice for Lady Bird? Not really. The reason she's interested in Danny is because of what he represents – he's not like everyone else in Sacramento. He's more East Coast, more New York (or at least 'Connecticut or New Hampshire', as Lady Bird specifies). Lady Bird's pursuit of Danny is consistent with the same desires and values that she has displayed since the very beginning of the story. Unlike Luke Skywalker's leap into the great unknown, her choice is not unusual. It's *typical*. And this, as we will see, is a very important part of her unique character arc.

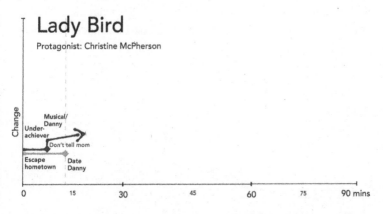

Lady Bird
Protagonist: Christine McPherson

Lady Bird uses the musical rehearsals as a chance to get closer to Danny and soon they are dating. He comes from a wealthy and very conservative family, but, like Lady Bird, he yearns to escape Sacramento and travel to Paris. She spends Thanksgiving at Danny's, which quietly hurts her mother, but Lady Bird doesn't seem to notice this. Danny starts to look like a total keeper. Until, on the opening night of their musical, Lady Bird catches him kissing another guy. She's confused and hurt, but also sad for Danny. They break up. While Lady Bird found a kindred spirit in Danny for a while, his sexual identity crisis isn't going to help her overcome her discontent. Their breakup marks the next major change in Lady Bird's *external* life.

Soon after, Lady Bird meets Kyle, a brooding anarchist/musician who is always reading a brainy book. She's smitten. This is the sort of guy she thinks she should be hanging with, and she chooses to pursue him. Of course, Lady Bird's choice here is, as we've seen with Danny, extremely typical of her existing desires, values and taste in guys. There is no *internal* change going on for Lady Bird at this point in the story. Why would she need to emotionally change? Why would that make her happier? How is that going to help her get into an East Coast college or be Kyle's girlfriend?

Before we move forward, let's back up a little. During Lady Bird's romance with Danny, her father loses his job. Because of the cost of college, this could be a major obstacle to Lady Bird getting her East Coast education. In another sort of story, this would be a major *external* change as the character tries to overcome this new conflict. But in this story, Lady Bird barely registers the problem. Why doesn't this event become a major change in the story? Because it's her parents' conflict, not hers. If you haven't noticed yet, Lady Bird, like most teenagers, is pretty self-absorbed. Her father said he'd help with her college application, so there's nothing for her to be concerned about – even if he loses his job. And sure enough, at the end of the Danny part of the story, the ever-faithful Larry delivers the documents she needs. The financial struggle of Larry and Marion does not shape the story; rather, it provides a background texture to the conflict and reinforces how self-absorbed Lady Bird really is.

So, back to the new guy, Kyle. He's super cool, dark and mysterious. He's also aloof and hard to approach. So Lady Bird befriends Jenna, one of the cool girls, to give her some social credentials and get closer to Kyle. It works. Lady Bird becomes friends with Jenna and starts dating Kyle. Unfortunately, when she drops out of theatre rehearsals to be with her new friends, Lady Bird neglects her friendship with Julie. They fight and, once again, Lady Bird doesn't see how her self-absorbed choices are hurting those close to her, including her long-suffering mother. This is reinforced when Lady Bird is suspended from school over an insensitive joke and discovers her father has had depression for years without her noticing. Soon, things aren't going well with her new friends either – Lady Bird is caught lying to Jenna about where she lives, and losing her virginity to Kyle is seriously 'unspecial'.

But despite the trouble Lady Bird is in, her choices throughout this act are consistent with her existing *internal* world –

61

grandstanding, showing off, acting out, lying, neglecting those close to her – all to get closer to a version of the idealised East Coast life she will soon be leading. Her choices are not *new or unfamiliar*. Again, they are *typical* (Marion would agree) and fail to reduce the growing conflict in her life.

But when Lady Bird gets news that she is on the waitlist for a New York College (a development that, again, she hides from Marion), it looks like her dreams are about to come true. It is here that a casual remark from a teacher regarding her entrance essay about Sacramento sees Lady Bird reflect on how much she is going to miss her hometown if she leaves. Lady Bird starts to 'pay attention' to the things that she loves. The *external* change of the waitlist and Lady Bird's *internal* choice to consciously 'pay attention' to the things she will miss mark out the transition to the next act in the story.

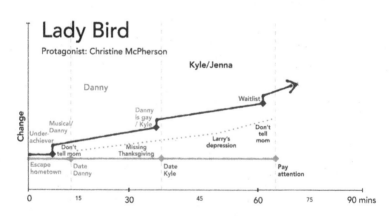

For the first time, Lady Bird makes a choice that is *not typical* of the character we've been following. Rather than trying to escape Sacramento, she's starting to take the time to appreciate it. This is particularly the case when Lady Bird decides to spend her prom night with nerdy Julie rather than Kyle. The two best friends reconcile and reaffirm how much they mean to each other. Even her relationship with her old boyfriend, Danny, is in a good place.

It is a sign that something in Lady Bird is shifting internally. She still wants to go to the East Coast, but she is starting to see her hometown from a different angle. She is changing at an *emotional* level.

Unfortunately, things with Marion aren't any better, particularly when she learns that Lady Bird is on a waitlist for an East Coast college. Lady Bird begs Marion's forgiveness, but even the news that she has been offered a college place in New York is not enough to reconcile mother and daughter. Despite her mother's pain, Lady Bird chooses to accept the offer and leave home, marking out the transition to the final act in the story.

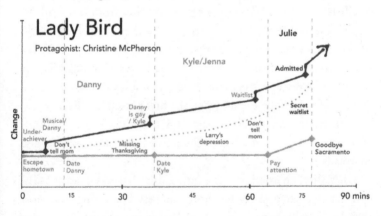

Lady Bird's *internal* choice to go despite her mother's pain is not unusual – this is what she wanted all along. But as the emotional ground beneath her has shifted, her decision is now laced with regret and a new perspective on her life in Sacramento.

63

While unpacking in New York, Lady Bird discovers a pile of unfinished letters from Marion that Larry secretly slipped into her suitcase. Larry says Marion couldn't find the right words to show Lady Bird how much she loved her, but these letters prove it.

The discovery of the letters opens Lady Bird up to finally appreciating how much her mother loves her. While the earlier parts of the story focused on Lady Bird's friends, this last part is all about Marion. It is the first time she has not had her mother by her side, and Lady Bird feels her absence keenly. The conflict between Lady Bird's *external* and *internal* world is at its greatest. Ultimately, this story has never been about boyfriends or best friends. It's been about mothers.

Later, at a party, Lady Bird finds a potential New York hookup cynical and shallow and starts going by her real name of Christine again. We get the sense that New York is not all she hoped for, and home, particularly her mother, is on Lady Bird's mind. Following an embarrassing hospitalisation for alcohol poisoning, Lady Bird calls Marion and leaves a message. In the touching final scene, she shares a story about how much she loved driving around Sacramento when she first passed her driving test. Lady Bird can finally appreciate how beautiful it was and how much she was going to miss it. She tells Marion she loves her and thanks her.

Lady Bird's name is not the only thing that has changed. The conflict that ate away at her from the very beginning, the sense that her mother was holding her back, that she had to escape Sacramento if she was ever going to realise her dreams, has now been resolved. Lady Bird can finally see the sacrifices and disappointments that have worn Marion down, and how her own self-absorbed choices hurt her. Most of all, she can see what a

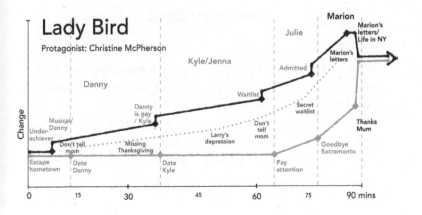

loving and loyal protector Marion has been and how much she took her life in Sacramento for granted. There's no doubt Lady Bird and Marion will fight again, but their enduring love for each other will go unquestioned.

Despite being very different films, *Lady Bird* and *Star Wars* share a story arc that marks out an *emotional change* in the main character as well as a sense that things are better, particularly on an *emotional* level, at the end of the story. But notice how different the shape of the arc in *Lady Bird* is when compared to *Star Wars*. Luke Skywalker's choices tend to be good ones that always reduce the conflict in his life. He's always heading in the right direction. Lady Bird's progress, however, is delayed. For a long time, she doesn't change at all and keeps making the same typical, self-absorbed choices. She totally neglected her most loyal friend, made some unfortunate boyfriend choices, and took her mother for granted for far too long. Luke Skywalker might have lost a few parental figures along the way, but Lady Bird's arc is more emotionally complex as she grapples with the impact of her poor choices.

Moonlight (2016)

Barry Jenkins' Academy Award–winning screenplay for *Moonlight* (from a story by Tarell Alvin McCraney) is a touching and deeply emotional portrait of a young boy finding his way in a turbulent world that does not understand him. While it is a story about a Change Character with an Optimistic Arc, the film, much like its main character, finds its own original path through the story.

The film is broken into three discrete, self-contained parts, separated by years. In Part One, entitled 'Little', we meet a young boy called Chiron who lives in Liberty City, Miami. It's a tough neighbourhood with a thriving drug trade. In the opening sequences, we see Chiron being chased by bullies who have given him the nickname of 'Little' and want to beat up his 'gay ass'. Immediately, we get the sense that Chiron's *external* world is hostile towards him. The bullies corner Chiron in an abandoned apartment block, but Chiron is saved by a drug dealer called Juan. When Chiron won't reveal his name or address, Juan, feeling obliged to help, takes the boy home to his girlfriend, Teresa. She gets Chiron talking and it's agreed he'll stay the night because he doesn't want to go home. This quickly establishes Chiron's *internal* life. He is painfully shy, meek and troubled.

In the morning, Juan returns Chiron to his single mother, Paula, who is relieved to see him, but we get the sense that Chiron is distant from her, perhaps even afraid. We don't have the full picture on Chiron's external and internal worlds yet, but the masterfully paced storytelling is giving us clues – this kid is generally terrified of his world.

The gentle drug dealer makes an effort to spend time with Chiron. This is an *external* change that challenges Chiron to come out of his shell and trust another person. The shy young boy chooses to accept the offer of friendship. In this case, it is an *internal* choice that is *new or unfamiliar*. In his quiet way, Chiron is changing *emotionally*.

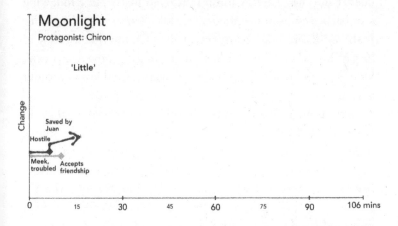

They go to the beach and Juan teaches Chiron to swim. Sensing Chiron's *internal* struggle, Juan counsels him to be proud and not to let anyone else decide who he is going to be in his life. Juan's words will echo through the rest of the story and reflect the slow *internal* change Chiron is experiencing.

At the same time, Chiron befriends another boy at school, Kevin, who teaches him to wrestle and stand up for himself. These scenes don't shape the narrative at this point but, like the scenes with Juan, reflect the *internal* change Chiron is going through that will resonate later in the story.

Despite his new friendships, things take a turn for the worse when it becomes clear that Paula, Chiron's mother, is using drugs again. Soon, the television has been hocked and Chiron is left to fend for himself as he has done before. While this is a clear problem for Chiron, it is a conflict that is already a part of his life, and it is why he is so distant from Paula. But a new problem is developing for Chiron.

Juan discovers that Paula is buying drugs from his gang, but he doesn't stop her. Later, Chiron retreats to Juan's place following a verbal attack from his mother. He asks Juan what a 'faggot' is. Juan's words are again reassuring, telling Chiron that it's okay to be gay. But when Chiron asks if Juan sells drugs, the dealer can't hide the awful truth. Chiron abruptly gets up and leaves without a word.

Even though Juan inspires a subtle emotional change in Chiron for a time, the realisation that his new friend is the source of his mother's addiction throws the young boy's life back into turmoil. From where he stands, offers of kindness and friendship from adults can't be trusted. Just like his mother's love, there is always a price to be paid. His choice to reject Juan's friendship is a resort to his old cautious ways. The conflict he's facing has grown and he's worse off than he was before. The *external* revelation of Juan's role in Paula's addiction, and Chiron's *internal* choice to pull away, mark the transition to the next act in the story.

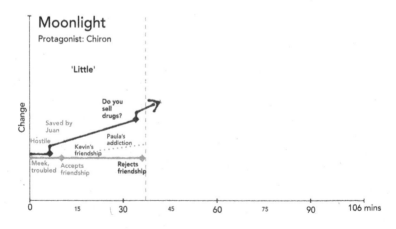

As mentioned earlier, *Moonlight* is broken up into three discrete, self-contained parts. Each part is like a one-act story where an *external* change happens (Juan's arrival), the character makes a choice (to accept his friendship), growing conflict leads to the climax (Juan's admission), and then a final decision is reached (to reject his friendship). Watch for this pattern.

In Part Two, entitled 'Chiron', it's a few years later. Chiron is now a painfully introverted teenager, quietly struggling with his sexual identity and, unfortunately, his *external* life is worse than before. Chiron's mother, Paula, is still hopelessly consumed by drugs and has resorted to prostitution to pay for her habit. The homophobic bullies are still circling, but they're bigger and more violent now, particularly one called Tyrell. Like before, the only place Chiron feels safe is Teresa's house, but Juan is now dead. Chiron appreciates her emotional support, even though his conflicted relationship with Juan lingers in their friendship. He is just as isolated and afraid as before, if not more so.

One night, while aimlessly travelling on the train, Chiron ends up at the beach where he learnt to swim with Juan. Sitting on the sand, he is approached by his old friend, Kevin (who taught him to wrestle in the previous part). Kevin has grown into a brash, strutting teenager and gives Chiron the nickname of 'Black'. Chiron, meanwhile, recently had a wet dream featuring Kevin, but, understandably, he keeps this to himself. The two friends haven't seen each other for a while, so they share a joint, relax, laugh and gradually open up to each other. Eventually, they kiss and Kevin masturbates Chiron to climax.

It's a tender moment and marks a dramatic change in both Chiron's *external* and *internal* worlds. After all this time, he finally has the chance to act on the feelings he's hidden his whole life. And he chooses to embrace the moment.

This is an *unfamiliar* choice for Chiron and signals an opportunity for Chiron to *emotionally* change. Afterwards, there is the sense that shy Chiron and brash Kevin will see each other again. For the first time, Chiron has hope that true intimacy, even love, might be possible for him. Despite the excitement he feels, there is also the conflict that accompanies any new relationship. He desperately wants this to work out. The pain of losing what he now has would be unbearable.

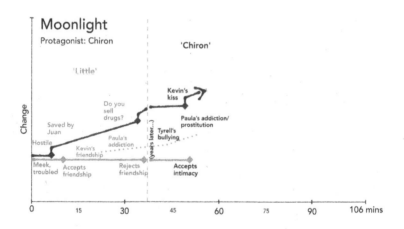

Unfortunately, the next day at school, Kevin is reluctantly recruited by Tyrell into a hazing game called 'Knock Down, Stay Down'. In it, Tyrell chooses another student and Kevin has to punch the victim until they can't stand up anymore.

Tyrell chooses Chiron. Despite how he feels, Kevin plays along with Tyrell's sadistic game and begins beating up Chiron. Meanwhile, Chiron, who was taught to be proud by Teresa and Juan, keeps standing up, even when Kevin begs him to stay down. Teachers eventually break up the fight. Later, Chiron is questioned but refuses to say who was responsible, even when he's accused of being weak and not being 'a man'. Instead, Chiron makes a different choice. A very *new and unfamiliar* choice.

When he returns to school, Chiron walks into class and breaks a chair over Tyrell's head. The bully cowers in fear as the other students struggle to hold back an enraged Chiron. As Chiron is arrested, his life descends into even greater pain and conflict. Any hope he briefly possessed has been snuffed out by Tyrell's game and Kevin's participation. How can he find love and intimacy when the people he gets close to – Juan, Kevin, even his mother – keep betraying him? These dramatic events and Chiron's *new and unfamiliar* choice to fight back increase the conflict in his life and throw us into the next act of the story.

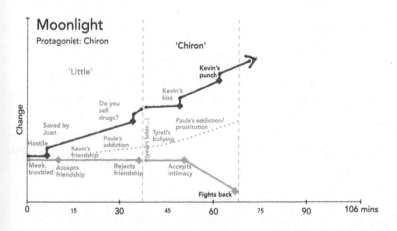

In Part Three, entitled 'Black', we meet a very different Chiron. He is now in his twenties, muscled and fearsome. He's a tough drug dealer and has fashioned himself on Juan, right down to his flashy ride and gold grills on his teeth. He's even spent time in jail. Chiron couldn't be more different to the meek boy we have become accustomed to. The *external* life he commands is dangerous and precarious, while his *internal* life is hidden under an elaborate disguise. He even goes by the name 'Black' now. Chiron and 'Little', it seems, are a distant memory. The radical *internal* choice Chiron made at the end of the last act – to fight back against the world – has led to even greater conflict. He may be feared and respected by those in his gang, but his true identity and, in particular, his emotional life, is completely hidden.

Despite these dramatic changes, Chiron is still haunted by his mother and has nightmares featuring her neglect and abuse. One night, Chiron gets a call from his old friend Kevin. It's a surprise, and they talk about the years that have passed, including what happened to Chiron. Kevin apologises for what happened and invites Chiron to the Atlanta diner where he works. He says he heard a song that reminded him of Chiron and wants to play it for him if he comes. Chiron doesn't commit, but later has a wet dream about Kevin, like he did when he was a teenager.

The call from Kevin brings up old conflicts for Chiron. But, after years of separation from those he once loved, after years of

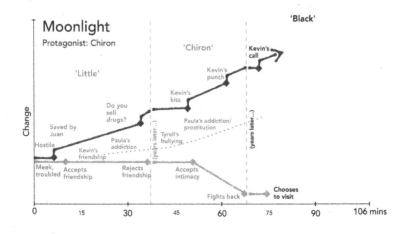

deliberate isolation in and out of jail, Chiron still chooses to take Kevin's call and visit. These are very *new and unfamiliar* choices for Chiron.

On his way, Chiron visits his mother, Paula, in a Georgia rehab centre where she works to keep out of trouble. He rarely visits her, but this time he makes the effort. It's a tense reunion and Paula finally admits she messed up and tells Chiron she loves him, even if he doesn't love her anymore. She apologises for everything. Both tearful, Chiron and Paula hug.

Despite everything that has happened between them, Chiron believes Paula when she says she loves him. This is something he could not do before. It's a touching and important reconciliation and a vital part of the emotional change Chiron is going through. But this is not the main event.

Chiron arrives in Atlanta and surprises Kevin when he arrives at the diner. Over a long and gentle conversation, the two friends catch up as Kevin cooks Chiron his chef's special. They cover a lot of ground but avoid discussing their intimacy on the beach as teenagers. Kevin says he married and has a kid but is now divorced. Chiron eventually admits he's a drug dealer. Kevin is shocked. Feeling judged, Chiron gets up to leave but Kevin plays the song that made him think of his friend. Chiron decides to stay and they retreat to Kevin's house near the beach. After more melancholic reminiscing about life, Chiron finally chooses to open up. Trembling and tearful, he tells Kevin that he is the only man who has ever touched him.

In the final moments of the film, we see Chiron lying cradled in Kevin's arms on the couch. It is a simple act of intimacy that, until now, has been impossible for him. While his *external* life may still be dangerous and precarious, Chiron has become more emotionally open. By doing so, he has created the opportunity to be understood and accepted by another person. Instead of hiding and isolating himself, Chiron is able to trust and be vulnerable. He has *emotionally* changed, giving him an Optimistic Arc that suggests his future will be better than his past.

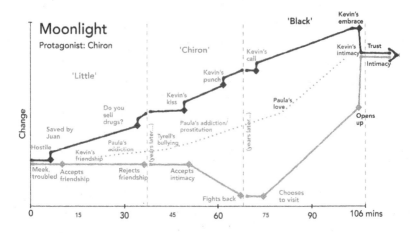

Moonlight is a quiet, nuanced and masterful piece of storytelling that is highly original in its structure. While it is broken up into three distinct parts, or 'acts' as Vogler and Field would call them, it defies convention with three self-contained mini-arcs that have their own 'beats' of external change, conflict and choice. In each section, Chiron struggles to emotionally change and twice slips back into old or more destructive ways. In the final section, Chiron makes early progress with his decision to visit Kevin and his mother, but the story creates emotional tension by holding off Chiron's final decision for the longest time. As the two friends talk, we can see Chiron's *internal* struggle to trust another human being and say the words that will set him free. When he finally opens up to Kevin, it's heartbreaking, exhilarating and authentic. The simplicity of the storytelling expertly disguises the complex character arc Chiron experiences.

Summary: Positive, transformative, resolved

In each of these films, the main character faces an *external* change that creates a *conflict* and forces them to *internally* change to resolve it. At the end, they are no longer the same character and their future looks brighter.

Each Change Character has their own unique journey within their Optimistic Arc. For Luke Skywalker, his emotional transformation was fairly gentle and gradual. He didn't fight against the change despite the challenges. Instead, he embraced his new life with the Force and never wavered. His choices always went in one direction – towards change and resolution.

In *Lady Bird*, Christine's journey was less straightforward. Her choices – her combative relationship with her mother, the kindred spirit she shared with Danny, her fling with brooding Kyle, her friendship with Jenna – were typical of the choices she always made. She needed to embrace her life in Sacramento and see it for the gift it was, particularly the love of her mother and best friend Julie. For most of the story, her choices did not reduce the conflict and often made matters worse.

Finally, Chiron's struggle with his identity goes well beyond the various nicknames he adopted throughout his life. Despite having positive influences in his life like Kevin and Juan, his fear of emotional honesty and vulnerability was entirely justified by the terrible betrayals he experienced at their hands. Only by opening himself up and forgiving their mistakes could Chiron finally begin to heal.

What gives these stories their Optimistic Arc is the fact

that the character's *internal* life has *changed* in a way that has *reduced the conflict* in their lives. Things might not be perfect, but whatever tomorrow brings, the future looks brighter and happier for the character. Luke is a triumphant hero who has matured significantly and transcended his humble origins. Lady Bird is pursuing her dreams and working on a better relationship with her mother. Even Chiron, who is still a closeted gay drug dealer living a dangerous life, has a chance at emotional peace and happiness that was impossible at the beginning of the story.

Some would argue these three stories all fit the structure of a Three-Act Hero's Journey. They are certainly shaped around an emotional change, but I doubt you could easily identify each of the twelve stages of the Hero's Journey, let alone agree on what they were. And do they break into three acts? As I've argued above, *Star Wars* is shaped around four major sections, or acts, while *Lady Bird* is broken up into five. Only *Moonlight* breaks up into three acts, but it is far from a conventional approach.

The tone of each film is different as well. The end of *Star Wars* is triumphant in a Hero's Journey sort of way, but *Lady Bird* is bittersweet and *Moonlight* is heartbreakingly tender. Maybe Luke Skywalker is a literal hero, but what about Lady Bird and Chiron? Are they heroes? I doubt they would think of themselves in that way. To explore more films that feature a Change Character with an Optimistic Arc, check out *Jurassic Park*, *Call Me By Your Name*, *Spiderman: Into the Spiderverse*, *The Farewell*, *Tootsie*, *The King's Speech*, *Toy Story*, *Children of Men*, *Jojo Rabbit*, *Arrival*, *Her* and *Carol*.

CHAPTER 3

'A storm is coming':
Change Characters with
Ambivalent Arcs

While an Optimistic Arc sees the character moving into a future that promises to be better than their past, the future of an Ambivalent Arc is not quite as rosy or certain. It's not necessarily terrible, and it can still be better than the past, but it's far from perfect. Crucially, despite how far they've come, there is ongoing conflict on the horizon that will emotionally test the protagonist. Success is by no means guaranteed.

In this chapter, we'll explore three very different stories about Change Characters with Ambivalent Arcs. The characters will face *external* change and *conflict*, but any *emotional* change they experience will not resolve all the problems in their life. There is still further to go.

The stories we'll examine are *The Terminator* (a classic sci-fi thriller), *The Social Network* (an astute character study) and *The Nightingale* (a brutal period drama from Australia). As we saw in the last chapter, each story will have a very different shape and quality as the characters choose a unique path to resolve the conflict in their lives. But things won't work out as well as they'd hoped. As the boy says to Sarah Connor at the end of *The Terminator* (spoiler alert!), 'A storm is coming'.

The Terminator (1984)

James Cameron's screenplay for *The Terminator* took what could have been a forgettable B movie and turned it into a long-running, multimillion-dollar franchise. Its premise – what if the robots took over? – is pure Hollywood sci-fi. What it lacks in nuance it makes up for with abundant chase scenes and dramatic tension. It also introduces an enduring female action hero – Sarah Connor.

The film opens in 2029 AD, in a world where monstrous skull-crushing robots are in the process of wiping human beings off the face of the planet. It quickly cuts to the present day (i.e. 1984) where a huge naked man (yes, naked) materialises out of a spontaneous lightning storm. He proceeds to kill a gang of hoods and steal their clothes. Elsewhere, another man materialises from a second lightning storm. He's smaller than the other guy, less homicidal and also naked (he's also kind of intense, but I'm pretty sure that wasn't in the script). The Little Guy asks someone what year it is before stealing clothes from a department store. What becomes clear is that Little Guy and Big Guy are both looking for someone – a woman called Sarah Connor.

When we meet Sarah, she is riding a moped and running late for her shift at the diner where she works with her best friend and roommate Ginger. Sarah is friendly and a hard worker, but she gets bullied by the customers, including a mischievous kid. From this brisk, efficient set up we get the sense that Sarah is carefree and kind-hearted (her *internal* world), but that she tends to get pushed around by others in her job as a waiter (her *external* world). Of course, there is more to her external world than this – there are two weird guys looking for her. How is she going to deal with that?

The Terminator

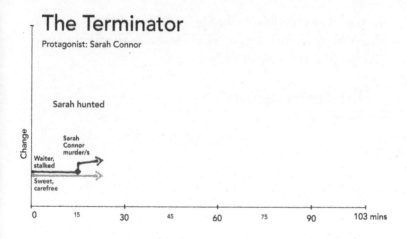

Protagonist: Sarah Connor

Sarah hunted

Sarah Connor murder/s

Waiter, stalked

Sweet, carefree

Change

| 0 | 15 | 30 | 45 | 60 | 75 | 90 | 103 mins |

Meanwhile, the Big Guy tracks down a woman who is also named Sarah Connor and kills her. Our Sarah sees the report on television but doesn't think anything of it. It's just a coincidence, right? She clocks off work and prepares for a night out with Ginger. Despite the *external* change in her life – the two guys, the murdered woman – Sarah doesn't react because she doesn't know about the threat yet. The audience is ahead of the character in true action/thriller style.

Sarah goes out to a nightclub and is followed by the Little Guy (actually, he's kind of normal-sized; it's just that the other guy is so huge). When she sees another television report about someone else called Sarah Connor being killed, she gets worried and tries to call the police, but their phone is busy. So she calls home, where the Big Guy has just killed Ginger, thinking she is Sarah Connor. Sarah leaves a message for Ginger and inadvertently reveals where she is to the Big Guy. He goes after her.

At the nightclub, the Big Guy tries to kill Sarah, but the Little Guy steps in and saves her. He tells Sarah that if she wants to live she should go with him. As the Big Guy shoots the hell out of the place with an arsenal of guns, Sarah chooses to go with the Little Guy, pushing the story into the next act.

The Terminator

Protagonist: Sarah Connor

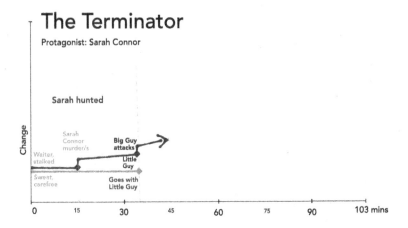

Sarah's choice is not particularly *new or unfamiliar* – she's doing what anyone in their right mind would do. While the situation might be *new or unfamiliar*, her *internal choice* is not. She's accepting help to escape from danger.

During a suitably destructive chase scene, Sarah learns that the Little Guy's name is Sergeant Reese and that he has been assigned to protect her. While escaping from their pursuer and hiding out in a car park, Reese explains to Sarah that he is from the future. Not only that, he tells her that the Big Guy is a robot called a Terminator. It wants to kill Sarah because she will give birth to a son who leads a rebellion against the robots in the future. Sarah is pretty overwhelmed (it's a lot of exposition to take in), and before Reese can say any more, they're attacked by the Terminator (aka the Big Guy). It all ends in a monumental pile-up with the cops surrounding them. Reese goes to take on the cops but Sarah stops him. It's a good choice by Sarah, one that probably saves their lives, and it is consistent with her established internal and external worlds. She's not a soldier like Reese and believes the police are on her side. As they are being arrested, the Terminator escapes, pushing the story into the next act.

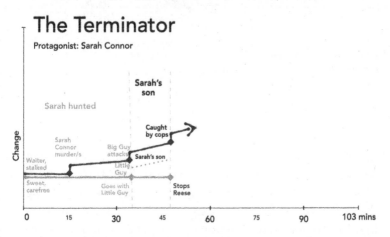

The Terminator

Protagonist: Sarah Connor

Once again, Sarah's choice is not *new or unfamiliar*. Despite how crazy this night on the town has been, it hasn't internally changed Sarah. She might have escaped with Reese, but she doesn't necessarily believe his story yet.

Throughout this act, Reese tries to explain his strange story about future robots, but the police, a forensic psychiatrist and Sarah all conclude that he is delusional. Meanwhile, the Terminator repairs itself in a dive hotel. Before too long, it attacks again. In a bloody shoot-out, the Terminator raids the police station. Reese (again) saves Sarah and they escape.

Again, Sarah's choice here is not particularly *new or unfamiliar*. She is still guided by her fairly typical understanding of the world, which does not include killer robots from the future. It's also worth

The Terminator

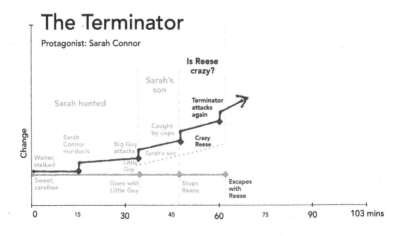

Protagonist: Sarah Connor

noting that, apart from the moment Sarah stopped Reese from attacking the police, her choices so far have been fairly 'reactive'. That is, she is not driving the narrative – Reese is the one making the big decisions. She didn't exactly have a choice when Reese urged her to escape the rampaging killer robot with him. While 'reactive' characters are not unheard of, they are generally frowned upon in mainstream Hollywood films. The industry wisdom is that audiences care more about characters who make clear choices and drive the narrative. Generally, that's pretty solid advice. However, I wouldn't discount reactive characters entirely (we'll do a whole chapter on them later). Indeed, I would argue that Sarah's reactive choices seem authentic next to the scale and strangeness of the danger she's facing. Sarah is an ordinary woman escaping an alleged killer robot from the future – and she has a lot to learn!

It's now night and Sarah and Reese run out of fuel. They decide to hide out in a drain where Sarah tends to Reese's wounds. Reese tells Sarah about her son, John Connor. Reese trained under John and volunteered to go back in time so he could meet the legendary Sarah Connor. Sarah is sceptical about being a 'legend' and claims she can't even balance her cheque book, let alone lead a rebellion. She doesn't want any of this. Reese shares a message from John that urges Sarah to face her destiny. If she doesn't, he will never exist and humanity will be destroyed. In a flashback, we see Reese looking at a crumpled photo of Sarah before it is burnt in a robot attack.

Sarah is starting to understand what is expected of her. But her *internal* world – her insecurities, her doubts, her ordinariness – is not ready to adapt. She's not ready to face her destiny.

The next day, Sarah and Reese find a hotel. While Reese is out, Sarah calls her mother to reassure her and makes the mistake of sharing the number of the hotel. What Sarah doesn't know is that the Terminator is on the other end of the line impersonating her mother. It now knows where Sarah is – and it's coming for her. It's a reckless choice that inadvertently worsens the situation. But it is all a part of Sarah learning what she is up against. Her choice is *typical* of an ordinary person who doesn't yet comprehend the danger she is in.

That night, Reese shows Sarah how to make bombs out of household materials. She wonders if he is disappointed by the 'legend' of Sarah Connor. Reese tells her about the photograph he used to have of Sarah, one that her son John gave him. In his typically intense manner, Reese confesses that he volunteered to travel through time for Sarah – that he loves her and always has. Despite the strangeness of his admission (some would say creepy) Sarah is moved and has sex with Reese.

Sarah's choice to call her mother and have sex with Reese captures an ordinary woman caught between worlds. One moment she makes a naive decision that puts them in danger, the next she seems to accept Reese's strange version of events.

Importantly, her choice to sleep with Reese is *new and unfamiliar* and signals the beginning of an emotional change in Sarah. The way she sees and understands the world is changing. As Sarah and Reese prepare to leave the hotel, the Terminator attacks. They narrowly escape in a truck, which pushes the story into the next act.

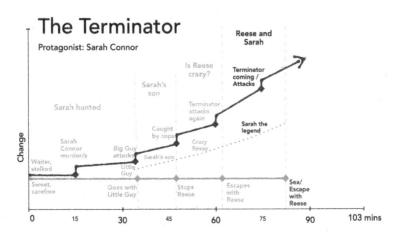

In another high-speed and super-destructive car chase, Sarah drives as Reese throws bombs at the Terminator. They're starting to work as a team and Sarah is getting a sense of what her future might look like. But, despite their efforts, the Terminator seems to be unstoppable. The chase ends with Reese mortally wounded. Sarah drags him into a factory. Reese is losing consciousness and Sarah starts barking at him like a military commander, ordering him to get up and be a soldier.

Her emotional transformation is escalating. She understands the danger and what is at stake now. It's not just her life, or her son's. The entire human race is at risk. Using their smarts, Sarah and Reese work together to blow up the Terminator. Unfortunately,

Reese is killed by the blast. Even worse, the Terminator is still alive. Sarah is all alone now. She can't rely on Reese to save the day. But thinking like the legend she is becoming, Sarah lures the Terminator into a compactor and crushes it to (robot) death. She's beaten it.

In the final scenes, a pregnant Sarah is driving across a desert with a gun in her lap and a tape recorder in her hand. She's recording a series of tapes for her son to explain everything, including the identity of his father. As she talks, a young boy takes a polaroid photograph of Sarah – it's the one Reese had. We realise that Sarah will give the photo to her son, John Connor, who will give it to Reese, his father (a classic time travel paradox). Sarah buys the photograph and drives off into an approaching storm.

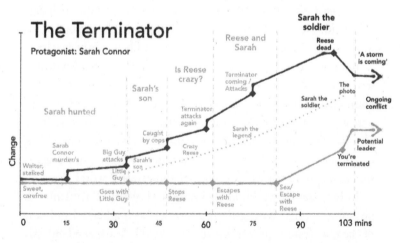

By accepting her strange destiny, Sarah defeated the Terminator (at least this version of it) and transformed from an ordinary waiter into the future leader of a rebellion. She may have gained a backbone, but Sarah also lost her carefree life, her best friend, her mother and her lover, and her trials will continue for a long time to come. Sarah's future does not look optimistic. There is a terrible battle approaching, and Sarah and her son John will be on the frontlines. Thanks to her emotional change, Sarah is stronger and more resilient now. But her arc is ambivalent, uncertain and unresolved. Sarah's story has only just begun, setting up a long-running franchise of films and television shows, each with a never-ending promise of more danger and thrills to come (although, unfortunately, with diminishing creative returns).

The Social Network (2010)

While Sarah Connor's arc sees her struggle to embrace her destiny as the mother of a revolution, the character of Mark Zuckerberg in *The Social Network* is quite the opposite. He *knows* he can change the world. He just has to persuade everyone else to get out of his way and let him do it. But is this what he really wants or needs?

In the opening scene of the Academy Award-winning screenplay for *The Social Network,* written by Aaron Sorkin, the main character, Mark Zuckerberg (a fictional version of the real person), has a combative dinner with his girlfriend, Erika. In it, he obsesses about how to distinguish himself in a highly competitive, cut-throat world. In these first few minutes of blistering dialogue, we learn a lot about Mark's internal and external world.

In his *external* world, he's a brilliant Harvard IT student, but he is not popular with girls and has not been accepted into any of the elite fraternities. In his *internal* world, Mark is relentlessly competitive, defensive, combative, dismissive of others and hides his deep insecurity behind an intimidating intellect. In other words, he has a massive chip on his shoulder. This is a guy who not only wants to stand out from the crowd; he believes he *deserves* to stand out. As you can imagine, he's a tough guy to be around.

Needless to say, Mark and Erika don't last long. They don't even make it to dessert before Erika dumps him. Mark lashes out by posting photos of Erika, as well as the entire female population of Harvard, on a website that he builds in a night. The site invites users to rate each girl's comparative 'hotness'. He calls it 'Facemash'.

Mark's choice to humiliate Erika and any other Harvard female that might attack him is, unfortunately, not a *new or unfamiliar* choice for Mark. This is very normal for him. What isn't normal is the response Mark's website gets. It's so popular that it crashes the Harvard server. He gets in trouble with the Dean and most of the Harvard girls hate him, but there's an upside – people now know who he is. As a result, he is approached by two wealthy brothers, the Winklevoss twins, who are making an exclusive social network for Harvard. They invite Mark to help build it to 'rehabilitate' his status around the college. He agrees.

But Mark doesn't help the Winklevoss twins. Instead, he stalls them and recruits his best, and only friend, Eduardo, to fund and

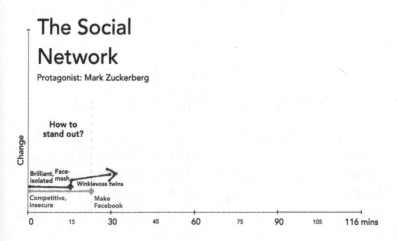

The Social Network

Protagonist: Mark Zuckerberg

create a rival social network called 'The Facebook'. Mark doesn't tell Eduardo about the Winklevoss twins. Mark's newfound notoriety (*external* change) and his decision to create his own social network (*internal* choice), mark the transition to the next act of the story.

He pulls a team together and uses Eduardo's money in his race to build a social network before the Winklevoss twins do. The story is interwoven with a series of flash-forwards where Mark, Eduardo and the twins are in dispute over the origins and ownership of the social network that will eventually become Facebook. Whatever the truth is, Mark outsmarts the twins and launches 'The Facebook' at Harvard with Eduardo as co-founder, pushing us into the next act of the story.

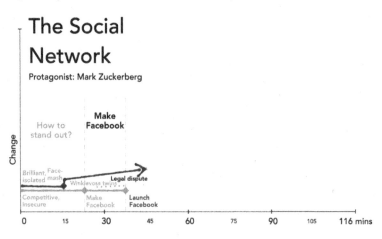

While Mark and Eduardo enjoy a new level of popularity around campus due to The Facebook, the Winklevoss twins debate whether to sue them. Making matters worse, Mark and Eduardo are at odds about the future of the site. Eduardo wants to monetise it with advertising, but Mark thinks it's too early, insisting they don't even know what they're selling yet. Mark is getting the reputation and status he craves, but a failed reconciliation with Erika, his ex-girlfriend, reminds him how far he still has to go. As a result, Mark becomes hell-bent on expanding The Facebook, which throws us into the next act of the story.

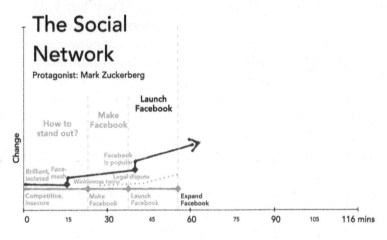

It's worth noting at this point that Mark's choices are not only driving the story, they are shaping the *external* changes in his world. He created Facemash, which attracted the Winklevoss twins, then he outsmarted them by launching his site first. In many stories, the *external* changes force the character to make an *internal* choice. But here, it's the other way around. Here, Mark's choices shape the world around him. Given how the real-life story of Facebook and Mark Zuckerberg is turning out, it's a prophetic artistic choice by the screenwriter.

It's also worth pointing out that Mark has not emotionally changed in the story yet. He's still the hyper-competitive, deeply insecure genius he was in the first scene. He doesn't feel the need to emotionally change. So far, The Facebook is giving him everything he wants – status, popularity, recognition. It might even make him rich!

Mark's drive to expand draws the attention of Sean Parker, the notorious founder of the music-sharing website Napster. He sees the billion-dollar potential of the social network and suggests they drop 'The' from the name. Mark brings Sean into the company despite Eduardo's reservations. Soon after, Mark moves Facebook to the West Coast, a decision opposed by Eduardo. As Facebook rapidly grows, the two friends and co-founders are again and again at odds with each other. As a lucrative angel investor joins Facebook, Eduardo freezes the company's accounts in an attempt to wrest back control. Mark is furious, claiming Eduardo's actions threaten the future of his once-in-a-lifetime invention. It's the first time we've seen Mark lose control of his *external* circumstances, and he doesn't like it. Despite this, the investor has offered to fully fund the company, and Mark invites Eduardo to sign some documents and celebrate.

The *external* change of the investor pushes the story into the final act, but Mark is always one step ahead. He's made a dramatic *internal* choice that Eduardo, and the audience, are unaware of, pushing the story into the final act.

During an investment round, Mark, with the help of Sean Parker, double-crosses Eduardo, effectively watering down his shares in Facebook to zero. As Facebook crosses a million users, Eduardo confronts Mark about his betrayal and threatens to sue him. It's a deeply emotional clash between the once-best friends and it rattles Mark. Soon after, Sean is arrested by police for drug possession, and Mark, for the very first time, wonders if he has partnered with the wrong people. Did he do the right thing? Did he just betray the only friend he's ever had? After everything that

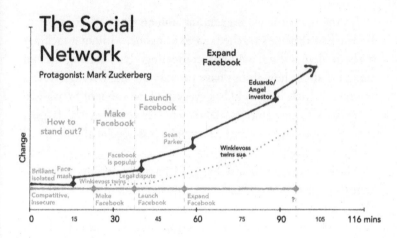

has happened, Mark is finally starting to *emotionally* change. But it's too late.

In the final scene, a flash-forward, Mark quietly invites one of the lawyers in the deposition to have dinner with him. She declines. Then he tries to 'friend' his ex-girlfriend, Erika, on Facebook. She doesn't respond.

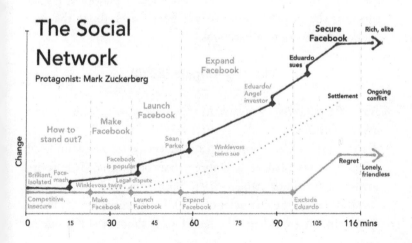

It's the first time we see genuine human emotion from Mark. It's the first time he's reached out to someone, without attacking, without demanding, without competing. He's having second thoughts about how things have turned out. There is regret. It's a moment of rich irony. He has everything he thought he wanted – reputation, recognition, riches. He has invented the largest, most powerful website in history, which is specifically designed to connect people – except him.

Mark is certainly a Change Character in the last few moments of the film. But his change comes too late to resolve the conflict in his life. His arc is unresolved, incomplete and deeply ambivalent. The writer, Aaron Sorkin, could not know how the real Mark Zuckerberg felt at the conclusion of this part of his life's story (the film was based on third-person interviews and the public record), which is why the conflicted and open-ended nature of Sorkin's approach is so effective. The character standing in for the real Mark is rarely emotionally open or vulnerable beyond his plea in the final scene that he's 'not a bad guy'. This admission is not only entirely plausible, it also captures the ongoing ambivalence people feel about the real Mark Zuckerberg and Facebook.

The Nightingale (2018)

Note: The following story includes depictions of sexual assault, rape and infanticide.

The concept of ambivalence can be tricky to get your head around. That's because it is more than one thing. Things are in flux, they're not stable, they're both good and bad. In *The Social Network*, the character of Mark has material wealth but is spiritually impoverished. The next film is almost the flip side of this. Prepare yourself. It's a brutal story. Harrowing. But hang in there, because there is power and strength in its ending. While the future may seem extremely bleak, the protagonist displays a courageous dignity that was not possible at the beginning of the story.

The film is the colonial drama *The Nightingale* by Australian writer/director Jennifer Kent (made in collaboration with Tasmania's Aboriginal community). Kent's first feature film, *The Babadook* (2014), terrified audiences with its nightmarish vision of motherhood. In this follow-up film, Kent produces a story that is even more disturbing but also extremely moving.

Set in remote Tasmania sometime in the nineteenth century, the story is about an Irish convict called Clare. In her *external world*, Clare is married to an Irish ex-convict, Aidan, and they have an infant who they love dearly. They have a hut and a horse and are slowly making a life in the new colony.

Clare's *internal world* is marked by strength and subtle resistance to authority. While she is not reckless enough to challenge Lieutenant Hawkins, the authority in the district, she does stand up for herself in front of the unruly men under his command.

When we meet Clare, she has finished her penal sentence and is awaiting the papers that will release her from the service of Hawkins. But Hawkins has taken a liking to Clare and has delayed signing the papers for three months. After a celebration to welcome a visiting officer, Clare takes the opportunity to ask Hawkins to sign the papers that will grant her freedom. But Hawkins taunts Clare, forcing her to sing for him and making unwanted advances. When Clare resists, Hawkins rapes her.

Clare hides the incident from her husband, Aidan, who insists he talk to Hawkins himself. But a fight breaks out between

Hawkins and Aidan, which is broken up by the visiting officer. Seeing the fight and the unruly condition of his men, the officer withdraws a promotion for Hawkins. Enraged, Hawkins and his men visit Clare and Aidan's hut. Another fight breaks out. Aidan is fatally shot. Clare is raped twice more. Their infant child is killed.

As I said, these are harrowing scenes. But there is nothing exploitative about them. They are depicted with unflinching seriousness. As we will see, this is an ambitious story, exploring a little-understood history.

After the attack, Hawkins and his men set out north to Launceston to make a direct plea for his promotion. Clare, meanwhile, arranges for her loved ones to be buried and makes a clear choice – she's going after Hawkins. He's going to pay for what he did. The *external* change of Hawkins' attack and Clare's *internal* choice to go after him push the story into the next act.

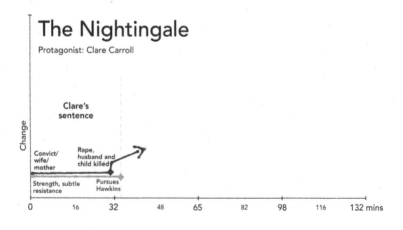

The Nightingale

Protagonist: Clare Carroll

But the Tasmanian wilderness is no place for a lone woman. At the insistence of a friend, Clare recruits an Aboriginal tracker called Billy, but not without some serious reservations – it's clear Clare is deeply prejudiced towards Aboriginals and even complains aloud that she might be eaten by him. Billy is no fan of Clare, either. He's suspicious of 'white bastards' like her and doesn't want any trouble. Clare lies and claims she is trying to catch up to her husband who is with Hawkins. A deal is struck and they set out.

At first, Clare guards Billy at gunpoint, but he is the least of her worries in the dense wilderness. Apart from the treacherous landscape, there are soldiers and chain gangs who are a constant threat for both Clare and Billy. There are also Aboriginal tribes who are waging an ongoing frontier battle against the settlers. It is literally a war zone.

Making matters worse, they are low on food, sleep-deprived and Clare is suffering painful mastitis from her surplus breast milk. Billy is able to steal food for them, but Clare struggles to trust him, even after he rescues her from a swollen river.

At night they talk, or more accurately, quarrel, and are surprised that they have more in common than they thought. Billy learns that Clare is Irish and hates the English. Her people were dispossessed, she's far from home, and she's a prisoner. Clare learns how Billy's people were also dispossessed; how he was taken from his family as a child, held prisoner, and taught the white ways. He also talks about how he struggled to retain his customs and longs to be free of the whites.

Despite their similarities, it is worth noting that Kent is careful not to let these experiences become equivalent in the storytelling. At numerous times, despite being a convict, it's made very clear that Clare is 'freer' than Billy. There's a war going on, and Billy's people are fighting for their land and their lives. There's a target on his back no matter where he goes. Whether Irish or English, from Billy's point of view, Clare is just another invader who can't be trusted.

Later, Hawkins and his men clash with an Aboriginal community after kidnapping and raping a woman from their tribe. Clare and Billy find the site of the battle and track a wounded soldier. It's the one who killed Clare's baby. Consumed with rage, she tries to shoot her child's murderer, but her gun fails. Clare is forced to bludgeon the soldier into submission, then stab him to death. It is a slow, bloody and brutal murder, and she is deeply shaken.

Billy realises Clare has lied about trying to find her husband and tries to leave. He doesn't want any more trouble. But Clare pleads with him and Billy learns she has lost her husband and baby to these men. Having lost his own family, he can relate. Billy stays and agrees to help seek revenge. Clare's brutal murder of the man who killed her baby (*external* change) and her decision to recruit Billy to help finish the job (*internal* choice) push the story into the next act.

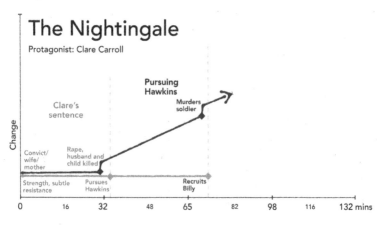

The Nightingale

Protagonist: Clare Carroll

Pursuing
Hawkins

Murders
soldier

Clare's
sentence

Change

Convict/
wife/
mother

Rape,
husband and
child killed

Strength, subtle
resistance

Pursues
Hawkins

Recruits
Billy

0   16   32   48   65   82   98   116   132 mins

While they now have a common enemy, Clare is by no means ready to accept Billy's ways. Despite her continuing mastitis, Clare rejects Billy's bush cure as 'hocus-pocus' and is wary of the bush tucker he gathers for them to eat.

Making matters worse, one of the chain gangs they escaped earlier catches up and discovers the body of the man Clare killed. She and Billy are now implicated in the murder of an English soldier.

Clare is also being haunted by nightmares of her dead husband and baby. Exhausted and traumatised, she deliberately throws herself down a dangerous slope, hoping the fall will kill her. Once again, Billy saves her and, afterwards, performs a healing smoke ceremony on Clare. Too weak to fight it anymore, she accepts the bush tucker he offers and applies the bush remedy that cures her mastitis.

When Billy finds the body of his uncle, the Aboriginal tracker who was helping Hawkins find his way, he is hungry for revenge. But Clare's resolve is waning. She's experienced first-hand the bloodlust that comes with revenge and has been repelled by it. When she is finally given a chance to put a bullet in Hawkins' head, she hesitates and is wounded before escaping into the thick forest.

Separated from Billy and Hawkins' men, Clare, lost and delirious, tries to drown herself in a river. When she wakes, Clare follows a black cockatoo, Billy's spirit animal, which shows her the way to a road that leads to Launceston. Having been repelled by the violence of her bloodlust, and finally following Billy's bush ways, she has escaped the dangers of the wilderness. She is emotionally changing. Clare's wounding and separation in the forest (*external* change) and her decision to open herself to Billy's ways and respect his people's knowledge (*internal* choice) push the story into the final act.

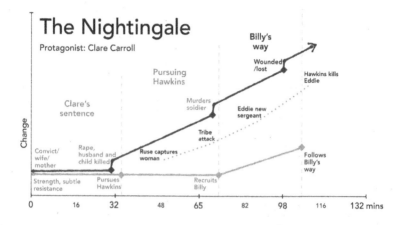

The Nightingale

Protagonist: Clare Carroll

Billy's way

Wounded /lost

Hawkins kills Eddie

Pursuing Hawkins

Clare's sentence

Murders soldier

Eddie new sergeant

Change

Tribe attack

Convict/ wife/ mother

Rape, husband and child killed

Ruse captures woman

Follows Billy's way

Strength, subtle resistance

Pursues Hawkins

Recruits Billy

0   16   32   48   65   82   98   116   132 mins

Paralleling Clare's story up to now has been a subplot involving Hawkins and his men as they make their way to Launceston. Here, Kent skilfully explores the cruel power dynamics within the colony by showing Hawkins using his privilege to threaten, humiliate and even murder his own men to maintain control. In this isolated outpost, on the edge of the world, the rule of law is optional for men as powerful as Hawkins. The struggle between the men reflects the themes of power and control at the heart of Clare's story.

Clare reunites with Billy on the road to Launceston where they narrowly avoid a massacre of Aboriginal prisoners, and Billy learns all his people have been killed. They make their way into town for supplies and cross paths with Hawkins, who has survived the wilderness. On the verge of securing his treasured promotion, Hawkins avoids making a scene and threatens to kill Clare if he sees her again. Defiant, Clare confronts Hawkins in the officer's bar where she reveals his murderous deeds in front of his superiors, declaring she is no one's property. She leaves having destroyed any chance Hawkins has of being promoted.

Clare and Billy retreat into the bush, but Billy, decorated in ceremonial paint and armed with a spear, returns later and kills Hawkins in his bed. Clare and a wounded Billy escape to a distant shoreline. Both sing in their native language, proud, strong and defiant. As the sun rises, they know that, while they will be hunted by the British, they are no longer their prisoners.

Given how distressing and unrelenting *The Nightingale* is, it never ceases to amaze me how moving and emotional the ending is. Perhaps it's the toughness of the storytelling, which doesn't pull its punches, that makes the ending so cathartic. And so ambivalent.

There is little doubt Clare and Billy's days are numbered. They will be hunted and, if caught, there will be no mercy, not in this place. And the killing will not stop. Many more women will be abused. Many more Aboriginals will be dispossessed and killed. There is a sense of impotence about their actions. They tried violence, they tried non-violence, and nothing was resolved.

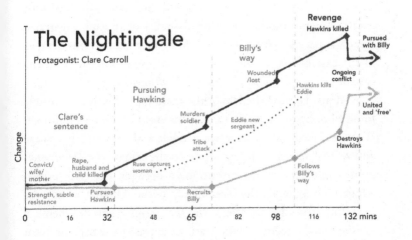

The Nightingale

Protagonist: Clare Carroll

Change

Revenge
Hawkins killed

Pursued
with Billy

Billy's
way

Wounded
/lost

Ongoing
conflict

Hawkins kills
Eddie

Pursuing
Hawkins

Murders
soldier

Eddie new
sergeant

United
and 'free'

Clare's
sentence

Tribe
attack

Destroys
Hawkins

Convict/
wife/
mother

Rape,
husband and
child killed

Ruse captures
woman

Follows
Billy's
way

Strength, subtle
resistance

Pursues
Hawkins

Recruits
Billy

0   16   32   48   65   82   98   116   132 mins

Despite this, Clare and Billy have secured a type of spiritual freedom. Clare has emotionally changed. She sees Billy as an equal now – even if the depth of their suffering is not equal – and has found an ally to begin the process of healing. Meanwhile, Billy has started the journey of taking back the culture that was stolen from him. As he declares to the rising sun in the final scene, 'I'm still here'. It is a powerful statement of survival and resilience that echoes from the past to the present day. Despite everything they have endured, Aboriginal people are still here.

Standing on the beach, Clare and Billy have almost nothing but their freedom (for now), their culture and each other. It's the opposite of the character of Mark in *The Social Network*, who has everything and no one. It is this faint light of hope, in a world of darkness, that allows the story to transcend the relentlessly brutal events of its narrative.

Summary: Bittersweet, nuanced, unresolved

Ambivalence is not a word you would normally associate with entertainment. But the open-ended quality of an Ambivalent Arc creates a space for the audience to imagine what happens next, as in the case of *The Terminator,* or what might have been, in the case of *The Social Network* and *The Nightingale.*

And just because the fate of the main character is not entirely resolved or happy, it doesn't mean the story has to be a bummer. We've watched these characters struggle and emotionally change and we're invested in their journey. In the case of *The Terminator*, we're itching for the next showdown between the transformed Sarah Connor and The Terminator (although maybe not the next four showdowns after). In *The Social Network*, there's a satisfaction in seeing Mark start to appreciate where he went wrong and where he could have been a better friend and human being. In *The Nightingale*, the devastating events are tempered by Clare and Billy's shared empathy and the depth of their cultures to keep them strong.

Watching a character struggle to change but still not get what they want has a bittersweet quality that can feel more nuanced and truer to life. It might not be a Hollywood ending, but an Ambivalent Arc can have its own sense of authenticity and truth. To explore more films that feature a Change Character with an Ambivalent Arc, check out *Portrait of a Lady on Fire*, *The Ice Storm*, *Brokeback Mountain*, *Donnie Darko*, *Thelma and Louise*, *Lost in Translation*, *The Irishman*, *La La Land*, *The Graduate*, *Spotlight*, *Marriage Story* and *Two Days and One Night*.

CHAPTER 4

'That's my family... It's not me': Change Characters with Pessimistic Arcs

Hollywood has often been referred to as the 'dream factory' – a multibillion-dollar industry that manufactures idealised visions of life for mass entertainment. Sure, they tell our stories, but they mostly tell us the 'dream' version, where things work out well or at least okay. But the truth is, Hollywood also has a long history of creating nightmare versions of life. Stories where things do not work out well or even okay. Where despair, death and torment haunt the characters forever. Where there is no redemption or relief from the conflict that invades their lives.

The slasher genre, for example, is built on the pleasure of watching characters you identify with getting maimed, murdered and dismembered in a satisfying rhythm of entertaining carnage. In horror films, if anyone is still standing by the end, we can assume they will be heavily sedated and in therapy for the rest of their days (or at least until the sequel). They are doomed. We know this even before we enter the cinema or press play on the remote. This sense of dread, fear and despair is what we actually look for. In fact, some of the most profitable films of all time are ones where most if not all the characters are utterly screwed by the end, such as *The Blair Witch Project*, *Paranormal Activity* and *Friday the 13th*.

Even outside horror genres, many celebrated and enduring Hollywood films are about characters who lucked out in the happiness lottery. These include *Citizen Kane, Sunset Boulevard, Chinatown, Apocalypse Now, Badlands, The Godfather, Taxi Driver, One Flew Over the Cuckoo's Nest, No Country for Old Men, Mystic River* and *Mulholland Drive.*

In this chapter, we'll be looking at three stories featuring Change Characters who, despite their best efforts to avoid disaster, end up with a decidedly Pessimistic Arc. They are the mafia classic *The Godfather,* the eerie science fiction of *Under the Skin* and the psychological mystery of *Burning.*

The Godfather (1972)

The Godfather, written by Mario Puzo and Francis Ford Coppola, is a film that has seeped into our collective consciousness. Even if you haven't seen it, it *feels* like you have. Many of its lines and sequences have been endlessly repeated and reused in popular culture. Just look at the self-aware references to *The Godfather* in *The Sopranos* and the sly parodies slipped into *The Simpsons.* Even Walter White's criminal and psychological descent in *Breaking Bad* contains echoes of *The Godfather.* It's not surprising. *The Godfather* is uncompromising in its ambition, both artistically and culturally, as it explores a dark history of violence and revenge. It is a brutal film, but it is not without tenderness as it depicts the everyday traditions that bind families together. *The Godfather* is not only the epitome of a Hollywood classic; it is the very definition of a tragedy and a perfect place to begin a discussion on Change Characters with Pessimistic Arcs.

The story starts in 1945 at the wedding of Don Vito Corleone's daughter. In the extravagant opening sequences, we meet a large ensemble of characters from the Corleone family, and it becomes clear that they are involved in a complex web of illegal activities, including extortion. One family member who seems to sit outside this is Michael Corleone, the main character. In Michael's *external* world, he is a college graduate and a recently returned war hero, and he's infatuated with a girl called Kay. He is glad to be home with his family and understands that his father does not want him involved in the family's illegal business. He's destined for greater things; in particular, politics and the Senate. In his *internal world,* Michael comes across as a carefree guy who is happily in love. He also respects his family and is devoted to them, especially his father Vito. He is determined to succeed outside the family business as Vito always hoped. When questioned by Kay about his family's reputation, Michael says, 'That's my family, Kay. It's not me'. Remember those words.

The first part of the film explores the machinations of the Corleone business as Vito deals with a proposal from the powerful Tattaglia family to form a partnership around a new narcotics operation. Despite his criminal history, Vito wants nothing of the grubby drug business, considering it beneath his family. His refusal to co-operate leads to violence and an attempt on Vito's life (*external* change) by a drug baron, Virgil Sollozzo, the man backing Tattaglia's plans.

While Michael has had little direct involvement in these developments, this is the world he was born into and it has consequences for him. During a date with Kay, he learns of the assassination attempt and is forced to retreat to the family home. There he bunkers down with his older brother, Sonny; Vito's consigliere, Hagen; and the rest of the Corleone gang. The first thing on everyone's mind, including Michael's, is how to defend Vito and the family. But Michael is not involved in the family business. How will he help? It's not clear what he can actually do – yet. The attempt on Vito's life (*external* change) and Michael's retreat to the family home (*internal* choice) mark out the transition to the next act.

The Godfather

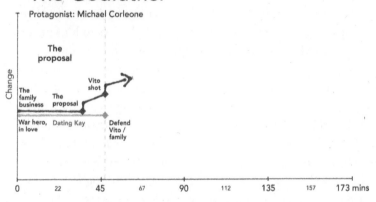

Thankfully, Vito survives the assassination attempt, and while Sonny organises retributions, Michael is kept at arm's length. Ever respectful of his father, Michael does as he is told, but his family's predicament is never far from his mind. He wants to help. The question is, how? With Kay missing him, Michael arranges to meet her in the city for dinner. But when they meet, Michael is distant. He's not the carefree guy we met earlier. He tells Kay he doesn't want her getting involved in his family's problems, and she gets the sense that Michael is changing (and so do we). Michael doesn't break off their relationship, but he says he doesn't know when he'll be able to see her again. It signals the beginning of an *emotional* change in Michael.

Later, Michael goes to the hospital to visit Vito but discovers that his father has been left unguarded. He immediately senses another assassination attempt by Sollozzo. With Sonny across town, and corrupt police officers co-operating in the attack, Michael has no backup – he has to get involved. Using his smarts, Michael recruits a visiting family friend, a humble baker, to pose as a guard with him at the hospital gates. The ruse works. The assassins retreat and Michael stands up to the corrupt police officers called to the scene. Michael is changing *internally*. He no longer wants to stand on the sidelines. As he says to his father in the hospital, 'I'll take care of you now. I'm with you now.'

As Sonny and Hagen argue about how to deal with this dramatic escalation (*external change*), Michael proposes a bold plan that would see him assassinate Sollozzo and the corrupt police chief who organised the attack on Vito. After all, no one will suspect him. He's a college kid. He's not a part of the business. Despite his family's initial scepticism, Michael convinces them that his plan will work. Finally, there is something he can do to avenge the attacks on his father and defend the family business. It's what he's been working towards throughout this entire act.

Michael follows through with his plan and guns down the family's opponents. Despite what he promised Kay, he has changed and become just like his family. The second attempt on Vito's life (*external* change) and Michael's decision to commit to his family and assassinate their opponents (*internal* choice) push the story into the next act.

Unfortunately, Michael's actions do not bring much peace as an all-out war is unleashed between the crime families. Fearing for his safety, the family exile Michael to Sicily. Back home, Vito is devastated to hear that Michael is the one who performed the execution. With the families now in open warfare, Hagen struggles to control Sonny, who is running things while Vito

The Godfather

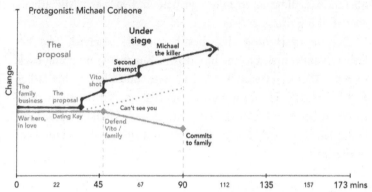

recovers. In an important subplot, Sonny viciously takes his anger out on his brother-in-law Carlo, who has been abusing Sonny's sister Connie (who we saw married at the beginning).

Meanwhile, a heartbroken Kay continues to ask after Michael who has not contacted her since the assassination. Despite his feelings for Kay, Michael meets and marries a Sicilian girl, Apollonia. It seems like an impulsive choice, but it suggests a greater motive in Michael. He is thinking of the family's legacy, of children, of their traditions. Like his choice to kill the family's opponents, he is committing to his family's future and his role in it.

Unfortunately, Michael's enemies have not forgiven his sins and Apollonia is killed in a car bomb that was intended for him. At the same time, Sonny's temper sees him easily targeted for assassination. Don Vito, knowing they are vulnerable, calls a truce and agrees to the demands of the other families. He will not stand in the way of their drug trade and will not break the peace. With his safety guaranteed, Michael returns home, joins the family business and proposes to Kay. He assures her that their operations will be completely legitimate in five years: 'My father's way of doing things is over.'

Despite everything that has happened, Michael, like his father, wants an end to the bloodshed. But there's no going back to his earlier carefree self. He has a responsibility to his father and his family. He must secure their future. Vito's capitulation to the other families (*external* change) and Michael's plans for legitimacy (*internal* choice) signal the transition into the final act of the story.

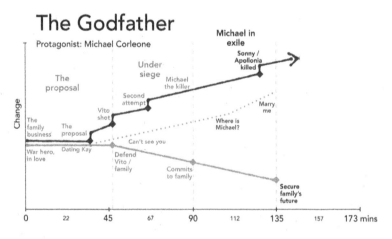

The Godfather

It is a few years later. Michael has been made head of the family business and plans to move to Nevada to buy legitimate casinos and hotels. He is also married to Kay and they have two children. It looks like he is a man of his word. However, despite his assurances to Kay, Michael and Vito suspect there will be more bloodshed during the move to Nevada. Sure enough, their Nevada associate refuses to sell, claiming the Corleone family is finished. But there is a sense that Michael has a plan to get what he wants. We don't know what it is yet, but he makes clear he's focused on securing the family's future. Meanwhile, Vito dies. At the funeral, Michael is invited by one of his senior capos to a meeting to sort out the Nevada dispute. Before he died, Vito warned Michael that whoever invited him to such a meeting would be a traitor and attempt to assassinate him.

Michael sets his plans in motion. During the christening of Connie's son, Michael's godchild, the Corleone gang set about ruthlessly executing the heads of all the other families and their opponents in Nevada (*external* change). After the christening, Michael has the traitor executed as well as Connie's husband, Carlo, who arranged for Sonny's assassination. When Kay learns of Carlo's murder, she begs Michael to swear he didn't kill his brother-in-law. Michael decides (*internal* choice) to lie to Kay and assures her that he had nothing to do with it. She believes him, but then she notices that Michael's men kiss his hand and refer to him as 'Don'. Michael has completed his transformation from uninvolved civilian to ruthless crime boss.

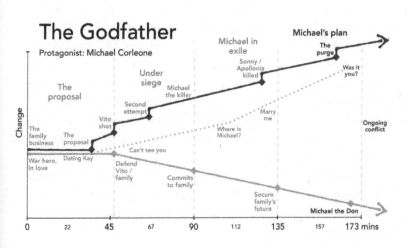

Michael is certainly a Change Character, but is it accurate to say he has a Pessimistic Arc? After all, despite the dangers, he beat his opponents to be the last Don standing. Isn't this what he wanted? Even if Michael has won the battle, he has not won the war – either with his opponents or with himself. Vito's greatest regret was that Michael was not able to escape the family business and lead a legitimate life. But will Michael be able to fulfil Vito's hopes with his own children, even though all of his choices have increased the conflict in his life? Without even taking the sequels into account, the feeling we get at the end of *The Godfather* is that Michael and his family will never escape their violent history.

Under the Skin (2013)

Note: The following story includes depictions of sexual assault and rape.

Written by Jonathon Glazer and Walter Campbell, and loosely based on the novel by Michael Faber, the world of *Under the Skin* is a strange and mysterious one. The film is a science fiction story set in a very recognisable contemporary world. However, unlike most sci-fi, there is very little dialogue and virtually no exposition telling the viewer what sort of world we are in, what its rules are, and what motivates its unnamed characters. It is only by watching what happens that we put the pieces together. And when we do, we are drawn into an eerie and unsettling experience with a strong contemporary relevance that lingers long after the closing credits.

Despite its economical storytelling, *Under the Skin* creates a complex inner life for its central character, an unnamed woman who rarely speaks as she moves through a coherent, nuanced and ultimately Pessimistic Arc.

In the opening sequences of the film, we meet the main character. She is cold and distant as she drives a white van around the streets of Glasgow, looking for a particular sort of man – ones who live alone and have few friends or family. When the woman finds a potential target, she asks for help in a surprisingly warm and friendly way and takes the man back to a dark, dilapidated house. The men expect to have sex with her, but instead, they become submerged and trapped in an infinite black void. The woman then leaves and looks for another victim. She works for a mysterious motorcyclist and has only just been recruited after her predecessor was killed. The woman moves through the world tentatively, as if it is strange and foreign and she is learning about it for the first time.

Despite being largely dialogue-free, the film effectively sets up the main character's *external* world. She is some sort of alien that has taken human form to kidnap unattached men. Why? We don't know yet. What we do know is that she is a form of bait, with a strict role to play, supervised by the mysterious motorcyclist. In her *internal* world, the unnamed woman is cold and indifferent to her role and largely unfamiliar with the human world, even though she mimics it very well.

We see the unnamed woman efficiently performing her missions to trap men in the void. Each time she does this, we gain a little more insight into her world and how it works. For example, the captured men are slowly consumed in the black void and turned into some sort of resource, possibly food, for the aliens.

However, during one unusually messy mission where she kills a man, the woman leaves an infant stranded on a beach. The child is not part of her mission and she appears indifferent to its fate. Even the motorcyclist, who arrives on the beach later to clean up any evidence, leaves the infant on the beach. However, soon after, while waiting in traffic, the woman appears to be haunted by the cries of a screaming child. She looks around to see a crying infant in the next car. She watches the child with curiosity.

It signals a subtle but significant *internal* change in our mysterious protagonist. For the first time, rather than being drawn to the men she is meant to be hunting, the woman notices a child. It introduces a *new and unfamiliar* element, and *conflict*, into the world she is learning about. Perhaps she's even wondering about the nature of her mission and why she is doing it. Regardless, the woman chooses to continue her missions, but it seems like a new perspective is seeping into her *internal* world. The *external* change of the child on the beach, as well as the woman's new *internal* curiosity about the child, push the story into the next act.

Under the Skin

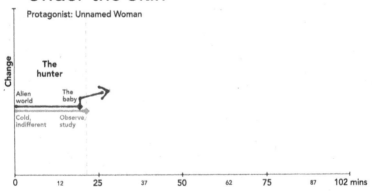

The woman's missions continue, but so does her *internal* change. She starts to focus on women on the street as well as men, as if curious about the difference. At one point, the unnamed woman falls heavily while walking, but she is helped up by complete strangers. Again, she seems bewildered by their actions and we sense her *internal world* struggling to understand this strange species. At one point, the mysterious motorcyclist examines the woman carefully, looking deep into her eyes as if he suspects a change is coming over her.

Later, the woman picks up a man with a severe facial deformity. She seems to connect and perhaps even empathise with the man and his sad story. After luring the man back to the void, the woman sees herself in a mirror, as if for the first time, and realises she looks like the people she has been watching on the streets. As a result, she rescues the man from the pit and escapes. The *external* change of seeing herself in the mirror, as well as the *new and unfamiliar internal* choice to rescue the man with the facial deformity and escape, throw us into the next act of the story.

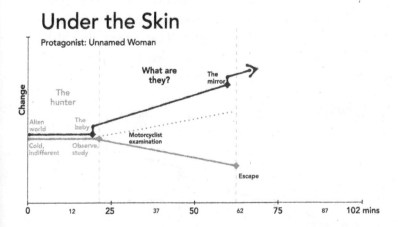

Under the Skin

Protagonist: Unnamed Woman

Unfortunately, her choice to run does not reduce the conflict in her life. As the unnamed woman escapes in her van, the motorcyclist quickly tracks down the escaped man and recaptures him. The motorcyclist joins up with a team as they search the countryside for the woman. The woman abandons the van and walks. At a café, she tries to eat a large slice of cake, just like the people she has been watching, but she can't stomach it and vomits.

Later, she meets a kind man who helps her catch a bus. Again, she is bewildered by the empathy shown to her and goes with the man back to his place. He prepares a warm bed and a cup of tea and gives her privacy. The kind man shows the unnamed woman around and we see her mimicking his actions, tapping along to music as if trying to understand this strange human. Alone at night, she looks at herself in a mirror, examining her body, discovering how it looks and moves. One night, the woman kisses the kind man and they begin to have sex until the man, unnerved, has to stop. There is a problem. Despite external appearances, she has no internal genitalia. No matter how good she is at mimicking this strange species, she will never be like them. She flees. The discovery of her strange, alien biology (*external* change) and her decision to leave the comfort of the kind man (*internal* choice) push the story into the final act.

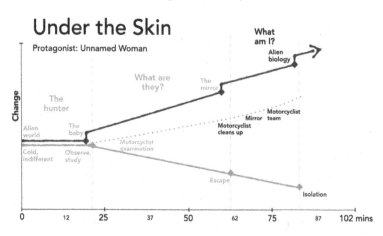

Under the Skin

Protagonist: Unnamed Woman

What am I?

What are they?

The hunter

Alien biology

The mirror

Motorcyclist team

Mirror

Motorcyclist cleans up

Alien world

The baby

Change

Cold, indifferent

Observe, study

Motorcyclist examination

Escape

Isolation

0   12   25   37   50   62   75   87   102 mins

114

Again, the woman's *new and unfamiliar* choice to escape is fraught with danger and risk – and the motorcyclists are still hunting her. When she reaches a remote forest she comes across a forester who offers advice on where she should and should not go. She finds a hiker's cabin and sleeps, but is woken by someone sexually assaulting her. It's the forester.

The woman runs but the forester corners the woman and tries to rape her. She fights back and, in the struggle that follows, the woman's skin peels off her back and reveals her alien biology underneath. She is smooth, largely featureless and inky black, like the void used to trap the men. The woman/alien slips her human skin off like a glove and holds her bewildered face in her hands. She has *internally changed*. Finally, she can see who she is under the skin and understands her alienness. Unfortunately, the forester returns and douses the woman/ alien in petrol, setting her alight. As the mysterious motorcyclists look for her, the woman's/ alien's body lies smouldering on the edge of a forest covered in snow.

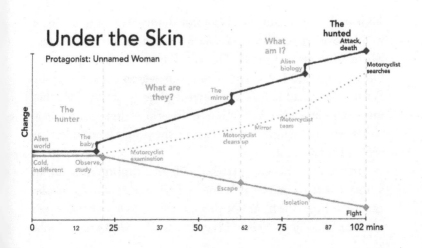

115

It is a dark, brutal and pessimistic end for the woman/alien. Despite her brave *internal* choices that allowed her to escape and realise her true nature, the conflict in her world was not resolved. The *external* world around her was one full of conflict – the mysterious oppressive motorcyclists, the sex-starved men she kidnapped, the rapist/forester. The eerie world of this film is one where you are either a hunter or the hunted. The spare use of dialogue and exposition creates space for the viewer to identify with the alien woman's disorientation, while at the same time recognise the inherent danger of her situation. Indeed, the bleak and recognisable setting seems to underline the writer's pessimistic outlook and give the film a grounded, contemporary relevance beyond its sci-fi premise. It is a place where emotional change might be possible, even for an alien, but freedom from sexual violence is not. *Under the Skin* is not for everyone, but it is a film that is not easily forgotten.

Burning (2018)

Burning is a haunting psychological drama that begins with a simple love triangle and transforms into a mysterious enigma where trust and truth are illusive. The screenplay, written by Oh Jung-mi and Lee Chang-dong, is based on a short story by Haruki Murakami. It is a masterful piece of storytelling that immerses the viewer in the internal world of Jong-su, a lonely writer who is trying to make sense of the people around him as well as his own past.

Jong-su is a Change Character with a Pessimistic Arc, but, in a story where truth, lies, delusion and fantasy constantly collide, can we be sure? The film's opening introduces us to our character's *external* world. Jong-su is in his early twenties, works menial jobs and comes from a poor farming family. He was raised by his short-tempered father who is currently facing a jail sentence, and his mother left when he was very young. In Jong-su's *internal* world, he is shy and reserved and harbours dreams of being a writer, but he isn't sure what he wants to write about.

One day, Jong-su bumps into Hai-mi, a friend from his childhood, but he does not initially recognise her. She explains to him that she has had plastic surgery. Shy Jong-su is instantly attracted to the beautiful and ethereal Hai-mi. In an intriguing café scene, Hai-mi talks about her interest in pantomime and make-believe as Jong-su listens intently. He's smitten. Then she asks Jong-su to take care of her cat while she goes on a trip to Africa.

They go to her tiny flat to meet the cat, whose name is Boil, but it's nowhere to be seen. Hai-mi explains that the cat tends to hide from strangers. Jong-su and Hai-mi start to kiss and have sex. It is a profound experience for shy Jong-su and signals the potential for a deep emotional change in him. His chance meeting with Hai-mi (*external* change) and decision to sleep with her (*internal* choice) push the story into the next act.

Burning

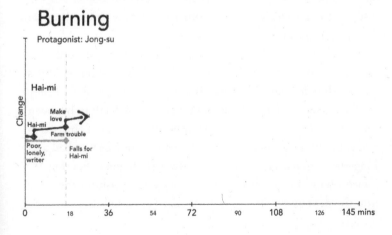

Protagonist: Jong-su

Jong-su returns to the family farm to take care of things while his father awaits trial for assaulting a state official. He keeps getting phone calls on the home phone, but the caller never speaks. In an important subplot, Jong-su's father is instructed during his court case to apologise to the state official to avoid a jail term. His lawyer also contacts Jong-su and urges him to persuade his father to accept the terms. But Jong-su doesn't visit his father. Instead, he travels to Hai-mi's house to feed her cat, even though he has never seen it. Infatuated with Hai-mi, Jong-su masturbates on her bed each time he visits.

One day, he goes to the airport to pick up Hai-mi, but she is not alone – she is with a wealthy and enigmatic young man in his late twenties called Ben. Over food and drinks, Jong-su learns that they met in Africa while waiting for a delayed flight. Hai-mi becomes emotional when recounting her travels, claiming the beautiful sunsets made her feel lonely and wish she could disappear. But Jong-su is more interested in the mysterious Ben and asks what he does for a living. Ben tells Jong-su that he wouldn't understand and cryptically says 'I play'. As he's leaving, Ben offers to drop Hai-mi home. Feeling inferior to the wealthy and sophisticated newcomer, Jong-su does not stop him.

This choice is fairly typical of Jong-su – he isn't as confident as Ben – and the encounter troubles him. What is Ben's relationship to Hai-mi? What is Jong-su to Hai-mi? Are they boyfriend and girlfriend? Did he imagine those feelings between them that day in the flat? He's quietly hurt and confused – and his conflict grows. The *external* change of Ben's arrival and Jong-su's *internal* choice not to assert his obvious affection for Hai-mi sees him slip back into his old ways, pushing the story into the next act.

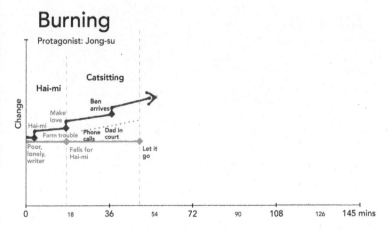

Jong-su returns to the farm and tries to gain support for his father through a local petition, but few people want to sign it. It seems that his father is not liked. When Hai-mi unexpectedly invites Jong-su to meet in the city, he is disappointed to see that Ben is there too. He begins to suspect that Ben is 'playing' with Hai-mi's affections. Having let it go before, Jong-su decides to reconnect with Hai-mi and find out more about his wealthy rival. It's a *new and unfamiliar* choice for shy Jong-su, and we get the sense he is *internally* changing.

It's worth noting here how Jong-su's strong *internal* choice helps solidify the direction of this new act in the story. As we've discussed, a new act in a story is normally proceeded by a strong internal choice by the protagonist. This choice gives the story direction. It indicates what the character will do about the conflict they're experiencing. But, Jong-su doesn't challenge Ben's relationship with Hai-mi, at least not initially. It's a weak choice that effectively underlines Jong-su's timid nature. If the rest of the story continued this way, Hai-mi and Jong-su would probably drift apart (and so would the story). However, given a second

Burning

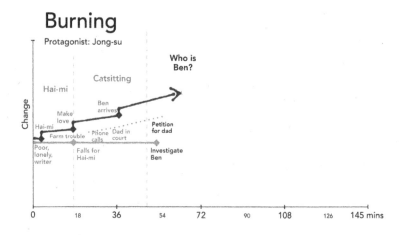

Protagonist: Jong-su

Change

Poor, lonely, writer

Hai-mi

Make love

Hai-mi

Farm trouble · Falls for Hai-mi

Catsitting

Ben arrives

Phone calls

Dad in court

Petition for dad

Investigate Ben

Who is Ben?

0   18   36   54   72   90   108   126   145 mins

chance, Jong-su takes the opportunity to quietly investigate his rival. It's a *new and unfamiliar* choice and signals he's capable of *internal* change.

During a visit to Ben's apartment, Jong-su finds a bathroom drawer full of women's jewellery. Whose is it and why does Ben have it? As a humble farmer's boy, Jong-su becomes suspicious of Ben's Gatsby-style existence and warns Hai-mi that Ben is using her. We see Jong-su's first pangs of jealousy towards urban sophisticates like Ben. Sure enough, during a night out, Ben and his friends slyly make fun of Hai-mi's naivety when she performs an African dance she witnessed while travelling. Jong-su catches Ben yawning as Hai-mi dances as if he is already bored of her.

Soon after, Hai-mi and Ben unexpectedly visit Jong-su at his family farm. As they drink, Hai-mi recalls how Jong-su saved her from a well when they were kids, but he doesn't remember the incident. They smoke weed and Hai-mi takes her top off and dances semi-naked as the sun goes down. Later, while she sleeps, Ben tells Jong-su that he likes to burn abandoned greenhouses for fun. In fact, he plans to destroy one nearby. Feeling unusually bold, Jong-su declares that he loves Hai-mi, but Ben just laughs at him.

The next morning, angry at how things are turning out, Jong-su scolds Hai-mi for her naked display. She is hurt and leaves with Ben. In the next few days, Jong-su tries to call Hai-mi, but she doesn't answer. At the same time, he maps the greenhouses near the farm but doubts Ben's claim about the fires, as well as everything else about him. Despite his growing suspicions about Ben, he has learnt little, and now Hai-mi is turning away from him. Things are not going well, and his choices, his paranoia, his angry outburst, are not helping. He is emotionally changing but failing to reduce the conflict.

Then, after days of trying, Jong-su receives a mysterious, unintelligible phone call from Hai-mi. He rushes to her apartment but the code has changed. Where is Hai-mi? Is she okay? Her mysterious call (*external* change) and Jong-su's decision (*internal* choice) to investigate push the story into the next act.

Burning

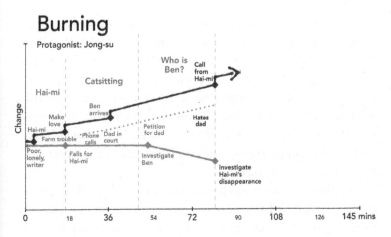

Jong-su keeps trying to call Hai-mi and persuades her landlady to let him inside the apartment. It is unnaturally clean, which is not how Hai-mi kept it. Her suitcase is still there, so she hasn't gone travelling. He looks for her at her classes, at work, but no one has seen her. He even follows Ben to a restaurant and asks if he has seen her, but he hasn't. When asked about the burning of the greenhouse, Ben says that he did it, but Jong-su disputes the claim. As Ben leaves with another woman, he admits that Jong-su was special to Hai-mi – she told him – and that it made him jealous. Convinced Ben is behind Hai-mi's disappearance, Jong-su follows him to a church, an art gallery and, ominously, a remote lake where Ben simply looks over the water. But there is no proof that he knows anything about Hai-mi's disappearance.

Jong-su also finds out from old family friends that Hai-mi's story about the childhood well is not true. Later, however, his mother contacts him asking for money and claims that she remembers a well near their house. Jong-su is bewildered. Who can he believe?

With his anger and confusion building, Jong-su is caught hanging outside Ben's place and gets invited in for a party. Ben is friendly and asks how the book is going, but Jong-su admits he doesn't know what to write about. 'The world is an enigma,' he says. During the party, Jong-su finds a pink watch in the bathroom drawer that is just like the one Hai-mi had. Also, Ben now has a cat that answers to the name of Boil, the name of Hai-mi's cat. As Jong-su leaves in bewilderment, Ben urges him to be less serious and have fun.

The discovery of the jewellery and the cat dramatically raise the conflict for Jong-su. But what will he do about it? Is Ben a killer? Can Jong-su believe anything Hai-mi said? He appears paralysed with confusion. Like Michael Corleone in the moments leading up to the purge in *The Godfather*, it is difficult to know what Jong-su is thinking or planning, if anything. Strangely, Jong-su leaves the party without confrontation – just like he did when he first met Ben. Is he reverting to his old timid ways? Or does he have a plan? It's hard to tell. The discovery of the jewellery and the cat (*external* change) and Jong-su's enigmatic decision (*internal* choice) push the story into the next act.

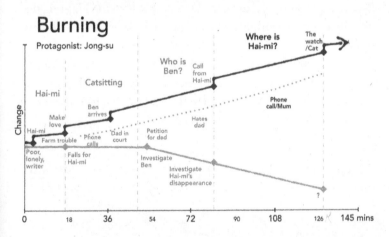

Sometime later, Jong-su's father refuses to apologise to the public official and is sentenced to jail. Jong-su sells the last cow on the farm and moves into Hai-mi's old apartment where he dreams of her and cries. One morning, he sits and starts to write. In the meantime, we see Ben in his luxury apartment putting make-up on his new girlfriend. It is an eerie scene, brimming with quiet threat.

Then, in the closing sequence, Jong-su invites Ben to meet him by a road. As always, Ben is friendly and expecting to hear news about Hai-mi. But instead, Jong-su stabs Ben to death and sets his body alight. Afterwards, Jong-su strips naked, burns his clothes and drives away.

Jong-su's journey from a shy and quiet aspiring writer to this violent killer is shocking but not altogether unexpected. Throughout the film, Jong-su harboured a quiet anger that was reflected in his fraught and distant relationship with his father and absent mother. He is poor, lonely and anxious, living on the fringes of South Korean life, and his growing jealousy of wealthy Ben was palpable throughout. Despite his love for Hai-mi, she lives in a fantasy world that he cannot completely believe. As his jealousy of Ben drives Hai-mi away, the world Jong-su barely had a grip on transforms into a puzzling enigma that he no longer understands. Hai-mi's disappearance and Ben's wilfully secretive life push Jong-su to despair and violence. His change is dramatic and his arc is deeply pessimistic. Or is it?

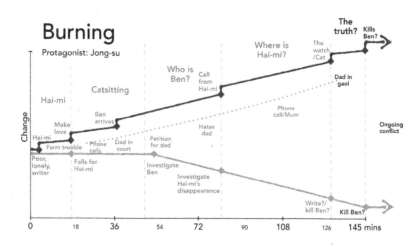

Just before Ben's apparent murder, we see Jong-su finally writing, like he always wanted to do. Does he finally know what he wants to write about? After this point, is the scene with Ben part of a story or an imagined reality? Is it making sense of the enigma Jong-su has been living through, one that will prevent the violence that has destroyed his father's life? If it is, then it gives the ending a very different tone, one that is more ambivalent. Or is this another fantasy, like Hai-mi's story about the well or the cat? Were they real or not? It is impossible to tell – which is exactly the point. Like Jong-su, the viewer is trapped in a finely tuned enigma that will never give up its answers.

Summary: Powerless, dark, despairing

These films offer stories that are mesmerising, compelling and highly original in their exploration of characters struggling to emotionally change in the face of escalating conflict. But their efforts are ultimately futile and their choices lead to despair as the world overwhelms and crushes them.

Let's face it, the world can be overwhelming. Sometimes we make the wrong choices. Unlike the Hero's Journey, things don't always work out. It's a very human experience. Some would say it's *the* most human experience. Through stories like these, we have the opportunity to live vicariously through another person's pain and empathise with their demise from a safe and sobering distance.

In many ways, this is what stories do best – they allow us to experience another person's life and empathise with the beliefs and values that drive them through their world, no matter how things turn out. Maybe we recognise their pain and feel less alone. Other times, we might better understand the strange choices that lie behind other people's actions. Or maybe we just feel more grateful for the life we do have. While stories with a Pessimistic

Arc may take the shine off a date night, they do us a favour. They connect us more deeply with others. To explore more films featuring a Change Character with a Pessimistic Arc, check out *Mystic River, Another Round, Animal Kingdom, The Vanishing, Black Swan, Beanpole, Snowtown, Seven, Sunset Boulevard, Gone Girl, Kiss of the Spider Woman* and *Macbeth.*

PART III

CONSTANT CHARACTERS

CHAPTER 5

'Maybe you should rethink those ties': Constant Characters with Optimistic Arcs

The next few chapters are about the unsung 'heroes' of storytelling – Constant Characters. In screenwriting books and courses, they don't get as much attention as Change Characters, partly because they don't fit the strict demands of the Hero's Journey. They don't *emotionally* change. They have essentially the same internal values, beliefs and desires at the end of the story as they did at the beginning. As a result, it's harder to make these characters fit into a prefabricated emotional arc because they do things their own way. They're square pegs in round holes from fade up to fade down. They're stubborn. Often infuriating. They don't fit into the world around them. In fact, it's the world around a Constant Character that usually changes, not the other way around.

Despite this, the characters you'll meet in the following chapters are some of the most inspiring, fascinating, surprising and tragic ever committed to screen. They also front some of the biggest box office successes in film history, such as *Jaws*, *Die Hard*, *Paddington*, *Back to the Future*, *The Hunger Games*, *Alien* and *Raiders of the Lost Ark*.

Constant Characters may be underappreciated in screenplay books, but audiences understand their value. In fact, I would argue that the majority of fictional characters we encounter are

Constant Characters. That's because television, which makes up most of our storytelling diet these days, is fundamentally built around them. And it makes sense. The character arcs in television unfold over years. If a television character changes too quickly in two or three episodes, then they become a different person and the story is over. They can't change again over the next three episodes and become someone else. If they did, we'd doubt the credibility of the character or conclude we were watching a spin-off of Doctor Who. If television characters change at all, they change very slowly. If Walter White had turned from Mr Chips into Scarface by the beginning of Season 2, the story for *Breaking Bad* would have flatlined and audiences would have tuned out long before his final bloody showdown. Don Draper doesn't really change at all. He goes from an urbane narcissist who sells cigarettes to a hippy narcissist who sells sugar water. And who wants to see Selina Meyers from *Veep* become a less terrible human being? Where's the fun in that?

Constant Characters have an inner strength and belief that protects them from the emotional assaults of the world around them. Often they succeed (*Hidden Figures, Just Mercy, Twelve Angry Men, The King of Comedy, Apollo 13*). Sometimes it sows the seeds of their destruction (*Uncut Gems, I Care a Lot, Chinatown, No Country for Old Men, There Will Be Blood, Citizen Kane*). And other times it's a bit of both (*The Report, The Hurt Locker, Ford v Ferrari, Nightcrawler, Amour*).

For better or worse, Constant Characters don't seem to learn a lot from the world around them. Despite this, there's a lot they can teach us about the breadth and depth of storytelling. Let's take a look at three Constant Characters with an Optimistic Arc – stories where being a stubborn pain-in-the-ass is actually a good thing.

Erin Brockovich (2000)

Susannah Grant's witty and stirring screenplay for *Erin Brockovich* is drawn from the real-life story of a potty-mouthed single mother who goes from destitution to high-profile lawyer in a few short years.

In the film's opening sequences, we meet Erin and learn that, in her *external* world, she is a single mother, twice divorced and unemployed. She has very little work experience, certainly not enough to be a doctor, which is the job she's applying for in the opening scene. She's had it hard in life and things only get worse when she has a car accident.

We get a key insight into her *internal* world when, during the court case for the car accident, Erin launches a hot-tempered, foul-mouthed attack at the rich lawyer who crashed into her. It becomes obvious that Erin can be sweet and charming when she wants to be, but distrustful and defensive when judged.

When Erin's case fails and she can't land a job, she demands that her lawyer, a grumpy but loveable guy called Ed, give her a job in his firm. In a terrific scene, we see the two sides of Erin – the ballsy firecracker who isn't afraid to say what she thinks, and the vulnerable single mother doing what she can to provide for her kids. Ed agrees to help and gives her a lowly admin job with no benefits.

The failed court case (*external* change) and Erin's gutsy decision (*internal* choice) to demand a job from Ed set up the next act of the story. It's telling how brazen Erin's choice is here. She's shaping the world to her will. Look out for more of this.

Erin Brockovich

Protagonist: Erin Brockovich

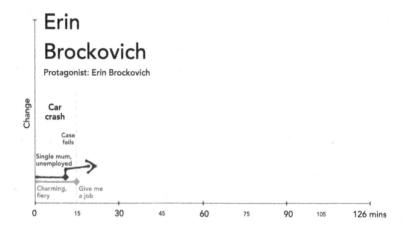

Erin tries to fit in around Ed's firm, but her brashness and questionable dress sense alienate her from the other women around the office. When Ed suggests she reconsider her attire, Erin snaps back that he should rethink his ties. It's a simple but effective example of Erin shaping the world around her (no prizes for guessing who is wearing better ties by the end of the story).

At the same time, Erin is struggling to find a babysitter for her kids and agrees to allow her next-door neighbour, George, a biker and part-time construction worker, to help. But she warns him it won't get him laid.

Her situation takes a turn when Erin comes across a case at work that intrigues her. It is a pro-bono job regarding real estate valuations in a small town called Hinkley. She finds medical records in the files and wonders what they have to do with real estate. Erin asks Ed if she can investigate it further and he distractedly agrees. The Hinkley case (*external* change) and Erin's decision to pursue it (*internal* choice) push the story into the next act.

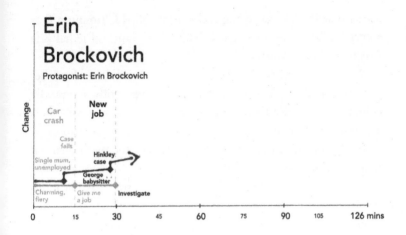

Let's stop for a second and consider those first two acts. They're quite short, each about fifteen minutes in length, but they each have a specific function that helps establish the story. The first sets up Erin's character and ends with her choice to demand a job. The second sets up the legal case that will shape the rest of the story and ends with her choice to investigate. You could look at these two acts as one and just call it the 'setup', but I think that hides the effectiveness of Susannah Grant's writing. The first act is mostly character (the internal stuff), the second is mostly about plot (the external stuff). Separating these two parts makes the details of character and plot easy to follow. Grant also holds back on an important subplot, Erin's relationship with George. She leaves this for the next act when we can pay attention to this important development and give it the emphasis it requires.

With Ed's apparent permission, Erin heads off to Hinkley for a week of research. She discovers that a corporation, Pacific Gas and Electricity, is mysteriously buying up houses in a small town and paying for residents' medical bills. Digging around, Erin learns that PG&E was using a chemical called Chromium 6 as a rust inhibitor, even though it had a wide range of lethal side effects, including cancer.

When Erin returns to work, she finds that Ed has fired her for disappearing for a week. She storms out with a typically colourful spray of offensive language. Erin unexpectedly finds a sympathetic shoulder with biker George, and the two grow closer. Ever distrustful, she tells him not to be too nice to her – it makes her nervous.

Soon after, Ed calls around with news that some chemical test results have arrived from Erin's Hinkley research. It sounds like a serious contamination has taken place and he wants to know about it. But Erin won't tell him until he rehires her with a raise and benefits. Once again, Erin shapes the world around her and gets her way. The arrival of the Hinkley research (*external* change) and Erin's decision to strongarm Ed (*internal* choice) push the story into the next act.

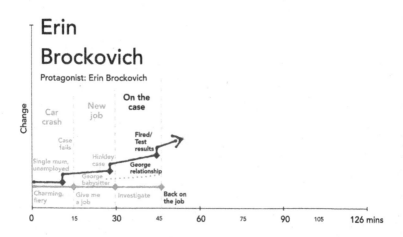

Erin Brockovich

Protagonist: Erin Brockovich

134

The next act is a big one – almost an hour of screen time. That's huge, but it's the heart of the story. In this act, we see Erin on the case, spending days, weeks and months driving all over Hinkley interviewing residents affected by PG&E's contamination. No one has made the connection between the PG&E plant and the illnesses that are killing people all over town. Erin has to persuade people to tell their stories so she can put the pieces together and prepare a case. Despite their distrust of outsiders, down-to-earth Erin is more than capable of winning the trust of the townsfolk. What she lacks in legal expertise Erin makes up for in people expertise. She knows these simple, working-class folk. She's one of them, and she is moved by their sad stories.

Throughout the act, despite the size and complexity of what she is tackling, it is Erin's inner qualities that are making the difference – her ability to connect to ordinary people, her dogged determination, her distrust of authority, her relentless hard work. Erin doesn't have to change to succeed; she just has to keep being who she already is.

But there are forces in her life that are trying to change her. George and the kids struggle to cope with her absence. Ed tries to reign in Erin's unorthodox methods. The other lawyers on the case make assumptions about her competence. The women in Ed's office judge Erin for her attire and special treatment. One by one, we see each of these obstacles come around to Erin's way of thinking. George learns to be a supportive boyfriend, her kids start to back their mother and the office ladies look out for Erin. Even grumpy Ed starts swearing to let off steam. Erin, however, is not changing. She's changing the world.

The case is coming together until a law firm Ed has recruited resorts to binding arbitration rather than a trial. A judge will decide the outcome with no jury or appeal. The Hinkley residents feel like they've been cheated by fancy city lawyers. It's up to an exhausted Erin to win them back. She needs signatures from ninety per cent of them or the case will collapse. This threat (*external* change) and Erin stepping up to save the day (*internal* choice) push the story into the final act.

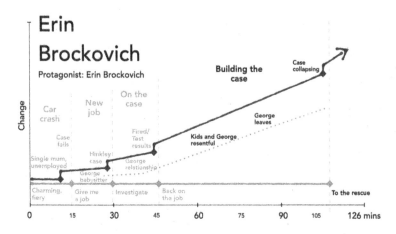

Erin moves into a Hinkley hotel with George and the kids so she can work 24/7. She's making progress, but there's still no smoking gun that will prove PG&E's parent company knew about the contamination. Without this evidence, they could still get away with it. But Erin's unique way with people uncovers an ex-employee who was asked to shred crucial documents – only he didn't shred them all. Erin and Ed present the signatures and the evidence to their astonished case partners. They win the case. It's one of the biggest settlements in US history.

In the final scene, Ed presents Erin with a cheque for her share of the proceeds, but he warns her that it's not what they agreed on. Erin, ever the suspicious hothead, berates Ed for cheating her until she realises the cheque is for a lot more than the agreed amount. For once, Erin is the one making assumptions and Ed loves every second of it. But make no mistake, this display of humility is momentary. Erin is still the same firecracker she was at the beginning.

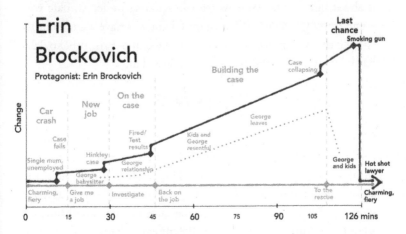

It is the David and Goliath scale of this story that makes it work. Whatever obstacle Erin comes across, no matter how big, she is willing to take it on, despite conventional wisdom telling her to leave it be. And most of the time she succeeds. Sure, there are moments of self-doubt, but mostly Erin is winning, and any setbacks are because of other people's incompetence.

Normally, this would be pretty dull to watch because the protagonist has just been kicking goals the whole time. There's no tension because it feels inevitable they will win. In *Erin Brockovich*, the tension comes from the scale of the battle. It's a real-life story and we know that Erin wins the case. What we don't know is *how*? The stakes are so high. She is so outgunned. How does this ordinary woman beat a giant corporation?

This brings us to the themes of the film and what makes Erin's arc optimistic. Her unique inner qualities enable her not only to resolve a great conflict in her own life but also in the lives of her clients. This is an inspiring story of resilience and self-belief in the face of doubt and prejudice. Erin's battle for herself and her clients is about fighting for your worth when others underestimate you – and never giving up. If Constant Characters have a tendency to change the world around them, then the name 'Erin Brockovich' has become synonymous with doing just that.

Moana (2016)

Constant Characters already have a good sense of who they are at the beginning of the story, even if they haven't taken the time to think about it yet. The story of the Polynesian princess Moana is a great example of this. Written by Jared Bush, *Moana* is about a young girl who is destined to be the queen of her small isolated island. The film draws on various Polynesian cultures and legends, and crafts an inspiring tale of courage and identity.

The story begins with a (fictional) Polynesian creation story in which the goddess Te Fiti makes islands in the ancient oceans of the world, thus creating life. But the mischievous demigod Maui steals Te Fiti's heart, a green stone, to give humans the power to make life. Maui is attacked by Te Kā, a volcanic demon, and the heart of Te Fiti is lost in the ocean and Maui is never seen again.

When we meet Moana, she is a tiny infant listening to her grandmother, Tala, tell this creation story. Her eyes are alight as her grandmother reveals that the heart of Te Fiti will one day be found beyond the reef that surrounds the isolated island where they live. In this opening image of the wide-eyed Moana, we gain a powerful insight: she longs for adventure.

In the next few sequences, we learn that Moana, in her

external world, is a princess, and that her culture and strict father forbid anyone from venturing beyond the reef. According to conventional wisdom, the island provides everything they need. In Moana's *internal* world, she longs to go beyond the reef and see more of the world she instinctively knows is out there. However, she also loves and respects her culture and father, and accepts her role as princess on the island.

But when a blight ruins the island's crops and fish supply, food becomes scarce. Moana's grandmother says the blight is a curse that was created when Maui stole the heart of Te Fiti. Someone must find Maui and restore the heart – and that someone is Moana. Grandmother Tala shows Moana a hidden cave and shares the secret seafaring traditions of their people. She also reveals that the ocean once showed Te Fiti's heart to Moana when she was an infant. Grandmother Tala gives Moana a beautiful green stone, Te Fiti's heart, and says the ocean chose her to restore it. Moana knows she is destined to go beyond the reef on behalf of her people. One night, she takes an old boat and sets sail. The arrival of the blight (*external* change) and

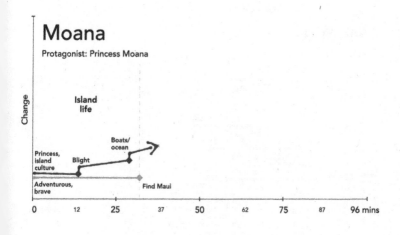

Moana

Protagonist: Princess Moana

Change

Island life

Boats/ ocean

Princess, island culture

Blight

Adventurous, brave

Find Maui

0   12   25   37   50   62   75   87   96 mins

Moana's decision to accept the challenge of finding Maui and restoring Te Fiti's heart (*internal* choice) push the story into the next act.

Despite a serious lack of seafaring credentials, Moana bravely navigates the oceans guided by a fishhook constellation that, legend says, will show her where Maui is. After surviving a storm, she finds Maui, but he is reluctant to help. He tells her that he lost his magical fishhook weapon in the fight with Te Kā, the volcanic demon. Without it, he can't transform into other creatures and beat Te Kā. Following a dangerous and hilarious attack by coconut creatures, Moana persuades Maui that he would be a hero again if he helped. Her appeal to Maui's vanity works and he agrees. But first, they have to get his fishhook back. Maui's unexpected refusal to help (*external* change) and Moana's clever decision to appeal to his vanity (*internal* choice) push the story into the next act.

Maui reluctantly teaches Moana to sail and they arrive at the lair of Tamatoa, a giant crab who has found Maui's magical

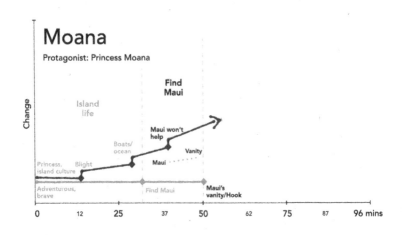

fishhook. Moana tricks Tamatoa and they escape with the weapon. But Maui finds he can't control the hook's shapeshifting powers anymore. He becomes discouraged and reveals he is an orphan that the gods adopted. They gave him the magical fishhook and made him Maui. Moana reassures him that the gods don't get to decide who he is – only Maui can do that. With this encouragement, Maui regains his shapeshifting powers and, with Moana on the boat's rudder, they set sail to restore the heart of Te Fiti.

Have you noticed who's doing the changing here? Sure, Moana can sail now, but is she really different from the adventure seeker we met at the beginning? Like Erin Brockovich, Moana is changing the people around her.

Moana and Maui arrive at the island of Te Fiti. With Te Fiti's heart in his possession, Maui once again takes on Te Kā. But the volcanic monster is still too strong and Maui loses, damaging his fishhook badly. One more hit and he could lose it forever. Maui gives up. Without his hook he is nothing, so he leaves.

Left all alone, Moana questions why the ocean chose her for this important journey. It's been a nagging question for Moana, but now it seems to be overwhelming her. A vision of her grandmother, Tala, appears and offers to lead her home, but Moana hesitates. She doesn't want to go back. She knows it is her destiny to go further than her people have ever gone and fulfil the ocean's calling. She realises something she has always instinctively known – the ocean's call is inside her and always has been. Maui's unexpected departure (*external* change) and Moana's recommitment to her destiny (*internal* choice) push the story into the final act.

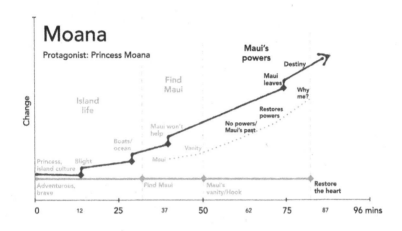

Moana

Protagonist: Princess Moana

Moana repairs her boat and takes on Te Fā. She outsmarts the demon and makes it past the barrier island to Te Fiti. But the island is gone. Moana now realises that Te Kā and Te Fiti are one and the same. The volcanic demon is the creation goddess without her heart. Maui returns to help Moana and sacrifices his magical fishhook in the battle. Trusting her destiny, Moana faces Te Fā and replaces her heart. Te Fā transforms into Te Fiti, the creation goddess. Life returns to the islands. Her people are saved. In the final sequence, Te Fiti rewards Maui with a new magical hook, and Moana, as chief wayfinder, leads her people past the reef and out to sea in a beautiful flotilla of boats.

Throughout the story, Moana's internal world revolved around curiosity, bravery and self-belief, qualities that were on display from the very first scene. Along the way, she transformed Maui's idea about who he was, as well as that of her people, and even resolved Te Fiti's identity crisis. The fact that Moana transforms a god qualifies her as a hero in the traditional sense, but probably not in the Hero's Journey sense. This is because she doesn't emotionally transform, nor does her grandmother, Tala, who has been a truth-teller from the very beginning. Moana has changed the world, not the other way around, giving her a powerfully Optimistic Arc.

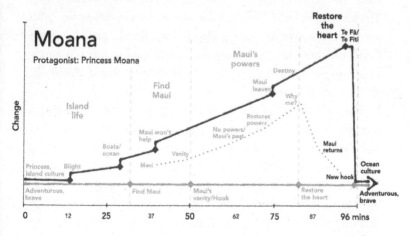

Thematically, Moana's arc describes a story about knowing who you are and trusting your destiny, no matter what is thrown your way. It's a powerful and inspiring theme and explains the film's popularity. However, it is more than a little ironic that a story celebrating cultural identity has been collaged together by a largely white American story team using several different Pacific Island communities. In a way, Moana's fictional island has become more famous than the under-represented communities it is based on. But this is Disney, after all. It's an early attempt at diversity from a cultural juggernaut that has an unfortunate history of cringeworthy stereotypes and cliches. Let's hope they build on this tentative start by employing more writers from a range of backgrounds who can write diverse stories that are as entertaining and smile-inducing as *Moana*.

A Fantastic Woman (2017)

Note: The following story includes depictions of sexual assault.

The screenplay for *A Fantastic Woman,* written by Sebastián Lelio and Gonzalo Maza, takes a deceptively simple premise – the death of a spouse – and creates a heartbreaking but ultimately uplifting portrayal of a woman defending her love and identity in the face of cruel prejudice.

The protagonist of the story is Marina, a professional singer and waitress. In the opening sequences, we meet Marina and her boyfriend, Orlando, a manager in a textiles factory. It's an unusual relationship in that Orlando is significantly older than Marina, and Marina is transgender. But they are confident and comfortable around each other. They have nothing to hide. Over a birthday dinner, Orlando gives Marina a note promising a luxurious resort holiday (after having mislaid the tickets he'd purchased earlier). They celebrate and dance together and are clearly in love.

So, in Marina's *external* world, she is comfortable and content in both love and life. She loves her singing. She loves her boyfriend. In Marina's *internal* world, she has the confidence and strength to pursue a fulfilling life despite significant societal obstacles relating to Orlando's age and her transsexuality.

Later that night, back at Orlando's apartment, Orlando wakes with a crushing headache. Marina hurries to get him to the hospital, but he falls down the stairs and injures himself. At the hospital, as Orlando is being attended to, Marina is treated with suspicion by the hospital staff as she gives her name and explains what happened to her partner. Eventually, a doctor reveals that Orlando has died.

Marina calls Orlando's brother, Gabo, to tell him the news. As she waits, Marina grows increasingly anxious and runs away from the hospital. To her surprise, she is intercepted by the police. Back at the hospital, the police have questions regarding the bruises on Orlando's body, a detail Marina has already shared with the doctors. They ask for ID to confirm her name and gender and want to know why she ran away. Marina is saved by Gabo, Orlando's brother, who asks that she be let go before the family arrives. He tells them that it's a 'sensitive situation'. The *external* change of Orlando's death sees Marina make an impulsive *internal* choice to run away. While it is not a particularly conscious choice, it does signal a transition to the next act and shapes how the rest of the story unfolds.

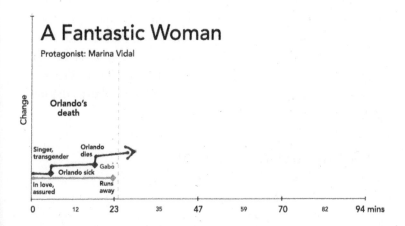

A Fantastic Woman

Protagonist: Marina Vidal

Marina goes to work at a bar but doesn't mention to her boss what happened the night before, even though they appear to be friends. While she's working, Marina is contacted by Sonia, Orlando's ex-wife, who arranges for the return of his car and apartment keys. A sceptical detective also visits Marina and asks questions about the bruises on Orlando's body. Her attitude to Marina is condescending, but Marina stands up for herself.

The next morning, Bruno, Orlando's son, lets himself into the apartment and intimidates Marina, questioning her gender and relationship with his father. He wants to take Orlando's dog, Diabla, but Marina insists Orlando gave the dog to her. During his visit, Bruno constantly calls Marina the wrong name, which she defiantly corrects.

On the way to drop off the car to Sonia, Marina sees a vision of Orlando sitting in the back seat. Afterwards, she finds a locker key in the car with a strange label – 181 – and decides to keep it. Perhaps this is where Orlando left the tickets for their dream holiday.

Sonia, like all the others, questions Marina's gender and relationship with Orlando, cruelly dismissing their love as a 'perversion'. She tries to bribe Marina and forbids her from attending Orlando's funeral or wake. Again, Marina bravely defends herself as she considers her options. Sonia's demand (*external* change) signals a shift into a new act as Marina debates what to do (*internal* choice).

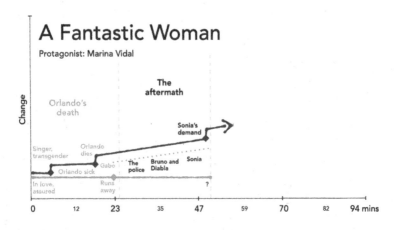

A Fantastic Woman

Protagonist: Marina Vidal

Despite Marina not making a clear choice about this new development, she has consistently defended her relationship with Orlando and her identity throughout the act, just as she did at the start. The pressure is building and, so far, Marina is holding firm.

Marina visits the detective from earlier and is humiliated when she is forced to undergo a physical examination. Apart from looking for evidence of a struggle, it is an attempt to intimidate Marina, using her transsexuality against her. But there is no evidence and Marina is released. Later, Gabo calls and offers to give Marina some of Orlando's ashes in return for not coming to the wake, but Marina hangs up on him.

Marina visits her singing tutor, who scolds her for missing her last lesson. But they have a loving relationship and, again, like her boss, Marina doesn't mention Orlando's death. We get the feeling Marina doesn't lumber people with her problems. She is strong and independent. A quality she has needed in order to survive.

Back at Orlando's apartment, Marina discovers that Bruno has come back and stolen Diabla, Orlando's dog. She's angry and makes a call to find out where the wake is being held. With the help of her sister, Marina moves out of Orlando's apartment and races off to the wake. As she enters, Sonia makes a scene and demands that Marina leave. When Orlando's daughter starts to cry, Marina respects the family's wishes and leaves. Soon after, Marina is abducted by Bruno and some friends who physically assault her and dump her in an alley.

Beaten and bruised, Marina goes to a bar and hooks up with a random man. They have sex, but it's obvious Marina is numb with grief as she sees another vision of Orlando. The sudden escalation of the assault (*external* change) sees Marina make a clear decision that takes us into the next act – she has to leave Orlando behind. She will not go to his funeral (*internal* choice).

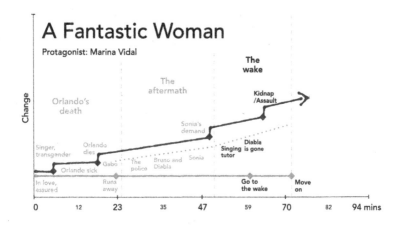

A Fantastic Woman

Protagonist: Marina Vidal

Back at her sister's place, Marina says she has turned the page. But later, while working at the bar, Marina sees a man with a locker key very similar to the one she kept from Orlando's belongings. She discovers the key is from a sauna. Even though she needs to move on, she wants a keepsake of her own from Orlando, perhaps even the tickets to their dream holiday. Marina goes to the sauna and poses as a man to gain access to the locker. But there is nothing inside. The locker is empty. She has no keepsake to remember Orlando. This unexpected discovery (*external* change) helps Marina realise that she can't simply move on. She decides to say goodbye to Orlando no matter what the risks (*internal* choice), pushing the story into the final act.

Marina catches a cab to the funeral. As she walks up the driveway, she is confronted by Bruno, Sonia and Gabo in a car. They tell her the funeral is over and ridicule her. Marina climbs on top of the car's roof and stamps her high heels, demanding to know where Diabla is. Orlando's family drive away in fear. It's an unusual display of anger from Marina, but it is short-lived

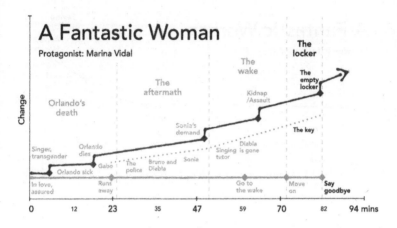

and doesn't suggest she is emotionally changing in any significant way. Rather, it reveals how frustrated she is with Orlando's family (they are pretty horrible to her).

At the funeral home, Marina sees another vision of Orlando. The vision leads her into the crematorium, where she discovers his body. Marina says her goodbyes and ends up being the last one to lay eyes on her love before he is cremated.

Later, we see Marina jogging with Diabla. Orlando's family has relented and given her the dog as a keepsake. That night, Marina prepares for an opera concert. She sings for an adoring crowd while her tutor accompanies her on piano. Marina has suffered a great loss, but she and her love for Orlando have survived.

A *Fantastic Woman* unfolds in five distinct acts as Marina faces escalating challenges, such as her attendance at Orlando's funeral, the hospital staff who are confused by her gender, the police officer who uses her birth name, Bruno calling her the wrong name, Sonia calling her a perversion and the detective ambushing her with a physical exam. But throughout these challenges, Marina is clear about her relationship and her gender

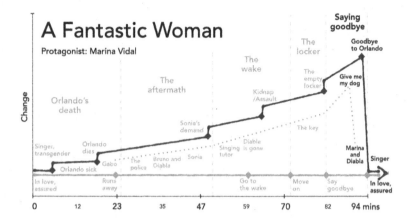

A Fantastic Woman

Protagonist: Marina Vidal

Change

Saying goodbye

Orlando's death

Singer, transgender

Orlando dies

Orlando sick

Gabo

The police

Bruno and Diabla

Sonia

Sonia's demand

Singing is gone

Diablo tutor

The aftermath

The wake

Kidnap /Assault

The empty locker

The locker

The key

Give me my dog

Goodbye to Orlando

Marina and Diabla

Singer

In love, assured

Runs away

Go to the wake

Move on

Say goodbye

In love, assured

0   12   23   35   47   59   70   82   94 mins

identity. She fights back with confidence and clarity about who she is and what she meant to Orlando.

Interestingly, Marina's big *internal* choices are not as articulated in each act break as they are in some of the other stories we've looked at. For example, it is not clear what Marina decides to do after Sonia bans her from the funeral. However, the narrative drive is not diluted by this. This is because we already know what Marina thinks. She knows who she is and what Orlando meant to her. It was established in the first sequence. Every choice she has made has underlined what we already know about her.

It is only after the assault in the alley that Marina backs off and decides not to go to the funeral. It's not because she doubts who she is or that she doesn't deserve to say goodbye. She's just tired of fighting. But this is only a temporary hesitation. Marina finds a way to be with Orlando one last time despite the obstacles in her way. As a result, she is a fantastic example of a Constant Character with an Optimistic Arc.

Summary: Resilient, courageous, inspiring

When a Constant Character's arc is optimistic and their stubborn attributes don't turn everyone against them, they have the potential to change the world. These characters have inner strength and self-belief, and they know that things will turn out well if only people could see the world as they do.

The tension in these stories comes from the conflict and pressure heaped on the protagonist while the audience wonders how they will withstand the assaults. But they do. And they make their world a better place as a result. No wonder these films can be so punch-the-air inspiring. To explore more films that feature a Constant Character with an Optimistic Arc, check out *Hidden Figures*, *Just Mercy*, *The Invisible Man*, *Die Hard*, *Paddington*, *Twelve Angry Men*, *Jaws*, *The King of Comedy*, *Apollo 13*, *Sexy Beast*, *Gladiator* and *Alien*.

CHAPTER 6

'Do you know why I am the way I am?':
Constant Characters with Ambivalent Arcs

As explored in the last chapter, Constant Characters have an inner resilience that enables them to take on the world. And while that strength often has the potential to change the world around them, sometimes that's just not possible. Or if it is, the results are far from perfect. Matters are left unresolved, conflicts linger, ultimate victory is far from certain – just like life.

In this chapter, we'll be looking at Constant Characters with an Ambivalent Arc through three very different films: *Winter's Bone* (a quiet, yet tough, drama about a desperate teenager), *Amour* (a heartbreaking story of enduring love) and *The Hurt Locker* (a tense character study of a soldier).

All of the lead characters in these stories have extraordinary inner strength. They *know* who they are. Their values, desires and beliefs are as immovable as a mountain. It is hard not to admire their perseverance and self-belief. But despite this, their situation is ambivalent at the end of the story. They haven't been able to resolve the conflict in their lives.

Perhaps because of these gritty, real-life qualities, all of these films are award winners – *Amour* won the prestigious Palme d'Or at Cannes and the Academy Award, BAFTA and Golden Globe Award for Best Film in a Foreign Language. *The Hurt Locker* won Best Picture and Best Original Screenplay at the Academy Awards. *Winter's Bone* was nominated for both Best Picture and Best Screenplay at the Academy Awards and won the Grand Jury prize at Sundance. Whatever the reason for their success, the inner resolve of these characters may explain why their stories are so unique and unforgettable.

Winter's Bone (2010)

The screenplay for *Winter's Bone,* written by Debra Granik and Anne Rosellini, and adapted from the novel by Daniel Woodrell, is a masterclass in quiet tension. The efficient simplicity of the drama, combined with the grounded poetry of the dialogue, elevates what could have been relentlessly grim material into a thoughtful and uplifting story of youthful courage.

The story is set in the rural mountain communities of the Ozarks, Missouri, and centres on teenager Ree Dolly. In the quiet opening scenes, we see Ree caring for two young siblings as well as her mute mother, who appears to have had a nervous breakdown. They are very poor and have little to eat. We learn that Ree's father has not been home for a long time and has recently been bailed for cooking crystal meth. A police officer informs Ree that he has disappeared after using the family home as his bail bond. If he doesn't appear in court in a few days, the family will lose their home. Ree quietly listens to the news and curtly tells the police officer she will find her father.

In these few short scenes, we gain a lot of insights into Ree's life. In her *external* world, Ree is desperately poor and isolated in a precarious family situation. In her *internal* world, Ree is smart, resourceful, fiercely independent, devoted to her family, suspicious of authority and emotionally tough. If you needed a big sister who had your back, Ree would be a great choice. With news of her father's disappearance (*external* change), the story quickly kicks into a new act as Ree sets out to find him (*internal* choice).

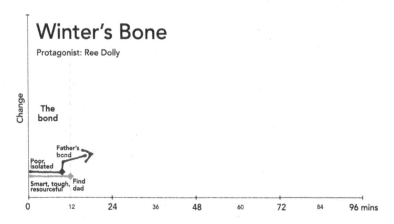

Winter's Bone

Protagonist: Ree Dolly

We see Ree visit a number of places hoping for news about her father's whereabouts. She tries to borrow a truck to get around but is refused, so she is forced to walk. She visits her father's violent brother, Teardrop, but he's uncooperative and threatening. Then she finds a colleague of her father, a drug cook, who is equally unhelpful. She keeps going and works up the courage to visit notorious crime boss Thump Milton. He too refuses to talk to her. One cousin tries to put her off the scent by claiming her father died in a meth lab fire, but clever Ree sees through his lie.

Despite being related to a lot of these people, Ree gets the feeling everyone knows something, but no one is talking. As she tries to care for her siblings, including teaching them to hunt for food, Teardrop visits to inform Ree that her father's car was found burnt out – with no sign of him inside. Ree senses the horrible truth – her father is dead. Drugged and vaguely threatening, Teardrop urges Ree to sell the family timberland before the bondsman takes it. But it's a big decision for the teenager. A tearful Ree begs her mute mother to tell her what to do, but she is no help.

By now, her father has missed his court date and a bondsman arrives to claim the house. Refusing to give up without a fight, Ree argues that her father is not hiding: he's dead. The bondsman gives Ree a week to prove it or the house will be taken.

Already, we've witnessed a tremendous sense of determination in Ree. Most teenagers would crumble under the sheer weight of this desperate situation. She knows she has to be tough, but she has no idea how tough she's going to need to be. The realisation that her father is dead (*external* change) and her choice to find evidence to prove it (*internal* choice) push the story into the next act.

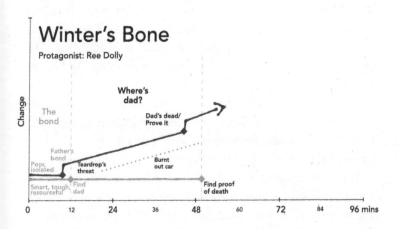

Ree goes to a cattle sale to confront Thump Milton, who she is sure knows everything about her father's death, but he refuses to see her again. Unperturbed, she goes to his house where a group of Milton women, her relations, attack Ree and brutally beat her. Teardrop arrives to take her home. On the way, he reveals that her father was killed because he was seen talking to the police. He doesn't know who did it but knows he'll seek revenge if he finds out.

It's interesting to note how Teardrop's attitude to Ree is changing here. At first, he was threatening and distant, but news of his brother's death and Ree's brave determination to save the family home seems to have had an effect on him. Teardrop is softening.

Back home, Ree desperately considers adopting out her siblings to Teardrop. She also tries to join the marines hoping for an upfront payment to settle the bond and save the family home. But she's not eligible.

An increasingly volatile Teardrop invites Ree to join him in finding where her father's body is buried. Unsurprisingly, no one will talk to a family that snitches. Frustrated, Teardrop vandalises a truck and threatens to shoot a cop who pulls them over. It's hopeless and Ree feels like she's at a dead-end. She mourns as she sorts through her father's belongings and burns the remaining junk.

Then, one night, the women who beat Ree arrive on her front doorstep. They will take her to her father's body (*external* change). Wary but desperate for answers, Ree agrees to go with them (*internal* choice), which pushes the story into the final act.

The women cover Ree's head in a sack and take her to an isolated pond. In a boat, they stop next to a tangle of branches. The women tell Ree to reach down and pull her father's body to the surface. Ree reaches down and drags up her dead father's arm. The Milton women tell her to cut off his hands with a chainsaw so she can prove her father is dead. Distraught, Ree can't do it but

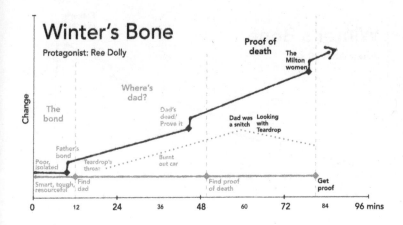

manages to hold her father's body up while the Milton women cut off his hands.

The next day, Ree presents her father's hands to the police in a sack. She claims they were thrown on the porch by a passing truck. The bond is cancelled. Unexpectedly, the bondsman returns a cash sum of money that was put up by an unknown criminal associate of her father. The house is saved and Ree has money to feed her siblings – for now, anyway. As they all sit on the porch, Ree assures the kids she will never leave them. Teardrop arrives and quietly reveals he knows who killed Ree's father but won't say who. With a sense of sadness and inevitability, Ree watches as Teardrop drives away, knowing he will seek revenge, and that it will probably be the last time she sees her uncle alive.

Over the course of *Winter's Bone*, we see Ree survive a journey to hell and back thanks to an inner strength she displayed from the very beginning. She started as a tough, resourceful teenager in a horrible but stable situation. She ended the story as pretty much the same tough and resourceful teenager in a slightly more horrible but stable situation. She has a home and money for the

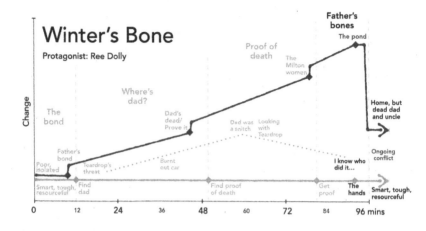

Winter's Bone

Protagonist: Ree Dolly

moment. However, she has no father, no income and still has to raise her siblings and care for her mother. What's worse, the only person she connected with on a deeper level, her uncle Teardrop, will soon be dead or, at the very least, in hospital for a long time. No, things aren't perfect. But they're not a total downer, either. There's a slightly uplifting quality to the end of Ree's story. Her courage and resilience have been inspiring.

As we saw in the subplot with Teardrop, it was Ree's bravery that inspired him to open up about his brother and help his niece. And Ree's distant relatives, the Milton women, were also swayed by her doggedness and eventually helped her find her father's body, despite the risk that she would snitch.

Ree's determined choices had an influence on the world around her, just enough to save her home and family. Apart from its themes of youthful resilience and courage, *Winter's Bone* also explores ideas of loyalty and family, leaving us with the feeling that Ree has earned a new level of respect from her community – respect she may be able to call on in the future.

Amour (2012)

Michael Haneke's screenplay for *Amour* is a heartbreakingly beautiful story of enduring love and dignity in old age. It is an unflinching story about an elderly man struggling with the deteriorating health of his beloved wife. Like *Winter's Bone*, the story's material, on paper, suggests a relentlessly grim night of so-called 'entertainment'. But the story is extremely moving, powerful and, ultimately, nurturing. Yes, it is sad. But many other emotions are swirling around that make this film unforgettable. It is a masterwork from a master storyteller.

The story opens with a flash-forward of a fire crew breaking into a Paris apartment. A foul smell has been reported. They find the dead body of an elderly woman lying on a bed surrounded by an arrangement of cut flowers. Typically unsentimental, Haneke is not interested in holding back any false suspense about where this story is going. It might be called *Amour*, but there will be no Hollywood ending in this film.

We flash back several months where we meet Georges Laurent, an elderly, retired piano teacher, who lives with his wife of many years, Anne. In these opening sequences, we see Georges and Anne going about their lives – attending concerts, eating together, telling stories – and it is obvious they are deeply in love.

From these scenes, we glean that Georges, the principal character, is moderately wealthy, relatively healthy and happily married (*external* world) as well as cultured, restrained but also emotionally attentive and deeply in love with his wife (*internal* world).

Then, one morning, while having breakfast, Anne experiences a minor stroke that leaves her briefly catatonic, mute and unresponsive. It is an eerie and disturbing experience for Georges (and the audience).

Sometime later, Georges discusses the situation with their self-obsessed daughter, Eva. We learn that Anne has been left paralysed on one side by an operation to clear her carotid artery. She is now confined to a wheelchair.

Anne returns home and, being generally afraid of doctors, makes Georges promise that he will never put her in a hospital or care facility again. He reluctantly promises. Anne's stroke and subsequent failed operation (*external* change), as well as Georges' promise (*internal* choice), push the story into the next act.

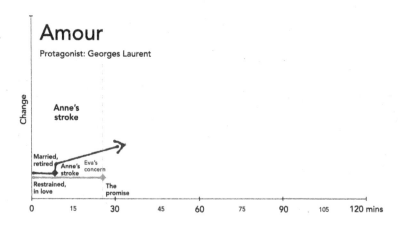

Georges works hard to attend to Anne's needs – cleaning her, feeding her, doing exercises, keeping her company. Anne tries to stay positive and not impose too much on Georges. The two seem to be making progress as they build a new routine – reading to each other, telling stories like they used to. But it's very hard.

One day, while Georges is out at a friend's funeral, he returns to find Anne on the floor next to an open window. They do not openly discuss it, but it appears Anne attempted to commit suicide by throwing herself out of the window. Later, as Georges discusses the bizarrely sentimental funeral, Anne abruptly says she doesn't want to go on. Georges gently urges Anne not to lose hope, explaining that he is not burdened by her. But it is clear that Anne's mood has deteriorated (*external* change). Georges' steadfast support (*internal* choice), despite Anne's grim admission, pushes the story into the next act.

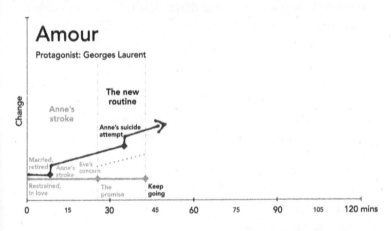

One of the most powerful qualities of this story is how much emphasis is placed on the struggle of everyday activities – getting out of bed, eating a meal, going to the bathroom, walking across the room. Haneke lingers on ordinary activities, underlining the mountainous obstacles they have become for Georges and Anne. The scenes are deceptively simple, but they are full of tension and suspense as we watch this frail couple wrestle with these seemingly impossible tasks. They also capture, without resorting to dialogue or clumsy sentiments, Georges' fierce and stubborn love for Anne. We can *see* it in his body as he lifts and holds her.

Life continues for Anne and Georges. A successful ex-student visits and is saddened by Anne's condition but cheers her by playing a beloved tune on the couple's grand piano. Georges gets Anne an electric wheelchair, which gives her more independence, but her rehabilitation is painfully slow. While she doesn't harass Georges with her thoughts of dying, it seems Anne's mood has not improved much.

Sometime later, Eva, their daughter, visits and is shocked to discover Anne has deteriorated dramatically. We learn that Anne has had another stroke that has left her demented and barely able to speak. Eva urges her father to put Anne in a hospital where she will get professional care, but Georges steadfastly refuses – he promised he wouldn't do that to Anne. Instead, he has arranged to get a nurse to help him three times a week. Georges' stubborn decision to honour his promise to Anne (*internal* choice), despite her deterioration (*external* change), pushes the story into the next act.

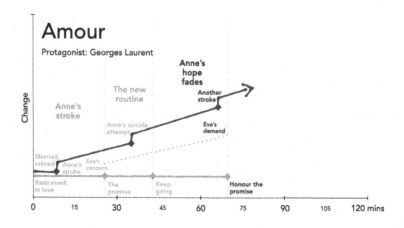

Georges soldiers on with the part-time help of a nurse. He feeds Anne in bed, sings their favourite songs to her, shops and cleans. Anne's moods are up and down; some days are better than others. One night, angry and frustrated, Anne spits her water in Georges' face. He impulsively slaps her but instantly apologises, ashamed of his actions.

During a visit from their daughter Eva, Georges locks Anne's room to protect her dignity. Eva is outraged and demands Georges send her mother into care. But Georges refuses. He has the help of a nurse and the care he gives is better than Anne would get in a hospital. Eva cannot argue with Georges' calm and determined reasoning. He tells her he will keep going until the bitter end.

Then, one night, Anne starts calling out in confusion and despair. Georges tells her a story and calms her until she sleeps. He then takes a pillow and holds it over Anne's face until she suffocates.

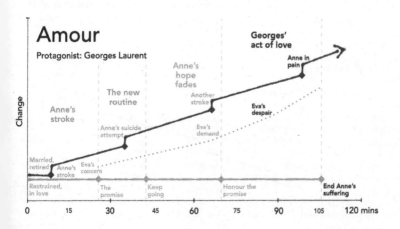

I still remember the gasps in the cinema the first time I saw this film. I may have been one of them. But Georges' actions made complete sense at that moment, and still do. It was inevitable this was how Georges and Anne's time together would end. It was an act of true love. The film is called *Amour* for a reason. Georges' decision to end Anne's suffering (*internal* choice) pushes the story into the final act.

Georges goes out and buys flowers. He carefully cuts them in the sink. He chooses a dress from Anne's wardrobe. He locks and tapes up the doorframe of Anne's room. He writes a letter. A pigeon flies into the apartment. Frail Georges catches it with a blanket and gently caresses it.

Later, while resting, Georges hears someone washing up. It's his beloved Anne. She tells him to get his shoes and jacket – they have to go. Georges does as he's told and follows Anne out the front door.

Back in the present, after the fire crew have left, Eva sits in the empty apartment, lost in her thoughts. What happened to Georges? Who knows. That's not what the film is about. What

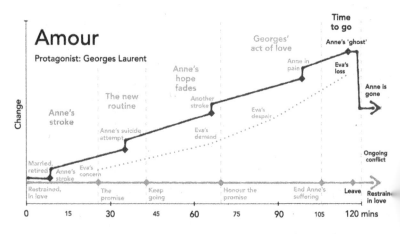

matters is what happened to Georges and Anne. The painful backdrop to their tender and enduring love gives the story a bittersweet quality that never resorts to sentimentality. Georges' determination to honour his promise to Anne, and remain true to the love they shared for so many years, shapes this heartbreakingly beautiful story, giving it a truly Ambivalent Arc.

But is Georges a Constant Character? Does he emotionally change? You could argue that Georges does change because he goes from refusing to end Anne's suffering to suffocating her. But Georges displays no guilt or regret at delaying Anne's death for as long as he could.

Throughout the story, Georges has displayed an incredibly calm and considered strength in a situation that would drive most people to despair. His daughter Eva, in her subplot, struggles to cope or to understand why her father makes the choices he does. From her position, his actions don't seem like love. Indeed, when Georges speaks of his friend's bizarre funeral, he frowns upon the sentimental displays of emotion. But that doesn't mean Georges doesn't feel love or emotion – it's just that his love is quiet and dignified, which is exactly what he gives Anne.

When she comes back to him, Anne is not some tormenting ghost demanding to know why he kept her alive. No, she is just as Georges remembered her when she was alive and they were in love. You won't find many characters more constant than Georges Laurent.

The Hurt Locker (2008)

Mark Boal's Academy Award–winning screenplay for *The Hurt Locker* was an unusual winner for Best Original Screenplay, as well as Best Picture. Set during the second Iraq War in a bomb disposal unit, it is a tense and claustrophobic film with a pervading sense of ambivalence about the characters and their story.

The film has an unusual episodic structure that is more like a detailed character study than a traditional story. It certainly doesn't conform to the Hero's Journey style of storytelling. The lead character, a reckless Sergeant called William James, is stubbornly unknowable – even to himself. There will be no easy emotional transformations for Will James. He's a Constant Character stuck in a deeply ambivalent cycle of risk and thrill-seeking. But all of this combines to create a unique cinematic experience that is not easily forgotten.

In the opening sequences, we meet Sergeant First Class William James, a bomb disposal expert who has just joined a new unit in the Iraq War. Unsurprisingly, James' *external* world is a pretty dangerous one. He's replacing another Sergeant who was blown up. But what is surprising is James' *internal* world – he is supremely relaxed about his new post and the dangers that come with it. One of the first things he does is remove a heavy protective cover from the windows of his quarters so he can enjoy some fresh air. He'd rather risk being blown up than miss out on a breeze.

As mentioned, *The Hurt Locker* has an unusual episodic structure.

The acts of the film are built around a series of tense missions that James and his team are sent on. Unlike many of the characters we've met so far, soldiers don't get to decide where they'll go and what they'll do next, and screenwriter Mark Boal is smart enough to take this into account.

Just because James doesn't choose the missions he goes on, doesn't mean he lacks the agency to make decisions. In fact, it is James' unorthodox *choices* that generate the conflict, shape and themes of this story.

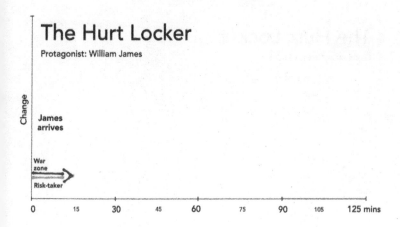

In the first mission, James and his colleagues Sergeant Sanborn and Specialist Eldridge are sent to disarm a suspected IED (improvised explosive device). Very quickly, James goes off-book. He declines to send in a remote robot first, unexpectedly sets off a smoke bomb to create a distraction, fails to communicate with Sanborn, who is trying to cover him, pulls a gun on an angry civilian, and more than once chuckles as if he's having fun.

James expertly disarms the bomb and they move on to the next mission. But he has already begun to alienate his team members. Sanborn and Eldridge label James a 'rowdy one' or thrill-seeker, and start counting the days until they are rotated out of the unit. These days provide a handy ticking clock within the structure of the film.

Meanwhile, a subplot is introduced in the next act that sees Eldridge struggling with the death of James' predecessor. An army psychiatrist encourages him to talk, but he's reluctant. The next mission is a difficult car bomb. The team is out in the open and the pressure of attack is imminent. Sanborn calls James back, but he refuses and removes his communications headset.

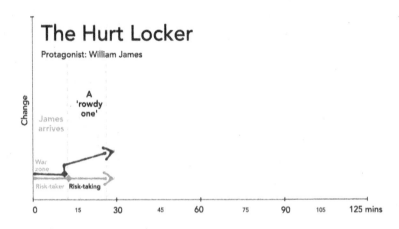

He wants to disarm the bomb no matter the risks. James succeeds against the odds. Sanborn is furious and punches James in the face, only to see him later revered by a commanding officer.

In another subplot, James meets an Iraqi boy selling DVDs while waiting for his next mission. He gives him the nickname 'Beckham' after the boy's favourite soccer player. At the same time, Eldridge opens up to the psychiatrist and worries that James is going to get them all killed.

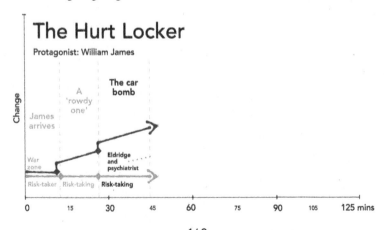

On the next mission, the team are sent to the desert to blow up some confiscated ordinance. As James prepares a pile of explosives, Sanborn contemplates blowing him up in an apparent accident. On the way back, the team and a group of mercenaries are attacked by snipers. They're cornered. James and Sanborn work together to save the unit. But when Eldridge struggles under the pressure, we see an unexpectedly supportive side to James.

Back at the base, the team drink and bond with a brutal play fight. Eldridge admits he was scared and James reassures him that 'everyone is a coward about something'. It's a telling line and gives us some clues about James' strange emotional world. What is he afraid of?

Sanford finds a box of bomb parts under James' bunk. James explains they're souvenirs from his hundreds of missions. They're all pieces of something that nearly killed him, including his wedding ring. Maybe this is what he's afraid of.

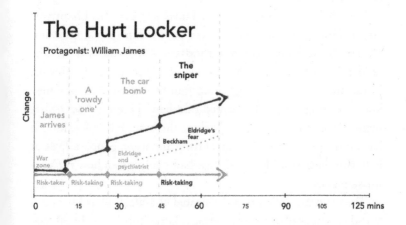

The Hurt Locker

Protagonist: William James

169

On the next mission, the team discovers a 'body bomb' – an explosive hidden inside the dead body of an Iraqi boy. James is sure the bloodied body is Beckham, his young friend. Instead of playing it safe, James insists on disarming the bomb and retrieving the body. He succeeds, but as they prepare to leave, the psychiatrist, who has joined the mission with Eldridge, is blown up by an improvised explosive. Eldridge is distraught.

As you can see, James is the character shaping these missions. His risky and unorthodox choices are generating a lot of the conflict, which fuels the story. And it's important to note that none of these choices is *new or unfamiliar* to James – this is his modus operandi. He's been emotionally constant so far.

While we are spending a lot of time with James, we still don't know a lot about him, other than the fact that he is a recalcitrant risk-taker. Why is he taking such risks? We don't know. But we're starting to get some hints. James calls home and a woman with a child answers. He doesn't speak, even though the woman appears to know it's James.

Haunted by the body bomb, James suspects Beckham was targeted by insurgents and used as a booby trap against his team. He leaves the base without authorisation and tracks down the residential house where he thinks Beckham lived. He breaks inside and holds an average Iraqi family at gunpoint. But they know nothing about a boy called Beckham. James realises he has made a mistake and escapes back to the base. His risk-taking is becoming more reckless and putting innocent people's lives at risk. But does he understand this? Not really, given how the next mission goes.

The team are called to a devastated city block to assess how a suicide bomber planned their attack. James thinks the bomb was remotely activated and that the perpetrators are watching them

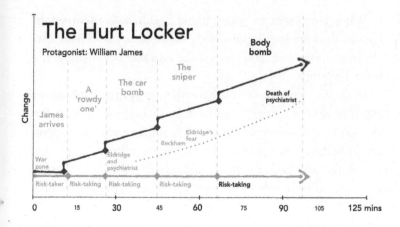

right now. He persuades Sanborn and an increasingly anxious Eldridge to follow him into a civilian area to investigate.

During a skirmish, Eldridge is kidnapped by insurgents. To save him, James shoots the kidnappers as they escape down a dark alley. Unfortunately, he also hits Eldridge, enough to warrant months of painful rehab. As Eldridge is flown out, he finally calls James on his recklessness, condemning his risky adrenaline fixes.

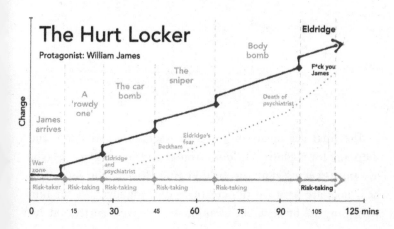

When James sees his young friend Beckham in the street, he ignores the boy, realising the body bomb wasn't Beckham after all. James is starting to appreciate the mistakes he's making. But is he changing?

In the final few days of their rotation, James and Sanborn are called to remove a suicide vest from an innocent Iraqi man. But the vest is too complicated and time is running out. James waits until the last second to escape and is almost killed.

On the way back to the base, Sanborn starts falling apart. He can't take the stress anymore. Yet James is as calm as ever. When Sanborn points out he almost died, James nods and asks him a strange question: 'Do you know why I am the way I am?' Sanborn says he doesn't. James says he doesn't know either.

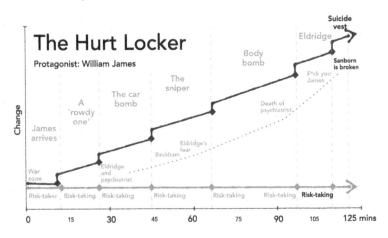

The final act opens in a supermarket. James is home and shopping for yoghurt. He looks strange and out of place. Maybe his thrill-seeking days are behind him. Maybe the only risks he'll take are between full-cream or diet yoghurt. We see him struggling to fit back in, cleaning the clogged gutters on his modest house, telling inappropriate war stories to his wife.

In a private moment with his baby son, James explains, almost to himself, where his head is at. He admits that there is pretty much one thing in the whole world that he truly loves. He loves it more than his wife and even more than his child. The story cuts to James back in Iraq, dressed in his bulky bomb disposal suit. He's smiling as he walks alone down a deserted street towards his next adrenaline fix.

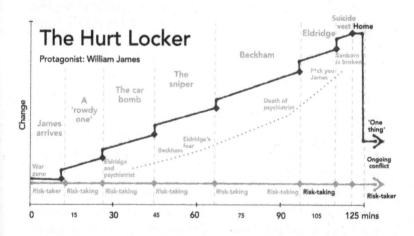

Structurally, *The Hurt Locker* is highly episodic, a series of discrete missions united only by James' increasingly dangerous behaviour. I think there is a good case to say this is a one-act story with James' choices serving one driving desire – his next fix. The story doesn't significantly change direction, and neither does James.

James doesn't emotionally change, but he almost does. He *knows* he has a problem. As a change, that's as minor as it gets. James' decision to return to a life-and-death existence says more about his inability to change than any fleeting moment of self-

173

awareness. Perhaps he'll be more careful and take fewer risks on this new posting. But he probably won't. The feeling we get is that he'll do the same thing all over again.

Of course, like many Constant Characters, his dogged choices have had an impact on the people around him – Sanborn is a psychological mess and Eldridge may or may not walk again. And what about the Iraqi family he held at gunpoint? What effect did his actions have on them?

In some ways, it is both a strength and weakness of the film that we are so locked into James' point of view. On the one hand, we rarely escape the pressure of the world he exists in, which is what makes the film so gripping. At the same time, we only see the Iraqi population through James' warped perspective. They are often depicted as dangerous insurgents, and rarely ordinary people trying to survive a war zone. Does *The Hurt Locker* indulge us in James' thrill-seeking behaviour from a safe distance, away from the real bombs and the real Iraqi people who form the cultural backdrop of the film? Probably.

I think the filmmakers are aware of James' deeply ambivalent point of view. He is hardly portrayed as a hero. In fact, in his own words, he's a coward. Emotional vulnerability and commitment are the bombs James can't defuse. He's only interested in his next adrenaline fix – and he knows it.

Summary: Tough, determined, dogged

As you've probably guessed, I love the complexity ambivalent stories offer up. When you combine them with a Constant Character, like Ree, Georges or James, it forces you to reflect on your own limits. Could you walk in their shoes? Can you empathise with their choices? Do they inspire you, challenge you, repel you? Depending on your own internal world, the characters we've met in this chapter are more than capable of doing all three.

A story that features a Constant Character with an Ambivalent Arc is likely to have a tough, gritty quality to it. The character may sometimes be hard to empathise with simply because of their unrelenting doggedness in the face of adversity. They're challenging people because they challenge the world around them. But it's also hard to take your eyes off them. Their fates may not always be pretty, but they have a depth and complexity that leaves most so-called heroes in the shade. To explore more films that feature a Constant Character with an Ambivalent Arc, check out *Melancholia*, *Promising Young Woman*, *A Hidden Life*, *If Beal Street Could Talk*, *Can You Ever Forgive Me?*, *The Report*, *Cold War*, *We Need to Talk About Kevin*, *Mustang*, *Take Shelter*, *Nightcrawler* and *Lean on Pete*.

CHAPTER 7

'We don't stop here':
Constant Characters with Pessimistic Arcs

It can be tough to watch Michael Corleone sliding down a slippery slope towards violence and murder in *The Godfather*. In part, this is because we've seen him change from a happy, carefree guy to a vengeful, blood-thirsty monster. The tragedy and transformation are there for all to see. But the fact that Michael *does* change makes it easier to identify with him and his choices. As we watch, we wonder if he will recognise the error of his ways because we know he's capable of kindness and love. But there is another type of character arc that can be more tragic than Michael Corleone's.

When it comes to Constant Characters with a Pessimistic Arc, stubbornness dooms them from the very first frame. We've never seen them as anything but a headstrong pain-in-the-ass. Are they capable of being any other way? Will they choose another course of action? Will they finally change the world around them, like Moana or Erin Brockovich? The answer is no.

In these stories, there is a pervasive and impending sense of disaster. The choices these characters make inevitably rub against the grain of the world they inhabit. And the world pushes back. Hard. Their end is never pretty. But are they fools? Are they recklessly blinkered? Are they always wrong? I don't think so.

As we'll see in this chapter a Constant Character with a Pessimistic Arc can sometimes be sincere in their convictions and right about the imperfect world they are fighting against. We'll be discussing *Mulholland Drive*, a mind-bending psychological mystery from David Lynch; *Inside Llewyn Davis,* a melancholic comedy from Joel and Ethan Coen; and *Sweet Country*, a tense Australian Western written by David Tranter and Steven McGregor. In these films, we discover that Constant Character with a Pessimistic Arc can be a careless fool, but they can also be unlucky, brave and even noble.

Mulholland Drive (2001)

You may be wondering how on earth I am going to discuss David Lynch's mind-bending film *Mulholland Drive*. How can we talk about character when the protagonist appears to have two different names and lives? And she's not the only one. Just about everyone in this bewildering film appears to have alternate lives playing out in completely different universes. What the hell is going on?

When I first saw this film, I had much the same reaction. I enjoyed every minute of it and, being a fan of Lynch's previous work, I was on the lookout for his trademark dreamscapes, puzzling characters and foreboding atmospheres. Not that it helped me any. I left the cinema shaking my head like someone had spiked my popcorn.

Like many Lynch films, this one is endlessly rewatchable. If you haven't seen it yet, avoid the spoilers below and soak up the bewilderment of your first screening. When you're ready, return to this chapter. You won't regret it. Unlike the mysterious blue box at the centre of the film, there is something inside this nutty story of Hollywood dreams and nightmares – and that's a Constant Character with a deeply Pessimistic Arc.

The story opens with a car accident on Mulholland Drive. A dark-haired woman emerges from the wreckage and stumbles, disorientated, down the mountain to the streets of contemporary Los Angeles. Here, the woman meets the protagonist of the story, Betty Elms, a sweet and friendly girl from Ontario who has just arrived in town. She is staying in an apartment owned by her Aunt Ruth and dreams of pursuing an acting career.

Betty is sweet, innocent and, let's face it, a touch naive (her *internal* world). She's from the country and trying to make it in Hollywood, the city of dreams (her *external* world).

Betty finds the dark-haired woman hiding in Aunt Ruth's apartment. The woman appears to have amnesia and doesn't know her name or what happened to her. She assumes the name 'Rita' from a movie poster of Rita Hayworth. Betty and Rita discover wads of cash and a strange blue key in Rita's handbag. Rita eventually remembers that she was going to Mulholland Drive. Betty suggests they call the police and 'pretend to be someone else' to see if there was an accident.

At the same time, we meet a host of other characters who, unknown to Betty, lurk ominously in the background of Hollywood life: a bungling hitman who steals a book of phone numbers and seems to be looking for the dark-haired woman, a nightmarish man who lives behind a diner and a hot-shot film director called Adam who is being forced by mobsters to cast an unknown actor called Camilla Rhodes in his next movie. It's all pretty strange. But hey, it's David Lynch! Rita's memory of Mulholland Drive (*external* change) and Betty's decision to help her (*internal* choice) push the story into the next act.

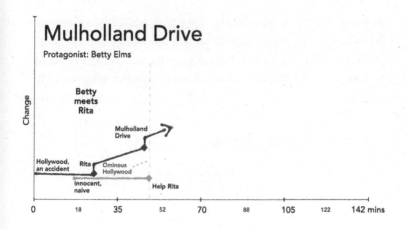

Mulholland Drive

Protagonist: Betty Elms

Betty and Rita hide the money and strange key. They go to a payphone to anonymously call the police. The payphone is at the same diner the nightmarish man lives behind, but they don't encounter him. Betty calls and discovers there was an accident on Mulholland Drive last night. While scanning the papers for more information, Rita sees a waitress with the name tag 'Diane'. She remembers a name – Diane Selwyn. Maybe that's her name. They look up Diane Selwyn's number but no one answers. But at least they're on the trail now.

Meanwhile, Adam, the film director, meets a strangely threatening cowboy who convinces him to cast Camilla Rhodes in his movie. Adam reluctantly agrees. At the same time, Betty rushes off to an audition, which she nails. While there, she crosses paths with Adam. They lock eyes. It's as if they have met before. Betty runs away in a panic.

Betty and Rita go to Diane Selwyn's apartment. When no one answers, Betty climbs through an open window. Inside, Betty and Rita find the decomposing body of a woman in the bedroom. Terrified, and fearing that her life is in danger, Betty

179

disguises Rita in a blonde wig. They look weirdly similar now. Betty and Rita have passionate sex and fall asleep. The discovery of Diane Selwyn's body (*external* change) and Betty's decision to have sex with Rita (*internal* choice) push the story into the next act.

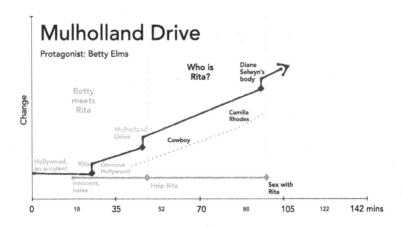

In the middle of the night, Rita insists they go to a strange theatre called Silencio. There, they watch a woman singing, only to discover it is a tape recording, or an 'illusion', as the creepy emcee declares. Betty discovers a blue box in her purse that appears to fit the blue key that Rita had. They rush back to Aunt Ruth's apartment. As Rita is about to put the key in the box, Betty disappears. Where did she go? Rita turns the key and opens the box. It is dark inside. Is there anything in there? The box clunks to the ground. Rita disappears too.

Still with me? Great. Because it's about to take a glorious left turn before it all comes together. The discovery of the blue box (*external* change) and the decision to open it (*internal* choice) throw this baffling tale into the final act.

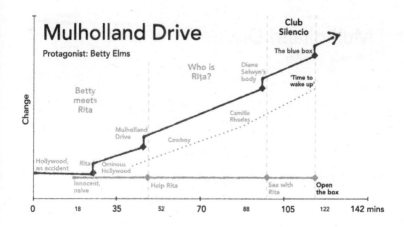

Betty wakes up on a bed. She is in Diane Selwyn's apartment. In fact, she *is* Diane Selwyn. Gone is perky, friendly Betty. She is now a sullen, depressed and failed actor called Diane Selwyn. In a series of flashbacks, we learn that Diane (Betty) was in a relationship with a fellow actor called Camilla Rhodes – who looks just like Rita! Camilla (Rita) was engaged to marry Adam, the director. When Camilla broke off their affair, Diane hired a hitman (the guy we saw earlier) to have her lover killed. He shows Diane a blue key that will signal he has killed Camilla. When Diane wakes, she finds the key on her coffee table – and Camilla is dead. Full of guilt and remorse, Diane spirals into a psychotic episode. Haunted by terrifying hallucinations, she collapses on the bed and fatally shoots herself. The room fills with strange smoke. A woman from the weird theatre whispers, '*Silencio*'.

As some of you may have guessed from the clues throughout the story, the first two hours of the film were an 'illusion' or, more precisely, a dream. In the dream section, Betty is starting afresh, pursuing a promising career in the city of dreams, then she comes to the rescue of a beautiful woman, Rita. They fall in

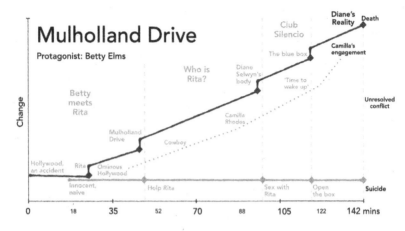

Mulholland Drive

Protagonist: Betty Elms

Change

Diane's Reality — Death

Club Silencio

Camilla's engagement

The blue box

Who is Rita?

Diane Selwyn's body

'Time to wake up'

Betty meets Rita

Unresolved conflict

Camilla Rhodes

Mulholland Drive

Cowboy

Hollywood, an accident

Rita

Ominous Hollywood

Innocent, naïve

Help Rita

Sex with Rita

Open the box

Suicide

| 0 | 18 | 35 | 52 | 70 | 88 | 105 | 122 | 142 mins |

love. But in this dreamscape, sinister forces are working against them – the hitman, the strange cowboy, the corrupt director, the rigged Hollywood system.

In the final section of the film, we see failed actress and spurned lover, Diane Selwyn, literally wake up from a dream – a dream where she was Betty and Rita was in love with her. But in the real world, Rita is Camilla Rhodes and she is about to get engaged to her director boyfriend. The gloss of Hollywood has been drained from this grim reality. Here, Diane has hired a hitman to kill Camilla. When Diane sees the blue key, she knows the deed is done. Unable to live with the guilt, she kills herself.

There are very few people who can pull off the old 'it was all a dream' manoeuvre, but David Lynch is one of them. His movies have always been obsessed with dreams, the unconscious and the fluidity of identity. What could have been a hackneyed trick played on the audience is instead a masterful, haunting and frequently terrifying meditation on dreams, ambition and spurned love.

Betty's dreams are the flip side of the nightmare Diane

is living. Almost every character is an expression of Diane's crumbling psychological state as they are recast in a dream version of her life. But she can't escape the nightmare she has created. Her spiralling inner world is made up of the same hopes, fears, desires and obsessions that got her into this mess in the first place. Unfortunately, Diane is a Constant Character, and her end is a pessimistic nightmare.

Structurally, *Mulholland Drive* breaks neatly into a four-act structure: Betty's first encounter with Rita, the search for Rita's identity, Club Silencio and Diane's nightmare reality.

While Betty's choices drive a lot of the story, it's worth noting that it is Rita who chooses to open the strange blue box that pushes the story into the final act. But isn't Rita just a manifestation of Betty/Diane's desires? For most of this movie, everyone we see is a part of Betty/ Diane's *internal* world. So when the box is opened, Diane wakes up, the dream world crumbles and a nightmare reality takes over.

The experience of watching *Mulholland Drive* perfectly captures Lynch's thematic intent as Betty, with exaggerated naivety, wanders through her dream landscape. It makes us want to believe in Betty's dream. We're drawn into her imaginary world and are given time to invest heavily in her relationship with Rita.

When the dream is taken away, we feel the same comedown as Diane. Her life is bleak and hopeless. She wants it all to end, which I suspect was the experience of a fair chunk of the audience who saw this film. But when framed as a dream/nightmare, the mysteries of this strange world come together in a surprisingly cohesive psychological drama.

Inside Llewyn Davis (2014)

Joel and Ethan Coen have made a career out of layered tragicomedies full of unforgettable characters and unpredictable storylines. Their screenplay for *Inside Llewyn Davis* is no different. If anything, it feels like they're close to perfecting their singular approach to storytelling that is part-fable, part-astute commentary and part-farce.

For our purposes, the story of struggling folk singer Llewyn Davis is an excellent example of a Constant Character with a Pessimistic Arc. As we'll see, the very structure of the screenplay underlines how inescapable Llewyn's fate is, giving the story a dark, melancholic humour. It's so sad that it's funny.

The story starts in 1961 at the Gaslight Café in New York's Greenwich Village where we watch folk singer Llewyn Davis singing for a small crowd. His performance is polished and soulful. But afterwards, he is beaten up in an alley by a man who is angry about something that happened the night before at the Gaslight. It seems that Llewyn misbehaved in some way.

Llewyn wakes up in a huge apartment owned by his rich friends, the Gorfeins. No one is home and Llewyn puts on an album he recorded with an ex-musical partner, Mikey Timlin, a mysterious figure who comes up frequently in conversations throughout the film. From Llewyn's melancholic demeanour, we get the feeling that Mikey is dead.

In these opening scenes, we can glean a few things about Llewyn. In his *internal* world, he is artistic, sensitive and melancholic, and seems to be grieving a loss, possibly Mikey's. Given his beating in the alley, he also appears to have a caustic side that gets him in trouble. In his *external* world, Llewyn appears to be a talented but unsuccessful musician who is down on his luck and itinerant. All in all, tragicomedy gold.

As Llewyn is leaving, the Gorfeins' cat escapes. Locked out of the apartment, Llewyn is forced to take the cat with him. He visits his record company, where he discovers his solo record hasn't sold, before visiting an old musician friend and lover, Jean. Llewyn hopes to sleep on Jean's couch for a few days, but her couch is already taken by another musician. Worse, she's pregnant and the baby is most likely Llewyn's (a dramatic *external* change for Llewyn). Jean is furious and wants Llewyn to pay for a termination even though it might be her current boyfriend's baby. Llewyn agrees to get the cash. Making matters even worse, he loses the Gorfeins' cat. Jean's pregnancy (*external* change) and Llewyn's agreement to get the money for the termination (*internal* choice) push the story into the next act.

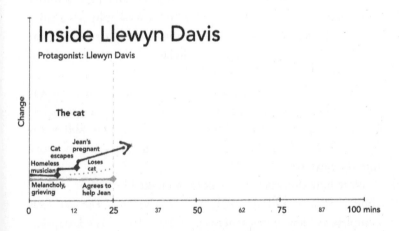

Inside Llewyn Davis

Protagonist: Llewyn Davis

Llewyn visits his sister in the hope of getting money from the sale of his parents' house, but the money is to keep his ageing father in a home for retired sailors. Llewyn's sister suggests that if Llewyn needs money, he could return to being a merchant sailor like his father. But it becomes clear that the only thing Llewyn hates more than his dad is being a merchant sailor, so he instructs his sister to throw out a box of old stuff from his sailing days. He's never going back there.

Llewyn calls the Gorfeins to reassure them about their cat, even though he has no idea where it is, and learns that he has been offered a paid recording session at Columbia Records. Llewyn races to the session with Jim, Jean's boyfriend, where they record a novelty song about space flight. Llewyn thinks the song is terrible and, desperate for money, takes his money upfront, rather than royalties on sales. He now has the money for Jean's termination. Then, by chance, he finds the Gorfeins' cat. Things are looking up!

But when he sees a doctor to book the appointment, he discovers he has credit from a previous lover, Diane, who didn't go through with a termination. Llewyn learns that he has a child living in Ohio. With his head spinning, Llewyn returns the cat to the Gorfeins only to end up in a fight with Mrs Gorfein when she sings Mikey's harmony during an impromptu performance. Even worse, the cat doesn't belong to the Gorfeins. Their cat was a boy, and this one, to quote Mrs Gorfein, 'doesn't have testicles'. Llewyn's discovery of his child (*external* change), as well as his fight with Mrs Gorfein over Mikey and the cat, push the story into the next act.

Note how this act break is not pre-empted by a clear *internal* choice, as it would normally be. Despite this, the act feels complete as Llewyn has kept his promise to Jean, his relationship with the Gorfeins has taken an unexpected turn, and he discovers that he's a father. What will he do next?

With everything that's happened, Llewyn really needs a break. So he decides to hitch a ride to Chicago (*internal* choice) where

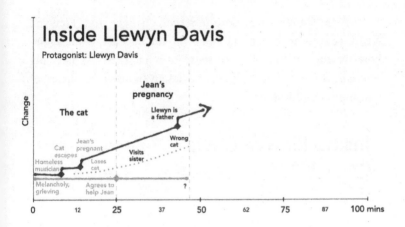

Inside Llewyn Davis

Protagonist: Llewyn Davis

he hopes to meet successful music manager Bud Grossman and finally make a living. His fellow passengers are the cat (the one without testicles), a mysterious beat poet called Johnny Five and a jazz musician called Roland Turner. It's a long, tense ride as Roland tells indulgent stories and harasses Llewyn with relentless insults about folk music. It's during one of these exchanges that Llewyn reveals that Mikey committed suicide.

In a strange confrontation, Roland threatens to place a Santería 'curse' on Llewyn to ensure that nothing will ever go right for him. Later, after he saves Roland from a drug overdose and Johnny Five is arrested, Llewyn abandons the cat and hitches to Chicago. There, he meets music manager Bud Grossman, who patiently listens to his singing and suggests he get back together with his old partner. Llewyn doesn't mention that Mikey is dead and, dejected, hitches a ride back to New York. On the way, he passes the town where his child would be living with his ex-girlfriend Diane. But he doesn't stop. Then, while taking his turn at driving, he clips a cat that runs across the highway. Is it the same cat he abandoned? Llewyn can't see as it limps off into the woods.

Bud Grossman's rejection (*external* change) and Llewyn's return to New York push the story into the next act. Note, again, how we do not have a clear sense of what Llewyn's next big *internal* choice will be, only that he has given up on his dream of making it in Chicago.

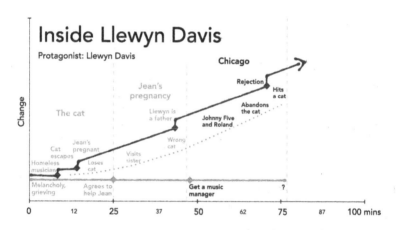

Back in New York, Llewyn visits the Merchant Marine's union. It seems he's chosen to throw in his music career and return to the merchant navy like his dad (*internal* choice). This is big, really big, and suggests an emotional change is taking place inside Llewyn. He's giving up music. But will this make him happy? Will he follow through?

Llewyn uses most of the money he saved from Jean's termination to pay his union dues and is booked on a ship leaving that week. Afterwards, he reluctantly visits his grizzled father and explains he's shipping out. Llewyn plays one of his father's favourite tunes on his guitar as his dad remains mute and quietly soils himself. Llewyn visits his sister to collect his pilot's licence and navy papers, but she's already thrown them out. Llewyn is distraught. Without his licence and papers, he can't ship out. Worse, back at the union, he can't get his money back either. He's penniless again.

Back at Jean's, Llewyn finds out she has arranged a set for him tomorrow night at the Gaslight Café. But Llewyn is adamant it will be his last. He's giving up music. Llewyn later discovers that Jean slept with the manager of the Gaslight, possibly to get him a gig. Drunk and angry, Llewyn heckles a sweet old lady singing at the café. He's thrown out.

With nowhere to go, Llewyn turns up at the Gorfeins' house. Apologies are made all around – Mikey has left a big hole in all their hearts. But there is good news. The cat came back! Llewyn is astonished to discover that it showed up one day and its name is Ulysses, a detail he never knew. And the novelty song that he recorded with Jim? It's become a big hit, but Llewyn won't get any royalties because he took a session fee. Oh well. He collapses into bed and sleeps. Llewyn's failure to rejoin the merchant navy (*external* change) and his return to the Gorfeins' push the story into the final act. But, as with the other act breaks in the story so far, there is no clear sense of what Llewyn will do next to escape his predicament.

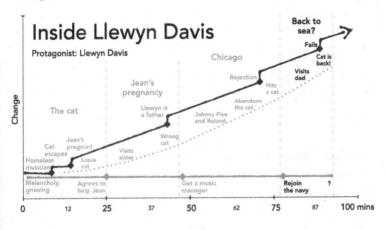

Llewyn wakes in the apartment the next morning but, instead of letting the cat out, he stops it before it can escape. That night, Llewyn plays the Gaslight Café. It's the same song we heard at the beginning of the film, with Llewyn playing with passion and conviction. Again, someone is waiting for him in the back alley. It's the same guy from the first scene. It's the same situation. As we watch Llewyn get beaten up again, we realise that the first scene was a flash-forward. He is, literally and metaphorically, right back where he started – penniless, homeless, unfulfilled and lonely.

It's likely that Llewyn will let the Gorfeins' cat escape again, just as he will keep sleeping on couches, making the same relationship mistakes and pursuing the same broken musical dreams. And he will always miss Mikey.

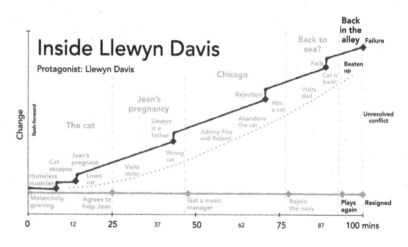

Inside Llewyn Davis is a perfect example of a Constant Character with a Pessimistic Arc. Thematically and literally, Llewyn is stuck in a loop, a recurring tale of hopelessness and despair, that he can never escape. His grief for the loss of his best friend and music partner has left a hole in his heart that can never be filled by anyone, not even himself.

Similarly, the relatively 'soft' act breaks, where Llewyn doesn't make a clear choice about how to tackle his problems, perfectly underline a sense of being overwhelmed. He eventually figures something out, but you never get the feeling he's in control of his story.

There is also a sense of resignation in Llewyn. He knows that he will never succeed. But, like William James in *The Hurt Locker*, this emotional insight isn't enough to change him in any significant way, certainly not enough to escape his cycle of hopelessness.

There is a melancholic beauty to Llewyn's tale that is surprisingly tender for the Coen brothers, but also for arcs of this type. With all the despair this sort of structure invokes, it's hard to see any light in all the darkness. But there is an integrity to Llewyn's pursuit of music, a fact that is celebrated by the many wonderful musical interludes throughout the film. He's foolish and vain, but he's also a crazy dreamer who just wants to write enduring music that makes life momentarily more bearable. You can't hold that against him.

Sweet Country (2017)

Note: The following story includes depictions of sexual assault and rape.

David Tranter and Steven McGregor's screenplay for *Sweet Country* is a gripping and powerful example of an Australian Western – a genre that features less gun-slinging than traditional Westerns and even fewer heroes. Inspired by the life of Tranter's great uncle, the story explores the dynamics of power and justice in a colonised country. Like many Australian classics, it's a tough-minded film that resists easy redemptions. But its ambition and gritty integrity shine through every dazzling cinematic frame.

At the centre of *Sweet Country* is Aboriginal farm worker, Sam Kelly, our final example of a Constant Character with a Pessimistic Arc. The story is set in the Northern Territory, just after the First World War, and we meet Sam in the opening sequences. He's in chains, a prisoner, his head bowed as he's watched by a crowd of people in a dusty street. Someone off-screen asks him if he understands what is happening. He nods.

Instantly, we're drawn into the story. Who is this man, why is he in chains, what has happened to him, what is about to happen? It's an excellent example of starting a story with a series of intriguing dramatic questions to pull the audience in.

The story then flashes back and we meet Sam again in a very different situation. In his *external* world, he lives and works with his wife, Lizzie, on a farm owned by a kindly preacher, Fred Smith. In his *internal* world, Sam is a quiet and observant man, and we get the sense that he shares Fred's gentle ways. Again, the dramatic question arises: how does someone as unthreatening as Sam end up in chains?

One day, Sam is asked to help a newly arrived farmer, Harry March, fix some paddock fences. Both Sam and Fred have reservations about Harry, who is a recently returned soldier from the First World War, but they agree to help anyway. It soon becomes clear that Harry is deeply racist towards Aboriginals like Sam and Lizzie. He insults them, neglects to feed them, drinks heavily and shoots his gun in a disturbing militaristic ritual at night. Sam quietly resists Harry's behaviour and doesn't cause a fuss. The next day, after sending Sam away to muster some cattle, Harry rapes Lizzie and threatens to kill her if she tells anyone. Returning home, Sam tells Fred about Harry's strange ways and they agree never to help him again. Lizzie does not mention Harry's degrading attack.

Throughout these opening sequences, the story expertly employs the use of brief, non-linear flashbacks that enigmatically deepen our understanding of the characters. We see ex-soldier Harry weeping by a fire at night, Fred savouring a few drops of precious rain, as well as Sam fighting back against an abusive farmer. The subtle storytelling technique encourages us to look deeper with these characters. They are more than they seem, particularly Sam. He may be quiet, but he's also strong and proud. He won't be pushed around unjustly by anyone, no matter what colour their skin.

Needing more help, Harry recruits a couple of Aboriginal workers from another farmer. One of the workers, a young boy called Philomac, is accused of trying to steal his watch. Harry chains Philomac up, but he escapes and hides on Fred's property, where Sam and Lizzie are minding the homestead. Harry arrives with a gun and accuses Sam of harbouring the fugitive. Harry starts shooting. He breaks down the door. But Sam is waiting with a rifle and fatally shoots Harry.

Knowing the dire implications of killing a white man, Sam and Lizzie escape into the outback. Meanwhile, Philomac steals a watch from Harry's dead body, an act of defiance after being unfairly placed in chains. Harry's dangerous attack (*external* change) and Sam's decision to defend himself (*internal* choice) push the story into the next act.

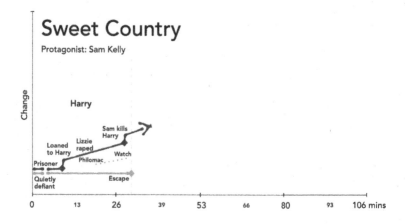

Sweet Country

Protagonist: Sam Kelly

An uncompromising policeman called Fletcher gathers a posse and sets out to hunt for Sam and Lizzie. Preacher Fred joins them to look out for Sam's welfare. It's a game of cat and mouse as Sam uses his knowledge of the harsh country to stay one step ahead of the authorities. He lures the posse into a gorge where they are attacked by a fearsome tribe of Aboriginals who kill one of the policemen. Preacher Fred, sensing Sam is innocent and has the upper hand, heads back to town, but Fletcher ploughs on, determined to capture his man.

Sam cleverly plants a scorpion in Fletcher's shoe, but the stubborn policeman struggles on, despite more of the posse turning back. Eventually, Sam lures Fletcher alone onto a desolate salt lake. Out of water and disorientated, Fletcher is close to death when Sam appears and gives him a water bag before disappearing into the heat haze again.

It's worth noting that while the central story revolves around Sam and Lizzie's escape from the authorities, a cleverly constructed subplot involving the young boy, Philomac, is playing out in parallel. In it, Philomac is coaxed into replacing one of his uncles as the head stockman. His white boss gives him a 'man's boots' and allows him to sleep in the stockman's shelter. But his uncle warns Philomac against embracing the white man's way too quickly – he himself was stolen from his family, lost his culture and started stealing. He can see Philomac heading the same way and warns him that being caught between two worlds is a dangerous place to be.

It's an intriguing narrative counterpoint to Sam's escape as it doesn't directly play into the main plot for most of the film. Rather, Philomac's story provides an extra dimension to Sam's story, subtly underlining the power dynamics at play between the Aboriginal and white communities, as well as within Aboriginal communities.

Back on the run, Sam seems to be winning against the police. But he has a problem – Lizzie can't keep pace as she is pregnant. When Lizzie is attacked by an Aboriginal tribe, Sam is forced to kill again to protect her. That night, Sam wonders if Fred's God is looking after them. Maybe he'll look after them if they give themselves in. The attack on Lizzie and her pregnancy (*external* change) forces Sam to decide to put his trust in the white man's law (*internal* choice).

Fletcher wakes up to find Sam and Lizzie sitting in the middle of the main street in town. They're immediately arrested and a trial will be overseen by a magistrate, Judge Sandhill.

It's important to point out that a trial is not something that Sam wants. He ran because he didn't trust he would get a fair trial in a white courtroom. Having no choice but to hand himself in, he hopes he's wrong. But from Sam's perspective, it's a desperate last resort. In other words, he hasn't internally changed what he believed at the beginning – that there's no justice for blacks in this country. His beliefs are constant. The trial is to take place

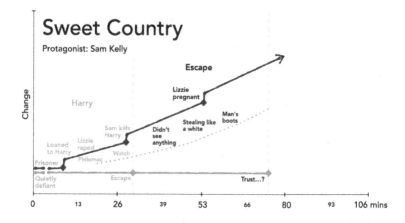

Sweet Country

Protagonist: Sam Kelly

in the open street because there is no church in this town, only a pub. As things get underway, a hanging platform is constructed nearby by the local townsfolk, as if the verdict is already in. But Judge Sandhill is a stickler for the law and fairness. He's able to establish from witnesses that Harry was drunk, that he had been chasing Philomac after chaining him up, and that he fired the first shot.

When Judge Sandhill tries to interview Lizzie, she is too distraught to reveal that she was raped by Harry. When questioned, Sam reveals Lizzie is 'in the family way'. With great difficulty and humiliation, Sam explains that he knows the child is Harry's because Sam can't have children. As the trial concludes, everyone watching, including Fletcher, Fred and Philomac, slowly put the pieces together – Sam killed Harry in self-defence. He only ran because he killed a white man. Simple as that. To everyone's shock, including Sam, he is cleared of all charges.

Fletcher dutifully sees Sam, Fred and Lizzie safely to the edge of town. It looks like Sam was wrong. The white man's laws set him free. They are just. But then a sniper's bullet slams into Sam's chest. He collapses and dies in Lizzie's arms with a devastated Fred muttering over and over to himself, 'What chance has this country got?' Sam dies believing what he believed at the very beginning – that justice is elusive for Aboriginals in a white world.

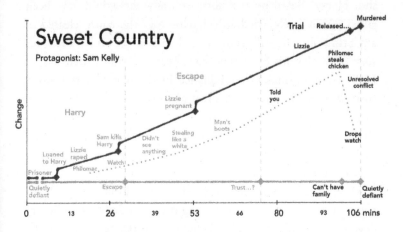

It's a devastating and shocking end to Sam's arc, but the story isn't quite finished. In a brief epilogue, Fred oversees the building of a church and Philomac sits by a river fondling the watch he stole from Harry's dead body. Having been assured by his white boss that Sam would be caught and punished, Philomac drops the watch in the water, recognising the violence and injustice it represents.

There's no doubt this is a gut-wrenching story. Sam's distrust of white culture is proved correct. Even though their courts unexpectedly set him free, the court of public opinion sealed his fate. Perhaps, for a brief moment, Sam believed things could be different – until the sniper's shot landed. In the end, as a character, his internal world remains constant as his story takes on a Pessimistic Arc.

It's worth reflecting, briefly, whether Sam's story would have been any different had he emotionally changed in some way. For example, what would have happened if he had not run and, instead, trusted the white system from the moment he shot Harry? Based on the story we know, he would have been jailed immediately, tried and, having told the truth, cleared of any crime. But he still would have had a target on his back. It's very likely that his fate would have been the same. There are no Hollywood triumphs over injustice in the world of this story. Instead, there are powerful forces at work – racism, oppression, dispossession – that shape Sam's Pessimistic Arc, robbing his choices of the usual agency we see in mainstream films. Sam can make choices, but in the colonised world he exists in, they do not have the same impact as they have for the white characters.

Despite the tragic nature of the story, Philomac's subplot plays an important role in widening the themes of *Sweet Country* beyond the confines of a simple fight for justice by exploring the ways cultural indoctrination has the potential to undermine a people's identity, culture and sense of independence. As Harry's watch drops in the river, there is hope that Philomac will escape Sam's fate to find his own way in the world.

Summary: Tragic, fateful, inevitable

It would be easy to assume that Constant Characters with a Pessimistic Arc bring unhappiness upon themselves. They resist the problems the world throws at them and, instead of finding alternatives, they charge on, constant in the belief that they are right and everyone else is wrong.

But that misunderstands the storytelling potential of this arc. As we've seen with these three examples, the tone of this type of story can vary dramatically. *Mulholland Drive* is not only an eerie and atmospheric puzzle, it also contains a sharp social commentary about the 'dream' of Hollywood and the powerful forces lurking beneath the surface. *Inside Llewyn Davis* is wryly funny and sweetly melancholic, and the pessimistic fate of Llewyn has an idealism at the heart of it that is almost noble. Sure, he'll never make it, but when he sings, he's trying to make this indifferent world a little more beautiful. And the devastating tragedy and injustice of Sam's death in *Sweet Country* is rescued from utter despair by the hope that Philomac might be saved.

Broadly speaking, they're all sad stories, but they're sad in very different ways. The constant nature of these three central characters, and their pessimistic ends, reveals a world that is harder and tougher and, in many ways, more authentic than traditional Hollywood fare. They're not so much an escape from the real world as an escape from the fantasy so much of our storytelling serves up. This is how they draw their power as stories.

Sometimes, when the world is getting us down, a story that is honest about how tough things can get can be a lifeline. It doesn't blindly say, 'Cheer up, buddy'. It says, 'I hear you'. To explore more films that feature Constant Characters with a Pessimistic Arc, check out *Uncut Gems, Chinatown, Apocalypse Now, I Care a Lot, There Will Be Blood, Mean Streets, No Country for Old Men, Leaving Las Vegas, Badlands, It Comes at Night, The Departed* and *Hell or High Water*.

PART IV

OTHER CHARACTERS
AND ARCS

CHAPTER 8

'I just don't know what
I'm supposed to be': Minimalist Arcs

So far, we've talked a lot about change, conflict and choice. These concepts are at the centre of understanding a character's arc. A *change* creates *conflict* that pushes the character to make a *choice*. These three concepts give shape to the story as the character's external and internal worlds are pulled apart in a struggle of wills. There's an elegant syntax to this approach that seems to capture a wide variety of stories. But are all stories shaped by change, conflict and choice? Do they all have big external changes that put pressure on the characters? Are stories always driven by a big conflict? Is the rise and fall of the story always shaped around the character's internal choices? And what *is* a choice anyway?

Before we start deconstructing the very language we're using and disappear down an existential sinkhole, let's take a quick look at a few well-known and much-loved movies that challenge the idea that stories are always about change, conflict and choice.

These films tell a story in their own way. And there's no disputing they tell a story in the common sense of the word. There are characters, stuff happens, more stuff happens, then the story ends. But instead of being shaped by *significant* changes, *big* conflicts or *dramatic* choices, the story is quieter, subtler and more nuanced than usual.

As a result, the stories have a flatter shape for the most part, and it's hard to see when change happens or when the conflict escalates or what choice the character has made to fix things (if they've even made a choice at all!). In many cases, these films can appear to be one long act with no breaks at all. I like to call them Minimalist Arcs. They are often quieter stories, where the emphasis is on the character rather than big plot points. They're about the smaller things in life, the little moments that seem inconsequential at first but have significance when seen as a whole. Like the title quote for this chapter suggests, characters with a Minimalist Arc aren't necessarily driven by powerful goals or overwhelming desires. Their choices are smaller, less directed, and more opaque, so it's harder to distinguish where one act ends and another begins. Instead, the impact of these stories sneaks up on you. It's all the little moments, thoughtful and well-observed, that accumulate throughout the film and hit you with surprising emotion at just the right moment.

But this doesn't mean that change, conflict and choice are not present in these stories. It's just that they are not *shaped* by these elements as much. And they are still about characters who either change or remain constant, and who usually have something resembling either an Optimistic, Ambivalent or Pessimistic Arc.

It's like the volume of the storytelling has been turned down, forcing us to listen carefully, to pay more attention, to spend time with these characters and just watch them, without wondering where the story is going. For this reason, I have not included diagrams in this chapter. The storytelling is so quiet and subtle that any diagram depicting their shape would appear uneventful in a way that misrepresents the strength of these stories.

When compared to the escalating pace of contemporary stories, Minimalist Arcs sound like radical mindfulness training or detox from a media diet of amusement park storytelling, binge TV and bite-size 'up next' streaming. You have to be in the right frame of mind for these stories, and they should probably come with a consumer alert. Warning: Minimalist Arc. Avoid large meals, alcohol or fatigue before consuming. But with a little bit of effort, these films can bring great rewards.

Lost in Translation (2003)

Sofia Coppola's Academy Award–winning screenplay is a marvel of minimalist storytelling. It tells the story of two lonely people who meet and spend a largely aimless week together in Tokyo. If you took Coppola's name off the front cover and sent the screenplay to industry script readers today, the results would be a hard pass at every turn. Why? Well, aside from the fact it would be considered xenophobic these days (a point we will discuss later), it also defies virtually every piece of advice ever offered to screenwriters.

There are no turning points or major plot developments, making it difficult to clearly identify any acts beyond a simplistic beginning, middle and end. The conflict in the story, if you could call it that, is internalised and low-stakes by movie standards. The choices the characters make are small and diffuse, rather than strong and clear. And the emotional climax of the film is deliberately left unintelligible.

And yet it *works*. But how? Let's take a closer look and see if we can figure this out. The story focuses on two characters – Bob Harris, an ageing movie star, and Charlotte, a melancholy college graduate, who are both staying in a Tokyo hotel. Bob is there to make a whiskey commercial. His marriage is in trouble and he's in the midst of a midlife crisis (his *external/internal* world).

Charlotte is travelling with her photographer husband, John. She's having marital trouble as well, and she's also in the midst of an early twenties 'what the hell am I meant to be doing with my life' crisis (her *external/internal* world). The two haven't met yet, but they clearly share an emotional orbit.

Over the first half an hour of the film, Bob and Charlotte cross paths in the hotel and slowly form a bond. They both seem to sense the other's loneliness as they wrestle with their relationship troubles and navigate the unfamiliar world of Tokyo (which includes, unfortunately, some tired cultural stereotypes).

By this point, we're over forty minutes into the film, almost halfway, and the two main characters have only just agreed to spend some time together. So far, so slow. Over the course of the next sixty minutes, the story follows Bob and Charlotte as they explore Tokyo together – hanging out in a nightclub, party, karaoke bar, sushi bar, hospital and strip club.

At the same time, they embark on excursions of their own. Bob plays golf, goes on a talk show, visits a spa and discusses renovations on the phone with his wife. Charlotte rides the trains, visits a temple and attends a flower-arranging class.

As you might guess from the above description, each outing doesn't exactly drive the plot forward or escalate the conflict in any overt way. These are very ordinary scenarios. Nothing particularly unusual happens in them. In fact, on the surface, it feels like almost nothing happens. The story spends a lot of time watching Bob and Charlotte spend time together. But it's not what's happening *externally* to Bob and Charlotte that's important. It's what's happening *internally*, at an emotional level.

While their *external* situations are fairly flat and uneventful, the longer Bob and Charlotte spend together, the more intimate their relationship becomes. At one point, they lie on a bed together drinking sake, watching movies and discussing their floundering relationships. They are obviously very fond of each other. Whatever *external* problems they have, the other person's company makes life more bearable.

The development of their relationship is a slow and incremental build. It emerges out of small and quiet moments rather than sudden or explosive ones. But where does this relationship go? If there is an escalating conflict anywhere in the arcs of these characters, it revolves around this question – Is their relationship platonic, sexual, paternal?

The only moment in *Lost in Translation* that might classify as a traditional turning point, or external change, happens late in the story when Bob sleeps with a cocktail singer and Charlotte is briefly angry with him. But the tension between them is quickly resolved and Bob and Charlotte spend one last night together at the bar.

The next day they say their goodbyes, both reluctant to give away how much they're going to miss each other. On the way to the airport, Bob sees Charlotte on the street. He stops the taxi and runs to her. She's crying. They embrace and Bob whispers something in Charlotte's ear. They briefly kiss and part ways. And that's it.

As you can see, the story of *Lost in Translation* is not shaped around big external changes that create distinct act breaks or developments. Instead, it's like one long build-up to the end. Similarly, Bob and Charlotte's choices are not particularly strong or directed. They don't have a specific goal or desire. They don't make big choices. All they know is that they want to see more of each other. To what end, they have no idea.

So if we can't map out this journey, what can we say about Bob and Charlotte's arcs? For a start, unlike the other stories we've looked at, there are two of them. But despite their obvious external differences, Bob and Charlotte's emotional journeys have a lot of similarities. In fact, their character arcs are essentially identical. They're certainly Change Characters, but, because of the restrained style of storytelling, we get the sense they're at the beginning of an emotional change rather than a fully realised transformation.

We also get the feeling that things are going to be better for Bob and Charlotte. Their arcs feel optimistic. They have a way to go, but we sense they will be okay thanks to this brief encounter. By the end of the story, Bob and Charlotte have emotionally opened up to each other and changed. They still feel lost, but at least they know they're not alone anymore. Someone understands how they feel. Someone cares.

Coppola uses Tokyo as an important backdrop to Bob and Charlotte's emotional arcs. Their shared sense of alienation and isolation is what draws them together as they struggle with the unfamiliar customs and behaviours of Tokyo. It's an extremely effective setting that highlights Bob and Charlotte's search for connection, meaning and authenticity in a bewildering world.

It's worth noting, however, that the story often resorts to ridicule and racial stereotyping to highlight Bob and Charlotte's emotional struggle. It's not called *Lost in Translation* for nothing. There are more than a few bum notes where I suspect Coppola was trying to give her characters a misanthropic view of the world, which often comes across as xenophobic and insulting. It's a legitimate criticism that has only sharpened over the years since its release. Despite this, there's still much to admire about this story. It deftly demonstrates a quieter and more spacious way to tell a story that doesn't rely on spiralling conflict, clear act breaks and articulated motivations.

Perhaps the best example of this approach is the ending. What did Bob say to Charlotte? The film never reveals it. Like much of the storytelling in the movie, what Bob and Charlotte are feeling, especially about each other, is left open. It is in the silences and stolen glances that *Lost in Translation* leaves space for the audience. Instead of revealing Bob's words, the minimalist storytelling invites us to do something much more interesting – *imagine* them.

Paterson (2016)

There aren't many films as minimalist as Jim Jarmusch's quiet comedy/drama *Paterson*. Actually, to call it a comedy feels like an overstatement, even though there are moments of wry comic genius. And 'drama' makes it sound like the story is dramatic. I can assure you that it's not. In fact, *Paterson* almost completely resists my earlier decree that if there is no conflict there is no drama and with no drama there is no story. On the contrary, this is an entertaining, funny, surprising and profoundly moving piece of entertainment.

Paterson tells the story of a shy amateur poet called Paterson who lives in the town of Paterson, New Jersey (I did say it was wry). Apart from writing poetry, Paterson works as a bus driver; he is married to Laura, who wants to be a country singer; and he has a bulldog called Marvin. Humble and retiring, he has never published or performed his poetry and has no plans to do so. This pretty much wraps up everything you need to know about Paterson's external and internal worlds.

The film is broken up into seven acts, one for each day of the week. It starts on Monday when we see Paterson go to work as a bus driver. While driving, he listens to the conversations of his passengers. Sometimes this inspires an idea for a poem, which he writes down on his breaks. When he goes home, he has dinner with Laura, takes Marvin for a walk and stops at his favourite bar for a quiet drink. This provides the structure for about ninety per cent of the film – Paterson wakes, goes to work, writes a poem, comes home, goes to the bar.

There are a couple of subplots involving Laura's ambition to become a country singer and Paterson's fraught relationship with Marvin the dog (they don't like each other). There is also an important subplot involving the notebook that Paterson uses for his poems. He keeps promising Laura he'll get it photocopied but never does. This covers about ninety-five per cent of the story so far.

As you can see, the story does have clear acts that structure the narrative, but they are not created by new or unfamiliar *external* changes or *internal* choices. They're just the days of the week. The sun comes up, the sun goes down. Yes, stuff happens in each act, but it's extremely routine. Nothing is *changing* in Paterson's external life.

Despite this, the unusual structure perfectly captures Paterson's life by immersing the audience in his daily rhythms. As he goes about the day, we are drawn into Paterson's quiet habits of observation and reflection. We're with him as he sees or hears something and starts to write a poem about it. This appears, word by word, on the screen, as if we're in Paterson's head. The poetry is simple and accessible, as well as beautifully observant. Even if you don't read poetry, it's hard not to enjoy Paterson's words. In a strange way, this is what creates forward momentum in the story structure, even though there's not a lot happening or changing in the story. We're drawn in as we look forward to Paterson's next poem.

Despite Jarmusch's deliberately undramatic structure, something eventually *does* happen in the story that is equally simple and devastating

Marvin eats the only copy of Paterson's book of poems. This happens on Saturday. Over the day, Paterson quietly mourns his loss. And so do we, the audience. It *hurts*. Like Paterson, we were invested in those poems.

On Sunday, the last day/act of the story, Paterson goes for a walk where he meets a tourist. The tourist has come to Paterson (the town, not the guy) because it is the hometown of renowned poet William Carlos Williams. Paterson and the tourist talk briefly about their love of poetry, although Paterson doesn't reveal that he's a poet. Before the tourist leaves, he gifts Paterson a blank notebook. Afterwards, Paterson sits quietly, thinking, watching the world around him. And starts to write. The end.

It's a sublime ending from a master of minimalist storytelling and demonstrates the subtle power of a simple, well-observed story. So what sort of character is Paterson? Is he a Change Character? Not really. He briefly mourns his loss, then quietly starts writing again. And we certainly don't get the feeling he's going to run to the copy shop after he finishes his next poem. If anything, in Paterson's mind, the loss of his poems only made them more special. He felt their loss and savoured that feeling, then he started again. He's a very satisfying Constant Character. We wouldn't want him to change.

What about his arc? Well, it's unashamedly optimistic. Despite his loss, we know Paterson will never stop writing. Maybe one day he'll perform his poems, or even publish them. Or maybe not. It doesn't matter. He's happy with his poems, his life, his wife, and even his dog (although that might be pushing it). So we can still describe Paterson in the same terms as the other stories we've looked at – as a Constant Character with an Optimistic Arc.

The minimalist structure of *Paterson* is not shaped by the usual forces of change, conflict and choice. Like *Lost in Translation*, looking at the story through this lens flattens the story's shape and misrepresents its strengths. *Paterson* is a strikingly original story because it largely resists these dramatic conventions and offers us, like Paterson, another way to see the world.

Call Me By Your Name (2017)

When we talk about 'conflict' in a story, part of the discussion is about the obstacles preventing the protagonist from getting what they want. The character has a desire, they choose a course of action, but something is in the way. It can be something *external,* like a mountain, an ocean, an enemy or an army. Or it can be *internal*, like fear, prejudice or a false belief. Obstacles are a vital ingredient when building a strong sense of conflict and tension – except if you're telling a story like *Call Me By Your Name.*

Adapted by James Ivory from the novel by André Aciman, *Call Me By Your Name* is a rich and deeply romantic example of minimalist storytelling. What's striking about this story, which tells the tale of two young men falling in love during a summer in Italy, is how few obstacles stand in the way of the protagonist. In this story, the protagonist wants something and gets it, with almost no effort whatsoever. The conflict in this film is so subtle and fleeting that it is almost non-existent.

And yet the characters and the world they exist in are utterly seductive. The film immerses the audience in a hot and languid Italian summer as the characters slowly grow closer. There are clear acts within the story, but they are not signposted with dramatic *external* changes or bold *internal* choices by the characters. Like its bucolic landscape, the shifts in the story are slow, quiet and gentle.

The protagonist of *Call Me By Your Name* is Elio, a 17-year-old Jewish-American living with his academic parents in rural Italy in 1983. Elio is a bookish teenager who is studying music and has a quiet confidence about him. When his father invites Oliver, a 24-year-old American graduate student, to stay and assist with his academic work over the summer, Elio is forced to give up his bedroom to the visitor.

Living in such close proximity, Oliver and Elio spend much time reading, eating, walking, riding bikes and swimming together as the summer unfolds. While Elio flirts with Marzia, a childhood friend, and starts a sexual relationship with her, it soon becomes clear he has eyes only for Oliver.

During a trip into town with Oliver, Elio hints at his attraction. Oliver warns against getting involved with each other, but later that night they kiss, and Oliver, again, is reluctant to go any further. Over the next few days, he tries to spend less time with Elio.

But it's not long before they arrange to meet one night and have sex. Afterwards, Elio, in a typically teenage response to intimacy, briefly withdraws from Oliver, but it's not for long. Soon they are meeting regularly to have languid sex and lie in each other's arms.

As the summer comes to an end, Elio's parents, sensing their intimacy, suggest that they go away on a trip together. Oliver and Elio spend three gloriously romantic days in an idyllic Italian town. At the end of the trip, they say goodbye at the train station.

Elio is heartbroken. A good and loyal friend, Marzia, is sympathetic and understanding about Elio choosing Oliver over her. Even Elio's parents are supportive. His father confesses he had a chance at a similar relationship when he was young but didn't follow through. He encourages Elio to cherish what he had with Oliver.

A few months later, Oliver calls with news that he is engaged to be married. As Elio and Oliver speak on the phone, it is clear that their feelings are still strong, but they accept that their relationship is not to be. Later, Elio privately mourns by the fire until he is called for dinner. He wipes his eyes and, finally at peace, goes to the table. It is a heartbreakingly beautiful end to a romance for the ages.

The story is told with very little conflict and even fewer obstacles. Elio and Oliver discover fairly quickly that they want to be together – and almost nothing stands in their way. Sure, they have a few momentary spats, but any lingering tension is resolved within the next scene or two.

What about Marzia, who Elio blatantly dumps for Oliver? Surely she'd be pretty sore about how she was treated? But she isn't. Marzia, as a long-time friend, understands who Elio is and recognises love when she sees it. No significant conflict there.

What about his parents? No obstacles there either. Not only do they know about the relationship, but they respectfully keep their distance and even encourage it. When they finally acknowledge the relationship, Elio's father is a dream dad who is open, honest and supportive of his son's feelings.

How about Elio himself? Wasn't he conflicted about his sexual orientation? After all, he did keep it a secret. But his secrecy seems to be more about protecting his parents' feelings than any inner conflict Elio might have been experiencing. In fact, Elio seemed extremely articulate and confident about his sexuality when he approached Oliver. Was Oliver even his first male lover? Perhaps not.

What about the cultural backdrop of rural Italy? It's a very traditional community with a patchy historical attitude towards homosexuality. But this aspect of the story is barely acknowledged aside from Elio and Oliver's chaste hug goodbye at the train station. It's like they live inside their own love bubble, protected from the typical conflicts and obstacles of the outside world.

Of course, Oliver's departure and eventual engagement bring great pain and conflict towards the end of the story. But, as Elio's character grows and matures, we get the feeling that he will learn from his pain and not be tormented for long. In other words, the only overt conflict in the story is quickly turned into something positive and worthwhile. Where's the drama in that?

None of this is a criticism. In fact, it's what I love most about this film. It is easy to make assumptions with any art form. There are conventions. There are ways of doing things. But art is most exciting when it breaks down our assumptions and shows us another way of seeing the world.

Using minimalist storytelling and little dramatic conflict, *Call Me By Your Name* builds an original and compelling Change Character who undergoes a gloriously Optimistic Arc. The world of Elio and Oliver does not emerge from conflict and struggle like so many of our stories. It comes from a deep longing for love. While there are several minor changes from the adapted book, both the source material and the resulting film immerse the audience in the lazy summer landscape of Elio and Oliver's romance and allows their love to grow slowly, sensitively and organically. To inject artificial drama into this setting would have broken the spell.

Summary: Quiet, intimate, character-focused

Good things come in small (minimalist) packages. As these three examples have shown us, a narrative does not necessarily have to resort to dramatic events, relentless conflict or clear and powerful character choices to tell a good story.

Of course, in a world dominated by a superabundance of blockbuster storytelling options, the standard advice is that an idea has to 'cut through', grab the audience by the throat from the first scene and never let up for a single second. But I think this advice misses something that audiences crave and that Minimalist Arcs offer in spades – intimacy.

By dialling down traditional dramatics, these stories immerse the viewer in the world of the characters. They linger where other stories will cut away. They quietly observe where others explain everything with an overwritten speech. They're not afraid of silence, stillness and space, which others fill with a car chase, an explosion or the imminent end of the universe.

Make no mistake, Minimalist Arcs still employ change, conflict and choice in their structure. They just do it in a way that emphasises an intimate connection to the characters and the world they live in. A powerful sense of place is a common feature of Minimalist Arcs – the Tokyo hotel and cityscape in *Lost in Translation*, the rundown streets of Paterson in *Paterson,* the sun-drenched fields of Lombardy in *Call Me By Your Name.* But what they lack in conflict they compensate with a detailed and delicate sense of character and place that elevates the intimacy of the drama. As a result, there is nothing small about the depth of emotion minimalist films can achieve. To explore more films that feature a Minimalist Arc, check out *Nomadland, Once, A Ghost Story, Before Sunrise, Echo, Down By Law, Alba, The Fever, The Straight Story* and *The Weekend.*

CHAPTER 9

'Are you coming with me?':
Dual and Ensemble Narratives

The Hero's Journey approach to storytelling places a 'hero' at the centre of each story, which makes sense. What else would you expect it to do? So far, we've focused (almost) exclusively on stories that have a strong central protagonist whose choices shape the story. This is a very common way to teach storytelling. Focusing on one central character makes it easier to understand the storytelling principles being explored.

But not all stories are centred on a single character. In fact, I would go so far as to say that the vast majority of stories we consume are dual-character or ensemble stories where multiple characters are being followed, each with their own discrete arc. That's because television drama is an ensemble format. These shows don't have a single story. They are a rich narrative tapestry with multiple story strands and character arcs that weave together over years, even decades.

Trying to keep track of all those story strands and arcs in a television show can be bewildering – even with a show you love. But, like single-protagonist stories, the principles of *change*, *conflict* and *choice* can help us make sense of it all.

To ease us into the task, let's stick with movies where we can count the number of character arcs on one hand and where stories only go for a couple of hours rather than years. But before we do this, let's nail down what we mean when we talk about Dual and Ensemble Narratives.

Stories are full of other characters – supporting characters, background characters, extras. The sassy waiter that serves the coffee, the ungrateful boss who holds the protagonist back, the uninterested spouse who takes the hero for granted. So what elevates a character from a supporting role into a lead character in an ensemble cast? It's very simple: point of view.

When the story focuses on a particular character and develops their inner life, motivations and choices, it is giving that character a unique point of view in the story. The writer is saying, 'This person is important. Pay attention to them'. Similarly, when a *change* in the story has an impact on that character and spends time focusing on them to the exclusion of others, the writer is saying, 'Pay attention to this person, this is who we are going to care about'. That's because the *changes* the character experiences, the *conflicts* they endure and the *choices* they make will *shape the story*. Obviously, there are dozens of other non-POV characters that populate a story. But their changes, conflicts and choices *don't* shape the story.

When a story is shaped around two or more protagonists, time is given in the narrative to develop each character's internal and external lives. Their combined changes, conflicts and choices work together to shape the story. Let's take a closer look at a classic dual-protagonist story – *Thelma and Louise.*

Thelma and Louise (1991)

Note: The following story includes depictions of sexual assault and rape.

Callie Khouri's Academy Award-winning screenplay for *Thelma and Louise* is a textbook example of a tight and compelling dual-protagonist narrative. Its iconic characters shocked and thrilled audiences with their bold yet authentic choices and wry humour. Despite being thirty years old, this film has lost none of its relevance and thematic power.

The story is about two friends, a submissive housewife (*external* world) called Thelma and a down-to-earth waitress (*external* world) called Louise. Despite being long-time friends, Thelma and Louise are very different people. Thelma has led a fairly sheltered life and longs to break free of her dull existence providing for her demanding husband (*internal* world). Louise is more grounded and cautious than Thelma, and much less outgoing. There's also a sense that Louise is hiding something (*internal* world*).

The story kicks off with a girls' weekend away where Thelma and Louise hope to let their hair down and enjoy some time away from the demands of their everyday life. But the trip takes a traumatic turn when a man Thelma was dancing with rapes her in a car park. Louise comes to Thelma's rescue and, in the ensuing altercation, fatally shoots the man. Unsure what to do, they hit the road.

One of the strengths of the screenplay is how the women's different personalities lead to different choices that combine to shape the narrative. Let's take a closer look at their arcs.

As you can see, Louise is a Change Character with an Ambivalent Arc who undergoes a dramatic *internal* change that doesn't completely resolve the conflict she is struggling against. The change starts relatively early in the story, with her choice to kill Thelma's attacker. This is, without a doubt, a *new and unfamiliar* choice for Louise. But while it is unfamiliar, it doesn't come out of nowhere. There is a hint that the decision was inspired

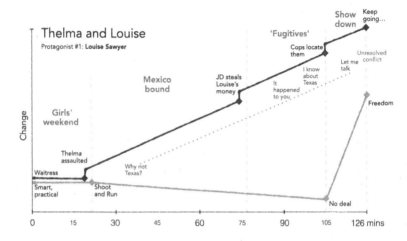

Thelma and Louise

Protagonist #1: **Louise Sawyer**

Change

Girls' weekend

Thelma assaulted

Waitress

Smart, practical

Shoot and Run

Why not Texas?

Mexico bound

JD steals Louise's money

It happened to you

I know about Texas

'Fugitives'

Cops locate them

Let me talk

Show down

Keep going...

Unresolved conflict

Freedom

No deal

0   15   30   45   60   75   90   105   126 mins

by an existing *internal* conflict for Louise. When Louise makes the equally unusual choice to escape to Mexico without going through Texas, the story deftly creates a huge obstacle for the characters to overcome (i.e. avoid Texas) while hinting at Louise's *internal* struggle (i.e. what happened in Texas?).

Another interesting aspect of Louise's arc is her unswerving determination to escape rather than give herself in, a choice she never reconsiders, despite Thelma's urging. Unfortunately, the choice to run only makes Louise look more guilty and increases the conflict she experiences with the police. But she doesn't trust the system and concludes that she will probably be jailed and executed, even if she was protecting her friend.

Nothing that happens to Louise after this point changes her mind. Even when she is contacted by a sympathetic detective who believes her story, she dismisses his offers of a deal. Even when she loses all her money (thanks to Thelma's recklessness) and the cops figure out where they are heading (Thelma again), Louise never contemplates turning herself in. Eventually, we discover why. Louise was raped too. The memory is so painful that she refuses to talk about it, even with Thelma. For Louise, the system will always be rigged against women like her.

However, in the final act of the story, despite the enormous trouble she's in, a new *internal* change comes over Louise – she starts to enjoy herself. She knows there's no going back, so she might as well embrace her new fugitive life. By this time, Thelma has also transformed from a submissive housewife into a daring and liberated armed robber who is as committed to escape as Louise. As a result, Louise doesn't feel as alone. She has Thelma, someone who understands her pain and why she can't go back to the life she had.

In the final moments of the story, as the women are cornered by the cops on the edge of the Grand Canyon, Thelma has a radical suggestion to avoid being caught – 'Keep going'. It's a stunning act of radical defiance that not even Louise has contemplated. She agrees, steps on the accelerator and drives into oblivion. It's a powerful and surprisingly subversive ending to a Hollywood film (even if the surging power ballad over the credits softens the impact).

The interesting thing about Louise's arc is that she makes only one big choice in the whole story – to kill the attacker and run (okay, that's two, but they happen pretty close together). She never wavers from her determination to reject the rigged justice system and escape to Mexico. It is only when Thelma makes her radical suggestion at the end that Louise sees an escape, a type of freedom she never imagined. So where did Thelma's radical suggestion come from? Let's take a look at her arc.

As you can see, Thelma is also a Change Character with an Ambivalent Arc. But Thelma's change happens later than Louise's and, in many ways, is more dramatic. After her attacker's death,

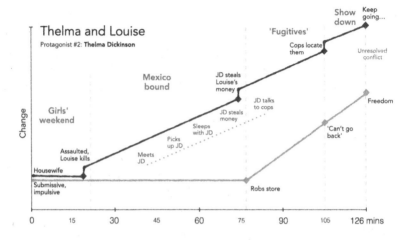

it is Louise, not Thelma, who makes the decisions. She's the one driving the narrative with the plan to escape to Mexico. Of course, Thelma makes a choice to stay with Louise, but it's a fairly reactive choice that doesn't shape the story.

However, when Thelma comes across the roguishly handsome hitchhiker JD, she is smitten. From here, her choices start to impact on the story and the seeds of her emotional change are sown. Feeling uncharacteristically liberated from her controlling husband, Thelma sleeps with JD and has the best sex (and possibly the first orgasm) of her life. She's on cloud nine – until she discovers JD has stolen all their cash. It's a devastating blow for Louise, and Thelma is forced to do something to get her friend back on the road to Mexico. Using a technique JD showed her, Thelma robs a store to get enough cash to make it to the border.

It's a radical departure for the normally compliant Thelma. Not only has she had sex with another man, but now she's a certified felon. And it doesn't stop there. When Louise is pulled over by a cop, Thelma pulls a gun on the officer and, with Louise's help, locks him in the trunk of the car. Later, Thelma and Louise join forces to blow up an oil tanker driven by a lecherous truck driver.

While Louise's emotional change grows slowly from an existing inner struggle, Thelma's change is more sudden and dramatic. She is becoming a completely new person as she makes a series of bold choices that burn down her previous life. As she says towards the end of the story, 'I feel awake… I don't remember ever feeling this wide awake'.

When Thelma and Louise are trapped on the side of the Grand Canyon, with the police ready to gun them down if they don't give in, Thelma's suggestion to keep going makes a lot of emotional sense. There is no going back to the prison of their old lives – both literally and metaphorically. Thelma and Louise are in control for the first time. By driving off the cliff and dying, they are transcending the misogynistic culture that oppressed them their whole life.

As you can see, *Thelma and Louise* expertly weaves together the arcs of its dual protagonists, giving them both meaningful choices that equally shape the overall story as well as each other's emotional arcs. Without Thelma, there would be no Louise, and vice versa.

But what about a story where the characters are less intertwined, where they have similar but separate stories? How do you manage an ensemble story where the arcs might be thematically connected but not dramatically interlocked?

Hidden Figures (2016)

Hidden Figures is based on the true story of three African-American women who overcame significant racial and gender barriers to play important roles in the US space programme. Its

Academy Award – nominated screenplay by Allison Schroeder and Theodore Melfi is fascinating, big-hearted and frequently very, very funny.

While *Thelma and Louise* is an example of a multiple-protagonist story where the characters' arcs have a direct impact on each other, the story strands in *Hidden Figures* are more discrete and run in parallel. As a result, the story in *Hidden Figures* feels bigger and more expansive than a tightly focused narrative like *Thelma and Louise*. By following three separate but related stories, the film creates a wide narrative canvas that explores big themes like racism, sexism, patriotism and self-belief. This is neither better nor worse. It's just different.

The story follows Katherine Goble, a human computer (someone who adds numbers all day), Mary Jackson, an aspiring engineer, and Dorothy Vaughan, an acting supervisor. They are all based on real-life women who worked in NASA's space programme in the 1960s.

While this is an ensemble story, Katherine's strand is the largest and most foregrounded. The biggest *external* changes that happen in the narrative, such as the Russians launching into space and the problem with the Friendship 7 launch, have the most impact on Katherine's story, so let's start there.

As we can see in the diagram, Katherine is a Constant Character with an Optimistic Arc. Her choices change the world around her on a number of levels – on a personal, professional and, most importantly, a social level.

Katherine's arc is broken into four acts. In the first act, she is introduced as a brilliant but humble mathematician working at NASA (her *internal* and *external* worlds). Katherine experiences an *external* change when she is given a new assignment to work on the Space Task Force, a special team tasked with launching an

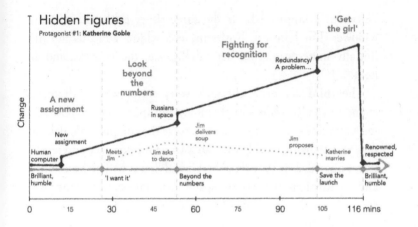

astronaut into space. The assignment is a big deal for Katherine because there are no women or African-Americans in the Space Task Force. Despite her talent, it's all pretty intimidating, and Katherine thinks she might be back working as a humble computer within a week. But when she speaks to her mother, she affirms that she really wants the job. So while Katherine might display some humble insecurities on the surface, when it comes to mathematics, she knows she can excel. Her *internal* choice to pursue this new opportunity pushes the story forward.

In the second act, Katherine faces many obstacles and prejudices because of who she is. A co-worker mistakes her for a cleaner; her supervisor, Paul Stafford, pays little attention to her talent and hides important information from her; and she is forced to drink from a separate coffee pot and use a 'coloured' bathroom across campus. Despite this, Katherine works hard, believes in her ability and eventually impresses everyone when she solves a perplexing maths problem that has dogged the team's launch efforts. As a result, she is given extra security clearance to examine the team's calculations. Even her grumpy boss, Al

Harrison, is impressed. At the same time, Katherine meets a widower, Jim Johnson. Katherine is a widow and, despite Jim initially underestimating her intelligence, the two become an item.

The third act of Katherine's story starts with a dramatic change – the Russians launch a man into space. It's a major blow for Katherine's team. They have to solve the complex calculations that will allow them to launch an astronaut into space and return him unharmed. If they fail, the United States will be humiliated and the Russians may win the space race. Harrison urges the team to 'go beyond the numbers' and that's exactly what Katherine chooses to do.

Again, Katherine must fight prejudice and the jealous undermining of Stafford, her supervisor, who insists on taking credit for her work. But Katherine fights back and is eventually allowed into the daily briefings that will give her the information she needs to develop the complex mathematics required. Her pioneering solutions to the team's problems – her ability to 'go beyond the numbers' – gains the respect of not only her boss, Al Harrison, but also Colonel John Glenn, the lead astronaut whose fate will be in their hands.

Unfortunately, just as Katherine is making progress, a new change impacts her story – an IBM 'computer machine' comes online that can perform all of Katherine's calculations in a fraction of the time. Her boss, Al, regretfully reassigns her to a new department. But it's not all bad news. With growing respect and admiration, Jim Johnson proposes to Katherine and they marry.

The final act of Katherine's arc starts with John Glenn on the launch pad, but there's a problem with the IBM computer's calculations, and John Glenn wants Katherine to doublecheck the numbers. He trusts and respects her. Katherine rushes to flight command with her calculations and Al Harrison lets her inside the hallowed room – another first for a woman. Katherine's numbers check out. The flight is successful. Thanks to the team, as well as Katherine's talent, the Americans launch a man into space. In the final scene, she co-authors a report while her prickly supervisor brings her a cup of coffee. She's won the recognition she deserved all along.

We can see that Katherine's choices changed the world around her. She changed her co-worker's attitude to women and African-Americans, she changed her boyfriend/future husband's attitude to women, and she even pioneered a new branch of mathematics that enabled space travel. But did Katherine emotionally change? You could argue that Katherine became more confident and assertive, but that would be a slight change. From her first day of work, Katherine was always pushing to do more, to see more, to be included in the Task Force, so it's hard to see how it's a significant change. I would argue that it was her constant, unswerving belief in her talent and value as a mathematician that allowed her to succeed, rather than any growth in confidence. This is what makes Katherine a Constant Character with an Optimistic Arc.

Katherine's arc provides the structure for the other character arcs in *Hidden Figures*. These stories have many similarities to Katherine's, such as a fight for recognition and respect, but they do not overtly impact on her central story. Let's take a look at the second protagonist, Dorothy Vaughan.

Using the existing act breaks as a guide, you can see that key changes in Dorothy's story weave around the 'tentpoles' of Katherine's story. And like Katherine, Dorothy is also a Constant Character with an Optimistic Arc.

When we meet Dorothy, she's under a car fixing the

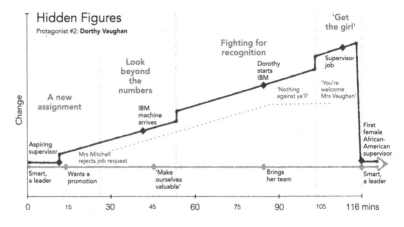

Hidden Figures
Protagonist #2: **Dorthy Vaughan**

'Get the girl'

Fighting for recognition

Look beyond the numbers

Dorothy starts IBM

Supervisor job

A new assignment

IBM machine arrives

'Nothing against ya'll'

'You're welcome Mrs Vaughan'

Change

Aspiring supervisor

Mrs Mitchell rejects job request

First female African-American supervisor

Smart, a leader

Wants a promotion

'Make ourselves valuable'

Brings her team

Smart, a leader

0   15   30   45   60   75   90   105   116 mins

starter motor. We discover that she is a strong and confident leader (*internal* world) who commands a large pool of human computers at NASA, all of them women and African-Americans (*external* world). Despite her obvious ability, Dorothy is only an acting supervisor, and her efforts to advance are opposed by Mrs Mitchell, her boss, who looks down on any ambitious African-Americans.

During the second act of the story, Dorothy experiences an *external* change in her circumstances when a new machine arrives at NASA – an IBM 'computing machine'. But no one knows how to programme this cutting-edge equipment. Dorothy, sensing the future potential, and threat, of the computer, comments to Katherine and Mary that they will have to make themselves useful (*internal* choice).

In the next act of the story, Dorothy slowly teaches herself how to programme the IBM computer. But with no support or encouragement from Mrs Mitchell, Dorothy is forced to do this secretly in her own time and even steals a book from the 'whites-only' section of a library to get the information she needs. At the same time, Dorothy teaches what she knows to her pool of lady computers so they can be ready when the machine finally comes online.

With courage and confidence, Dorothy becomes the first person to programme the machine to make a calculation – something no one else at NASA knew how to do. With this success, she recruits her team of human computers to programme the machine. It is a triumphant moment for Dorothy and her team, and a crucial advance for the Space Task Force.

Of course, Dorothy's choice to bring the IBM computer online has a direct impact on Katherine's story when she is made redundant. But the story doesn't make this a point of conflict between Dorothy and Katherine, even though it could have been. Instead, it leaves the two narrative strands in harmony. Within a few scenes, Katherine is called on again when the IBM calculations need checking – and Dorothy is right beside her, barracking for Katherine to do what she was born to do. In the final act of the story, Dorothy is approached by Mrs Mitchell and given the supervisor position she always wanted.

Like Katherine, Dorothy is a Constant Character with an Optimistic Arc. Rather than go through an *internal* change, she changed the world around her – except maybe Mrs Mitchell, whose attitude to African-Americans changed little.

But while Dorothy's story has many similarities to Katherine's – a triumphant struggle again prejudice – the two aren't as tightly wound together as Thelma and Louise. Dorothy's story runs parallel to Katherine's, strengthening its themes from another angle and reflecting the cultural backdrop of the film.

The final story strand in *Hidden Figures* is Mary Jackson, also a real-life person. Let's see how her story weaves around Katherine's and Dorothy's. Like Katherine and Dorothy, Mary is a Constant Character with an Optimistic Arc. And like the other protagonists, Mary's struggle is about recognition and respect.

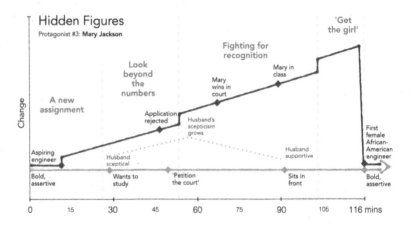

When we meet Mary, she is a talented but frustrated computer on Dorothy's team. She dreams of being an engineer (*internal* world) but is all too aware of the obstacles, both sexist and racist, that stand in her way, something her politically aware husband constantly reminds her about (*external* world). When Mary is transferred to a team working on the design of the space capsule, she is encouraged by her boss to apply for a permanent position with the engineers.

In the second act of the story, Mary applies for an engineer's position but is informed by the condescending Mrs Mitchell that she will have to attend a course at an all-white college to qualify. It's just as Mary suspected. The system is designed to hold women and African-Americans like her back. But with Dorothy's encouragement, Mary petitions the court to be allowed to attend the college classes.

In the third act of the story, Mary and her husband are disturbed by a violent attack on a bus carrying African-American protestors. Despite her husband's growing doubt that her efforts will come to anything, Mary attends court to argue her case. It goes well and the judge grants permission for Mary to attend a night course at the college. Mary's success sees her husband's hardened attitude soften as she proudly attends an all-male, all-white college course – and sits at the very front of the class.

Mary's story is more contained than the others, but her presence in the narrative is vital. She brings a fighter's spirit to the story, which contrasts with Katherine's humble outlook and Dorothy's pragmatic approach. Each character struggles against a different version of the same enemy – systematic prejudice against women and African-Americans – but they approach it in different ways. Each story reflects the ideas and issues of the others, but they are not bound together dramatically. In other words, you wouldn't be able to tell Thelma's story without Louise, but you could tell Katherine, Dorothy or Mary's story without the others and it would still work.

However, by bringing the three historically separate stories together and setting them against the backdrop of the fight to win the space race for America, *Hidden Figures* makes a wider point about inequality and patriotism in the United States. The results are powerful, entertaining and fascinating.

While some will dispute the historical liberties taken in the film, the most unbelievable thing is that it took almost sixty years for the story of these women to make it to the big screen – a fact that only strengthens the film's central argument.

Let's take a look at our last ensemble film, one where the characters have very different arcs, ranging from optimistic through to pessimistic.

Shoplifters (2018)

Written by Hirokazu Kore-eda, the Palme d'Or–winning *Shoplifters* is a layered narrative that features no less than six interwoven character arcs. It tells the story of a family of shoplifters living on the edge of poverty in Tokyo. Despite the large ensemble, the masterful storytelling affords each character a rich and unique inner life, creating a tender and nuanced tale that challenges our assumptions about what makes a family.

One of the striking features of *Shoplifters* is the emotional range created by the different arcs experienced by its ensemble. Unlike *Thelma and Louise* and *Hidden Figures*, the characters in *Shoplifters* do not all have one sort of arc. They are mostly all Change Characters, but the shape of their emotional arcs is varied and complex.

The family at the centre of the story includes Osamu, a day labourer; his wife, Nobuyo, who works at an industrial laundry; Aki, a young woman who is employed at a hostess club; Shota, a young boy; and Hatsue, an elderly woman.

When we meet the family, we assume that they are related to one another. But as the story unfolds, we slowly realise that is not the case. Osamu and Nobuyo are in a relationship, but they are not married and not Shota's biological parents. They are living together in Hatsue's house even though they do not appear to be related to her. Aki calls Hatsue 'grandmother' and Nobuyo 'sister', but both can't be right. Another important character is a young girl called Yuri, who the family has just taken in because she was being abused by her parents.

So how did this odd family end up living together, etching out a meagre living working menial jobs and shoplifting? It's an intriguing dramatic question that pulls us into the narrative.

Rather than map out all six arcs, I'll briefly outline the stories of three characters and where the differences between their journeys are most pronounced. Let's start with the young boy, Shota, who plays a fairly central role in the narrative.

For Shota, the arrival of little Yuri creates jealousy and tension (*external* change). Osamu encourages Shota to call Yuri his 'sister' and to call him 'father', but Shota is reluctant. He has been taught to shoplift by Osamu, but he begins to feel conflicted about teaching Yuri to do the same. Osamu insists that shoplifting is okay because no one 'owns' the goods until they're purchased, but Shota starts to doubt this warped logic. He sees through the lies that justify his stealing and the illusion of his 'family'. To prevent Yuri being caught shoplifting, Shota sacrifices himself and is caught by the police (*internal* choice).

His capture leads the police to discover that Yuri has been reported as missing. The 'family' are arrested and we learn that Osamu found Shota locked in a car in the hot sun and saved the boy. The police tell Shota that his so-called 'family' was going to escape and leave him behind. Later, Shota, now living in an orphanage, visits Osamu, who confesses they intended to leave him behind. He also tells the young boy that he no longer needs to call him 'father'. As the story ends and they part ways, perhaps forever, Shota whispers the word 'father' as Osamu runs after his bus.

In Shota's arc, his sense of family is challenged when Yuri joins them, leading him to question who his family is and what they do in order to survive. While he has escaped his precarious life of shoplifting, there is the sense that Shota misses his strange family and forgives their actions, knowing that they genuinely loved him. This makes Shota a Change Character who experiences an Ambivalent Arc. His life is more secure, but he feels less loved.

Hatsue, the old woman who owns the house, has a very different arc. She is the matriarch who cooks, cleans, tends to the emotional and physical needs of her extended family, and naturally embraces Yuri's arrival (*external* change). Hatsue gets on with everyone but is closest to Aki. We learn that Hatsue receives money from the son of her deceased ex-husband. The son is Aki's father, and we get the feeling she is an outcast that Hatsue has secretly taken in (*internal* choice). One day, as Hatsue watches her 'family' playing in the water at the beach, she mutters to herself, 'Thank you'. That night, she dies in her sleep.

Unlike Shota, Hatsue's arc is one of peaceful satisfaction. After being abandoned by her husband, she has slowly built a new 'family' with fellow outcasts who have filled her later days with love and companionship. She welcomes the addition of Yuri into her home. In contrast to Shota, Hatsue is a Constant Character with an Optimistic Arc.

Finally, let's look at Nobuyo's arc. When Yuri joins the family (*external* change), Nobuyo reasons that it is only kidnapping if they ask for a ransom. She is fiercely protective of the young girl and dismisses the idea of returning Yuri after she appears as a missing person on the news (*internal* choice). When she is blackmailed by a co-worker who has seen her with Yuri, Nobuyo threatens to kill the woman if she tells anyone – and we get the feeling she means it. When the family is arrested by police, a terrible truth about Nobuyo is discovered. She murdered her abusive husband when he discovered she was having an affair with Osamu. Nobuyo and Osamu went into hiding and were taken in by Hatsue, forming a family with her and other outcasts.

At the end of her story, Nobuyo asks Osamu to bring Shota to the prison where she is being held. She tells the young boy the details of the car they found him in so he can find his real family.

Nobuyo tells Osamu they are not good enough for the boy. She says goodbye to Shota and leaves.

The abuse Nobuyo suffered at the hands of her ex-husband led her to protect Yuri. Despite being an act of love and kindness, her choice led to the unravelling of her new family and a long prison sentence. Realising her mistake, she emotionally releases Shota so he can return to his real family. Nobuyo is a heartbreaking Change Character with a Pessimistic Arc. Her painful past and lonely future are captured in the kind smile she offers Shota before she says goodbye.

As you can probably gather, *Shoplifters* is a deeply emotional viewing experience that takes you from tender joy to devastating sadness. A large part of the film's power is the number and variety of character arcs that the audience is asked to invest in. Each character feels unique, authentic and compelling simply because their story is so different from the others. Only superior writing could make six distinctive characters feel like they belonged together as a family.

Summary: Layered, varied, expansive

Dual and Ensemble Narratives are very common in film and ubiquitous in television. Each protagonist has a unique point of view that explores their inner life and the emotional stakes for them in the story. Often, these stories are plotted tightly together so that the changes and choices of one character ripple through the other character arcs in the film. See *Thelma and Louise*, *Parasite*, *The Favourite*, *Queen and Slim*, *Marriage Story*, *Mad Max: Fury Road*, *The Shawshank Redemption*, *Cold War*, *Apollo 13* and *Toy Story*. Sometimes, the stories are less interlocked but feature similarly shaped arcs, creating a consistent tone throughout. See

Hidden Figures, Love Actually, The Royal Tenenbaums, The Hours and *Nashville*. And other times there is contrast between the multiple stories, each with a different feel and tone, which creates a rich storytelling experience. See *Shoplifters, The Ice Storm, Contagion, Fargo, Traffic, Pulp Fiction* and *Magnolia*.

While Dual and Ensemble Narratives may appear more complex on the surface, each character arc is still shaped by the principle of external change, conflict and internal choice. By giving each character a clear point of view, and their own arc, the audience is able to follow multiple stories at once without getting lost. At the same time, this approach creates a broader narrative canvas that expands the emotional and thematic possibilities available in each story.

CHAPTER 10

'I'm Losing All My Leaves'
– Reactive Characters

So far I've put a lot of emphasis on the importance of *choice* in understanding a character's arc. This isn't surprising. In Western storytelling traditions, the concept of choice is at the heart of understanding both character and story. Choice makes the intangible *internal* world of the character tangible as they try to impose their will on the *external* world.

Each time a character chooses what to do about a dramatic change in their circumstances, it moves the story forward. If those choices are big enough, they create a natural act break in the story as the character tries to see through their decision and grapple with new challenges in an escalating cycle of change, conflict and choice. Will their internal choices change or remain constant? Will their arc be optimistic, ambivalent, pessimistic? The character is actively shaping their circumstances, showing their grit, fighting back, taking control because their choices *matter*.

But what happens when a character's choices don't matter. What if their choices make no difference? What if they're not in control? What if they don't understand what's going on and have no idea what they should do next?

Earlier we saw an example of this in *The Terminator* where, for most of the story, the protagonist, Sarah Connor, not only has no idea what is happening but has little control over her choices. Other characters, Reece and the Terminator, are shaping what happens. It is only towards the end of the story that Sarah starts to understand what is expected of her and takes control – *'You're terminated!'*

This sort of character is often called a 'reactive' character. This is because their choices are short-term, spontaneous, knee-jerk responses to the problems they face. They're just 'reacting' to the next thing that gets thrown at them. They're not 'proactively' thinking through the consequences of their actions and following through with a clear goal or a clear result in mind.

As mentioned earlier, the general industry wisdom is to avoid reactive characters. That's because reactive characters can sometimes feel weak, aimless or just plain hopeless. They lack the necessary agency or insight to take control and shape their destiny. They're flaying about like a kite in a hurricane. They can kinda feel like *losers*. Who wants to watch a story about a loser? Audiences want to watch stories about winners! At least according to the wisdom of industry insiders (I assume they'd also know exactly what to do if confronted by a killer robot from the future).

But sometimes the nature of a story *requires a reactive character.*

Sometimes the conflict facing the protagonist is so large, so strange, so unfamiliar – like a killer robot from the future – that a large part of the story involves them just catching up to what is going on. And even when they are able to make a meaningful choice about what to do, sometimes it's hard to see what impact it will have. Maybe, like Sarah Connor, they will finally take control at just the right moment. While other times they will be crushed by a force that they could never hope to overcome. Or maybe everything gets resolved without their help at all.

Reactive characters are less frequent in Western storytelling traditions, possibly because of our worship of powerful, motivated individuals who shape the world to their needs (i.e., the Hero's Journey). Traditionally, choices matter. But that doesn't mean reactive characters have no place in our stories.

In this chapter we'll be looking at three exceptional and celebrated films each featuring a highly reactive protagonist. They are; the comedic anarchy of *The Big Lebowski*, the unnerving horror of *Midsommar*; and the emotional labyrinth of *The Father*. In each example, the reactiveness of the protagonist is a strength, rather than a weakness, of the narrative structure.

The Big Lebowski (1998)

Written by Joel and Ethan Coen, *The Big Lebowski* initially baffled audiences and critics alike with its rambling crime/caper stoner comedy riff on LA in the early nineties. But over time this eccentric shaggy-dog story has become one of the Coens' most enduring, and endlessly quotable, films.

At the centre of the story is Jeffrey 'The Dude' Lebowski, a carefree, bathrobe bedraggled, White Russian swilling, dope-smoking, ten-pin bowling, unemployed dropout (*internal/external* worlds) who, as we'll see, is the epitome of a reactive character. The feeling you get from The Dude is that proactive, decision-making has never been, and never will be, one of his strong suits.

The story kicks off with The Dude returning home to his cosy LA bungalow where he is assaulted by two thugs who keep calling him 'Lebowski' and claim his wife, Bunny, owes money to a porn king called Jackie Treehorn. But it's a case of mistaken identity as The Dude points out that no one calls him Lebowski ('I'm The Dude!') and he isn't married to anyone called Bunny. The thugs leave – but not before urinating on his rug. The Dude tells his bowling buddies, Walter, a Vietnam veteran, and Donny about the attack. At Walter's impassioned suggestion, The Dude decides to claim compensation for his soiled rug from the real Jeffrey Lebowski, a wealthy millionaire – after all, 'that rug really tied the room together'.

Now, this sounds like a choice right? And it is. But the idea to claim compensation from the millionaire Lebowski comes from Walter. Before that The Dude didn't see the point in complaining. Nevertheless he does complain to the millionaire Jeffrey Lebowski, an irritable man who berates The Dude for being a lazy layabout and throws him out. On his way, The Dude takes one of the expensive rugs from Lebowski's mansion.

Again, this sounds like a choice (and it's a pretty smart one actually). But does this choice put The Dude back in control? Ah, no.

As soon as The Dude returns home to enjoy a White Russian on his new rug he's attacked again – but by different thugs who, this time, steal his rug instead of urinating on it like the other guys. When he wakes up, The Dude is unexpectedly recruited by Jeffrey Lebowski, the millionaire, to deliver a ransom for his wife Bunny who he claims is being held hostage by the same people who attacked him (the first time that is, c'mon keep up!). The Dude agrees to the job but suspects that Bunny is only pretending to be kidnapped in order to pay off her debts to Jackie Treehorn. Walter joins The Dude on the drop but insists on swapping out the ransom for a 'ringer', an empty case full of dirty underwear. He also has a machine gun. Needless to say things don't go to plan and the kidnappers escape. The Dude is terrified they will now kill Bunny. Making matters worse, thieves steal his car with all the ransom money in it.

Over the rest of the story, as The Dude tries to figure out what's going on, he is; recruited by Lebowski's daughter, Maude, to recover the ransom money her father stole from a family trust; attacked by a group of latex clad 'Nihilists' armed with a marmot who claim they are the kidnappers; dragged by Walter to threaten a teenager who they think stole the ransom money (they're wrong); attacked by the original thugs again; drugged by the porn king Jackie Treehorn; beaten up by a Malibu police chief; tailed by a private investigator hired by Bunny's parents; and seduced by Maude to secretly impregnate her.

Suffice to say, whatever 'choices' The Dude makes up to this point in the story don't help him take control of whatever the hell is going on. He is largely being carried along by other people's plans and decisions – Lebowski's plan to pay the ransom, Maude's plan to get the ransom back (and become impregnated), Walter's insane ideas, the threats of the Nihilists, the drugging by Jackie Treehorn, the attack of the thugs (the first and the second).

But somehow, against the odds, The Dude figures out what is going on – the Nihilists are friends of Bunny and have attempted to extort money from Jeffrey Lebowski. But Lebowski double-crossed them and gave them an empty ransom bag (i.e., the 'ringer' was a 'ringer'). It seems Lebowski, having grown tired of Bunny, kept the ransom money for himself in the hope she would be killed. But, instead, Bunny returns home having gone on an unannounced holiday to Palm Springs.

So even though The Dude figures out the mystery, it's of little consequence – Millionaire Lebowski never admits guilt and Bunny returns home unharmed because she was never in danger. In the final act of the story, the Nihilists attack The

Dude, Walter and Donny at the bowling alley demanding the ransom money. Donny, who has had little to do with any of this, suffers a heart attack and dies. The Dude and Walter scatter his ashes and go bowling. The End.

So what was the point of all of that? It's a good question and one many audience members, including myself, were asking after seeing this nutty film for the first time. It just seems so random (and I haven't even talked about the mysterious cowboy, the numerous dream sequences or Maude's 'vaginal art'). The Dude, the so-called hero of the story, is swept along like the 'tumbling tumbleweed' we see rolling through the opening credits. And perhaps that's the point.

The Dude's utter lack of control and reactive choices capture his quiet philosophical 'live and let live' attitude to most things in life. He's not comfortable with responsibility or with making big decisions. He just wants to smoke some weed, drink a few White Russians and bowl a couple of frames. And despite everything that happens to him, The Dude holds firm to these internal values that he knows to be true (for him anyway – he wouldn't think to push them on anyone else). As a result he's a Constant Character with an Optimistic Arc. He's not like Walter. He's not like Jeffrey Lebowski. Or Maude. Or Jackie Treehorn. These people know what they want and know how to get it. But The Dude, not so much. Taking control, being in charge, making meaningful *choices*, that's for suckers. As he says 'The Dude abides'.

Midsommar (2019)

The screenplay for *Midsommar,* by Ari Aster, is a strange and unsettling psychological catharsis that explores ideas of grief, ritual and community while also effectively chartering the last days of a destructive relationship. At its heart, this is a story about control – specifically, giving over control to others. What better story to feature a reactive character?

The story centres on Dani, a psychology student who is grieving the death of her parents and mentally ill sister in a murder/suicide orchestrated by her sister. Understandably, Dani struggles to cope and worries her grief will be too much for her already emotionally distant boyfriend Christian (her *internal/external* world). Unknown to her, Christian was intending to break up with Dani but, following her family's death, he hasn't yet mustered the courage.

When Dani learns Christian was planning to go on a holiday to Sweden with some university friends, Christian feels compelled to invite her along. Only Pelle, Christian's Swedish friend, thinks it's a good idea that Dani comes. He believes the trip, which involves a midsummer celebration at the ancestral commune where he grew up, will be good for Dani as she deals with her grief.

In Sweden, Dani, Christian and his friends arrive at the commune which is called Hårga. Here they are welcomed by Pelle's extended family and enthusiastically invited to join in the festivities which only happen every ninety years. Things start out innocently enough with a mushroom trip in a field but Dani doesn't want to participate until Christian subtly pressures her to join. The experience gives her a panic attack but the community are warm and attentive to Dani's needs. In fact, their village is an idyllic utopia of communal living, cooking and harvesting. Of course, some of the community's everyday rituals are unfamiliar and a little odd to Dani and the other visitors but they're mostly open to learning and understanding.

Unfortunately, the first day of celebrations takes an unexpected turn when two elders deliberately throw themselves off a cliff and fall to their deaths in a gruesome and bloody sacrificial ceremony. Dani and the others are horrified and some want to leave. But Pelle convinces Dani to stay, assuring her that the elders' sacrifice was given willingly and that it is an important part of their culture and sense of family. Pelle feels strongly that Dani deserves a home and family after losing her own and warns that Christian, who has forgotten Dani's birthday, can never provide this. Christian also urges Dani to stay after he decides he is going to study the Hårgan community for his university thesis.

As you can see, Dani has generally been swept along by other people's choices – Christian's choice to go to Sweden, his (reluctant) invitation to her, Christian's pressure to join in the mushroom trip, Pelle's urging to stay as well as Christian's. She is, in a sense, making choices but they are largely initiated or made by someone else.

Things continue the same way over the next few days as the ceremonies continue and Dani is coaxed to join in with little understanding of what is involved or what is expected of her. Thankfully there is nothing as graphic as the elders' leap from the cliffs but one by one the other visitors start to disappear in mysterious circumstances – an English couple who were disturbed by the celebrations reportedly leave early; an obnoxious friend of Christian's inadvertently urinates on a ceremonial tree and disappears; another friend takes photographs of a sacred book without permission and also disappears.

As Dani tries her best to be polite and participate in the ceremonies she experiences a growing sense of unease with what is going on around her. Most disturbing, Christian becomes the target of Maya, a Hårgan girl, who has developed affections for him. Dani notices and seems to be increasingly aware of Christian's lack of commitment to her.

In the penultimate ceremony, Dani is asked to join a female-only Maypole dance which will determine which of the women will be crowned the May Queen. For hours Dani and the other women dance around the Maypole until only one exhausted dancer is left standing – it's Dani. She is crowned the May Queen.

As Dani is prepared for the final ceremony, Christian is drugged and taken away where he has sex with Maya, the Hårgan girl, in a fertility ceremony. On her return, Dani discovers Christian's infidelity and is distraught. Does this act of betrayal finally inspire Dani to take control, to reject her manipulative, coercive boyfriend? Let's see.

In the final ceremony, the community explain their rituals are designed to encourage fertility and new life by sacrificing nine lives – four outsiders, four willing community members, and one life selected by the May Queen. As the victorious May Queen, Dani has the power to choose who will be the ninth sacrifice. And, having finally recognised his uncaring, unfaithful and manipulative behaviour, she chooses Christian.

As Dani watches on with the Hårgans, Christian and the eight other sacrifices, including his four missing friends, are burned alive in a ceremonial house. While they burn, the community bellows in an act of ritual screaming, a gesture of their oneness with the sacrifices. As the ceremony reaches it's climax, Dani smiles joyously. She is finally at peace. Her choice has released her from Christian's control, as well as her grief, and delivered her to a new family with the Hårgans.

As you can see, Dani proves to be a highly reactive character who has little agency in the mysterious world of the Hårgans. Essentially, Dani makes only one meaningful choice of any consequence in the events of *Midsommar* – choosing Christian as the final sacrifice. The rest of the time, Dani's choices are manipulated by either Christian's subtle coercive control or pushed on her by others (e.g., Pelle's urging to come to Hårga, his pleas that she stay, the community's persistent invitations to join in). But her release from Christian via the community's rituals feels like a double-edged sword. Has Dani escaped one form of control, only to be trapped again with the strange and suffocating expectations of the Hårgans? Does her new family offer freedom or a prison?

It's hard to tell from the open-ended tone of the story, trapped as we are in Dani's euphoric point-of-view. But there is enough in this unnerving story to have serious doubts about Dani's prospects for taking control of her life again, making her a Change Character with a troublingly Ambivalent Arc.

The Father (2020)

Based on a play by Florian Zeller, and adapted by Zeller and Christopher Hampton, *The Father* is a masterful exercise in immersive as well as non-linear storytelling. It also features a compelling example of a reactive character. Very little can be taken for granted in this tale about the ravages of dementia as its protagonist is plunged into an escalating, and highly reactive, struggle with reality.

The story focuses on Anthony, an elderly man who we meet living in a London flat by himself where he is frequently visited by his daughter Anne. We learn early on that Anthony's latest in-house carer has recently quit and that Anne is anxious about finding another. It seems Anthony has had quite a few carers and they've all quit because of his difficult behaviour. Anthony assures Anne that he doesn't need a carer and that he will be fine by himself. Anne reveals that she might be leaving London to go and live in Paris with a man she has met. Anthony is confused and doesn't recall anyone in Anne's life since her marriage to a man called James fell apart. He also longs to see Anne's sister, Lucy, who never visits him. He's not sure why.

Later, Anthony finds a strange man in his living room. The man says his name is Paul and claims that he is married to Anne. Anthony scoffs at this nonsense and tells Paul that Anne is going to Paris to be with someone else. He thinks it's a ploy to get him to leave his flat and move him into a nursing home. Paul doesn't know anything about Paris and claims that this is not Anthony's flat. Paul insists that Anthony has come to live with Anne and him after his last carer quit. Anthony is becoming agitated when Anne returns home – but it's not Anne. It's someone else altogether. Someone Anthony (and the audience) doesn't recognise even though the woman insists she is his daughter. Anthony asks about Paul, who seems to have disappeared, and says he claimed to be Anne's husband. Anne has no idea what he's talking about and claims she's not married.

As you can see, Anthony, and the audience for that matter, is having trouble with some basic details about his reality, like whose flat he is living in, who his daughter is, what her husband's name is and even if she's married or not. As the narrative moves forward it also becomes clear that Anthony is not even sure *when* this is all happening as the story circles back to previous events and plays them out again – a lost watch, the arrival of a new carer, a chicken served for dinner, a verbal and physical attack from Paul (or is it James?). The execution of this disorientation is beautifully handled in the storytelling as it immerses the audience in Anthony's unreliable point-of-view. As a result, it's hard for him to make clear and proactive choices about anything because the world is constantly shifting and is not as he remembered it. Luckily, for us the audience, we have the luxury of being able to slowly piece together what is happening to Anthony, where he is and, most importantly, who everyone is.

First the mystery of what happened to his missing daughter, Lucy, is revealed – she died many years ago following an accident. The audience discovers this when Anthony finds himself lost in a hospital and wanders into her room as she lies in a neck brace, clinging on to life. Later, Anthony finds himself in a small room in a nursing home. At first Anne, his other daughter, is there, showing him around, asking him what he thinks of the room and reminding him she is going to Paris. She promises to visit often as Anthony asks again where Lucy is. Soon Anne is gone and another woman is there – it's the one who said she was Anne. But now she is Katherine, a nurse. And the man who said he was Paul, Anne's husband, is there too but now his name is Bill and he's a nurse too.

As Katherine calms an increasingly distraught Anthony, the audience understands that he has always been here in the nursing home, right from the very beginning of the story. Now, in advanced dementia, time, space and people are in a constant state of flux. Anthony is not even sure who he is anymore – *'I'm losing all my leaves...'* But Katherine is kind and reassuring as she expertly soothes Anthony, bringing him back to the present, the sunny day outside and thoughts of the lovely walk they will take later.

It's a supremely realised story that handles its difficult material with immense empathy and sensitivity. A version of Anthony's confusion and disorientation is experienced first hand by the audience by way of a non-linear narrative structure that is neither forced nor gimmicky. The approach organically underlines Anthony's helplessness, leaving his choices reactive and ineffectual and rendering him a Constant Character with a Pessimistic Arc.

Summary: Overwhelmed, helpless, impulsive

Reactive characters are certainly the lesser heroes of Western storytelling. They're rarely in control, are usually utterly confused and their choices frequently fail to make any difference at all. But, as we've seen, that doesn't mean their stories always have to be a 'bummer' (as The Dude would say). Sometimes things work out just fine (e.g., *The Big Lebowski*) or maybe they *finally* make a choice that helps solve their problems (e.g., *Midsommar*). Of course, a reactive character's arc can also end in tragedy as they become overwhelmed by their changing circumstances and fail to make choices that can hold their world together (e.g., *The Father*). Crucially, in each of the examples in this chapter, the nature of the story *benefited* from having a reactive protagonist. Their very reactivity underlined key themes in the story about being helplessly swept up by powerful forces outside their control.

It should be pointed out that while reactive characters often appear out of control and helpless, it doesn't mean that their choices are somehow random. Their choices, no matter how weak or short-term, are still informed by their internal values, beliefs and desires. The Dude's 'live and let live' ethos comes through loud and clear in his haphazard choices. Dani's low self-esteem is a factor that keeps her from escaping either Christian or the increasingly bizarre ceremonies. Anthony's pride sees him desperately clinging to the idea that he can take care of himself and will never leave his flat. While their choices in these examples may be ineffectual and, at times, weak, they still reveal a great deal about the character's intangible inner life. In other words, choice, or the lack of it, remains a fundamental building block to a reactive character's arc.

It's also worth noting that most characters, in any story, display a certain amount of 'reactivity', particularly in the early stages of the narrative when they're trying to understand the nature of the conflict they're facing. Is Louise really thinking through the consequences of pulling the trigger in *Thelma and Louise*? In *Moonlight*, does Chiron care what will happen after he hits the bully with the chair? Probably not, but very soon after both characters put into action a meaningful and motivated choice – Louise heads for Texas and Chiron becomes a gangster. As actors often say about their craft, 'acting is reacting'.

To explore more films that feature a Reactive Character check out: *Fruitvale Station*, *The Witch*, *The Game*, *The Hitchhiker's Guide to the Galaxy*, *Sex, Lies, and Videotape*, *The Third Man*.

CHAPTER 11

'I Like to Watch'
– Passive Characters

What do we mean when we describe someone as 'passive'? Implied in the word is a lack of drive or direction, of inertia, a sense of looking on listlessly as others make a decision and take control of a situation. It seems to be passive is to do nothing, to not act, to not make a choice.

The opposite of passive is, of course, 'active', which is all about doing something, making decisions, making *choices* – all of which, as we've found, is at the very heart of Western storytelling traditions.

But here's a question – why are we so obsessed with active characters when most of us spend the vast majority of our lives largely *passive*? Think about it. When we're a kid we don't get to make big choices and take control of our lives. That (ideally) is our parents' job. Then as we move through adolescence we start to make some big decisions, many of them very bad ones. But often it feels like other people's decisions trump ours – a parent's divorce, sudden unemployment, being forced to move towns, an illness in the family. Then, later, we find we have a job, and a partner, and possibly children. If we're really lucky, we may have made a clear and deliberative choice about *one* of those things. But most likely we find ourselves in a job we're kind of indifferent to (at best), with a partner who may or may not be 'the one' and a child who we care deeply about but, if we're honest, wasn't entirely planned. So far so passive. And for the vast majority of us this doesn't really change. Sure some of us are planning for the good life when we retire but, well, life has a habit of getting in the way. Towards the end, we're often in the hands of other people's decisions, even down to the choice of when we die. Bummer.

And maybe this is why Western storytellers generally avoid passive characters. When your whole world view is shaped by the idea of mighty individuals shaping the world around them to their desires, a story featuring a passive character is not only pretty uninspiring but threatens to undermine the philosophical bedrock of the entire culture – *What, you mean I'm not in control of life, that it will all go on without me, that I'm not the centre of existence?* Perhaps this is why our stories often resort to big powerful, super concentrated examples of ordinary people facing adversity and making big powerful choices to wrest back control of their lives. Perhaps, the instinct of the storyteller is to show us how great life could be if we'd just make better choices!

But as we've seen by the many examples in this book, audiences don't always want a story that feels like it's written by a motivational life coach. They often want their stories to feel like they come from a friend who understands what life can throw as us.

Which is why, in this last series of case studies, I wanted to find a place for passive characters. Like reactive characters, passive characters are largely discouraged in film and television because they lack the prerequisite energy and direction to take control of a typical story. However, as we'll see, passive characters offer a truly unique spin on a story that can be surprising, inspiring and, sometimes, even weirdly familiar.

Before we dive in, let's clarify what we're talking about here. The main difference between a passive character and an active one is that active characters (and reactive ones too for that matter) are at least *trying* to take control of their situation. They may be failing but they're trying. However, a passive character, either through circumstance or choice, does not seek to get involved. They will often be on the sidelines, watching others make choices, but rarely, if ever, making a strong one of their own. While this may not sound very dramatic, that doesn't automatically mean that a story featuring a passive character will be dull or unexciting. Quite the contrary. A passive character can be the axel around which the entire story spins as the tension mounts and the stakes get higher. Will they finally be forced to make a choice? Or will they pass the duty onto others? Will all be lost, or found?

And as we'll see, just because a story is about a passive character doesn't mean we won't be able to relate it to our own lives. In fact, in many ways, passive characters are almost *too real* as they expose the fantasy underlying many of our stories. They have the potential to reveal how powerless, unmotivated, uncommitted or cowardly we can be in real life. These unique qualities give passive characters the potential to shatter illusions and challenge complacency in ways their more active counterparts could only dream about.

The three films we will be examining are; *Being There* (1979), a classic social satire which both disarms and bites; *Dead Poet's Society* (1989), a stirring portrayal of courage in the face of crushing conformity and; *Los Silencios* (2018), a delicate and observant study of a displaced community where nothing is as it seems. With each of these examples, the overall passivity of the main character is central to appreciating the story's themes and ideas.

Being There (1979)

The gentle comical whimsy of *Being There* obscures a darker vein of angry social satire in this classic film starring Peter Sellers (in what many consider his greatest role). The screenplay is based on the novel by Jerzy Kosiński and is adapted by Kosiński and Robert C. Jones.

The story centres around Chance, an elderly man who tends the garden of a wealthy benefactor in a large mansion in Washington, D.C. In the opening sequences Chance is woken by the sound of the television coming on in his cosy old-worldy room. After watching television for a while, he goes about his quiet morning routine of putting on a neat suit and bowler hat, having breakfast by himself, and then performing his duties around the mansion, including tending the garden and dusting. In each area he works there is a television which Chance watches constantly, even in the garden. As Chance watches he imitates what he sees. When a character on television tips his hat, Chance does the same as if learning to do it for the first time. It becomes clear that Chance, while an ageing man, is the intellectual age of a young boy. He is quiet, polite, kind and dedicated to his duties in the mansion. In short, he seems very happy and contended (his *internal/external* worlds).

But things take a turn when Chance is informed by Louise, the maid, that the 'Old Man', the owner of the mansion, has died and that the estate will be closed down. Despite the dramatic news, Chance is seemingly unaffected and goes on watching television. When the attorneys representing the estate find Chance in the abandoned house some time later he reveals he has never been outside the walls of the mansion and has nowhere else to go. Nevertheless the attorneys confirm he has no legal claim to the estate and heartlessly turf him out onto the streets.

So far so passive. When confronted with the earth-shattering news his employer (and possibly father figure) is dead, Chance does not have the capacity to comprehend its consequences, nor to make any choices about what he should do. As a result, the attorneys are able to take advantage of Chance's willingness to cooperate, which raises the dramatic question – how will he survive in the big wide world?

The neighbourhood outside the mansion is a rundown ghetto of crumbling apartment blocks and Chance, with a briefcase and dressed impeccably in tailored old clothes from the mansion's attic, is confronted by a world he has only seen on television. Using what manners and customs he's picked up from television, Chance looks for something to eat but it's clear he's out of his depth. While transfixed by a television screen projecting his image in a shop window, Chance is injured when a limousine backs into him. The occupant of the limo is Eve Rand, wife of wealthy and influential businessman Ben Rand, who insists Chance come back to her mansion and see their private doctor. When Chance introduces himself as Chance the gardener, Eve mishears and thinks his name is 'Chauncey Gardiner'. Chance doesn't even seem to notice the mistake.

At the mansion, Eve introduces Chance to her husband Ben who is very ill with anaemia. When asked about himself, Chance honestly answers that his 'Old Man' died and his house was shut down by attorneys. But Ben misunderstands and thinks that Chance's *business* was shut down by the sorts of meddling attorneys and regulations he rails against on Capitol Hill. When Chance is asked what he will do next he explains that he hopes to 'work in the garden' again because he's very good at it. After a few sideways glances between everyone present Ben interprets

Chance's words – he's just like every businessman who yearns to 'tend the flinty soil' with his hands and 'water it with the sweat of his brow'. Ben instantly likes Chance, whom he thinks is a wise and insightful businessman, and invites him to stay while he recovers. Chance, of course, agrees.

Again, Chance has not really made any significant decisions yet. He's not in control of what is happening and appears to have little comprehension of what anyone is talking about. Luckily, his kind and polite manner, not to mention his impeccable suits and evocative descriptions of the garden he likes to work in, are opening up a surprising number of doors – which says a lot more about the self-involved people Chance is meeting than him.

Soon after, Ben invites Chance to meet the President of the United States who is seeking advice for an upcoming economic statement. When asked what he thinks about introducing 'stimulus growth' into the economy, Chance, assuming they're referring to the garden again, offers an analogy about letting the seasons take their course. Ben and the President are impressed and interpret that they should not intervene in the economy and should, instead, encourage a free market. The President quotes Chance's advice word-for-word in a high profile speech as the CIA try to find out who the incredible Chauncey Gardiner is. Despite finding no record of him, Chance's influence grows.

Before long he is offering his gardening/economy analogies on national television as well as attending an important banquet with the Russian Ambassador in Ben's place. When Ben's health declines, he gives Eve permission to find love again in Chauncey, an offer she is only too willing to pursue during an intimate, and hilarious, encounter in Chance's bedroom where he admits he 'likes to watch'. In the story's closing scene at Ben's funeral, his influential pallbearers discuss Chauncey Gardiner as the best candidate for the next President of the Unites States. Meanwhile, Chance has strayed down to the pond where he tends to a tree before stepping onto the pond and, literally, walks on water.

While the story of *Being There* is clearly shaped around Chance, his 'choices' have been largely shaped by other people – the attorneys, Eve, Ben, the President. His gentle personality means that Chance is largely passive as he obediently goes along with the suggestions of others, not fully comprehending the meaning they take from his simple descriptions of the garden and his fascination with television. The dramatic result is a story that somehow balances whimsy with caustic satire of the wealthy and powerful.

Make no mistake, while Chance may be the source of the humour in the film, he is not the butt of the joke. That honour goes to the vain and self-absorbed elites who interpret his words as their own preconceived wisdoms. They hear only what they want to hear, regardless of what Chance intends. As a result, the fate of the nation is in their, and ironically his, hands.

Consistent and contented, Chance is a Constant Character with a very Optimistic Arc (future president!). His passivity is central to *Being There's* satirical skewing of a culture that was, at the time, in the process of dumbing down political debate into a series of soundbites and catchphrases. With citizens, presidents and pundits alike increasingly relying on television and the internet for information, it's a process the whole world have only continued to refine.

Dead Poet's Society (1989)

This film has the strange honour of forever inserting an obscure Latin phrase into the minds of a generation of cinemagoers around the world – *'carpe diem'* or *'seize the day'*. If there is one thing a passive character struggles to do it's 'seize the day', making this semi-autobiographical screenplay by Tom Schulman, which went on to win the 1989 Academy Award for Best Original Screenplay, a perfect case study in the power of a passive character.

The story is set in 1959 at the fictitious Welton Academy, an elite boys school in Vermont. Through the eyes of shy newcomer Todd Anderson, the early sequences establish a school community that is built around long-held traditions, rigid conformity and uncompromising discipline. Through his outgoing roommate, Neil Perry, Todd is introduced to a close-knit group of friends including Knox Overstreet and Charlie Dalton (his *external/internal* worlds).

Todd and the boys also meet their new English teacher, John Keating, an ex-student from Welton and a Rhodes scholar. Keating is younger than the other teachers and it becomes clear his methods are also more unorthodox after he orders his students to tear out the introduction to their poetry text book. Keating argues the ideas in the introduction are too stifling to be of any use in reading poetry so 'rip, rip , rip!' he urges his students. It is a difficult request for Todd and the other boys, accustomed as they are to following the rules, but they do as the passionate teacher tells them. They also adopt a playful nickname for Mr Keating, 'O Captain, My Captain', from a Walt Whitman poem, which he encourages. Soon they are embarking on a range of strange but weirdly enlightening English lessons that challenge the students to find their own voice, think for themselves and squeeze the marrow out of life, or, as Keating tells them, 'seize the day'. But it's not easy for chronically introverted Todd who suffers from a stutter and struggles to speak at the best of times.

It's worth noting how the screenplay, and the resulting film, supremely directed by Peter Weir, manages to keep a retiring character like Todd in the foreground of the story. In almost every scene, everyone is talking but Todd, yet we see and understand them largely through his point-of-view. The story (and directing) lingers on Todd's perspective, subtly emphasising his passivity in the majority of the scenes, particularly those with the larger-than-life Mr Keating. It's a masterclass in point-of-view.

When Neil discovers that Mr Keating was a member of an unofficial group called the 'Dead Poet's Society', he recruits the others, including Todd, to reform the club. Guided by a book of poems from the old club, the boys meet at night in a nearby cave where they recite old poetry and even dare to write some of their own. It's an intoxicating transgression for the normally obedient boys who take on Keating's advice and 'seize the day' elsewhere in their lives – Neil auditions for a local theatre production of 'A Midsummer Night's Dream' and lands a major role as Puck; Knox falls for Chris, the girlfriend of the football captain, and tries to win her over with poetry; while Charlie becomes a boundary-pushing-proto-beat-poet when he brings booze, cigarettes and girls to one of the secret club meetings. Everyone is 'seizing the day' – everyone except Todd, of course, who comes to the club but mostly watches on and listens to the exploits of the others.

Later, Mr Keating pushes Todd to come out of his shell after he fails to bring an original poem to class. Sensing the soulful young poet hiding inside the boy, Keating challenges him with a creative improvisation in front of class that stuns everyone, including Todd. His roommate, Neil, giddy from landing the lead in the play, also pushes Todd to 'do something' if he wants to be in the Dead Poet's Society (even Neil can see Todd is passively cruising through this whole experience). Despite this, Todd remains on the margins and even discourages Neil from continuing with the play until he gets permission from his strict father. Neil is adamant, however, that acting is his future, not medicine like his father wants. Being on stage is where he is truly happy and he won't ignore that.

Notice how Todd is surrounded by highly 'active' characters seizing the day all over the place – Neil defies his father and pursues an acting career; Knox pursues Chris; Charlie keeps pushing boundaries at school and Mr Keating pushes the boys to express themselves. It is the strong *internal* choices of these characters that is shaping the narrative – yet do-nothing Todd remains the emotional heart of the unfolding story. Why? Perhaps because the longer Todd does nothing, the more we expect him to *do something*. There is dramatic tension in this dynamic. How can he just stand there when everyone else is having the time of their lives! But his failure to act only helps to emphasise the crushing shyness and insecurity that imprisons Todd's character.

Things come to a head when Neil defies his father and performs in the play to a standing ovation. But Neil's incensed father retaliates by arranging to send him to military college where he will study to become a doctor as planned. Neil, distraught that he will never realise his acting dreams, commits suicide with his father's gun.

The school community is in shock, particularly Todd. An investigation is held and the members of the Dead Poet's Society, including Todd, are pressured to say that Mr Keating encouraged their misbehaviour, even though the teacher was unaware of the meetings. Soon after Mr Keating is sacked.

On his way out, Keating returns to the English room to collect his personal belongings and discovers a class in progress with the disgraced Dead Poet's Society. He doesn't make a scene and collects his things. But Todd can no longer stay silent at the injustice and, to the howls of the fill-in teacher, stands on his desk and calls to the departing Keating, 'O Captain, My Captain'. Following Todd's brave example, soon most of the class are standing on their desks in a stirring tribute to the teacher who has changed their lives forever. Tears in his (and our) eyes, Keating thanks the boys and leaves.

Todd's unswerving passivity throughout the story has made his courageous choice in its closing moments all the more profound. His choice goes to the very heart of the film's themes – *seize the day* – and achieves its power because it comes from the least likely candidate amongst the Dead Poet's Society. It was harder for Todd to 'do something', which is why it's so moving when he finally does. Despite the character's passivity, the writing and directing, as well as an outstanding debut performance from a very young Ethan Hawke, ensures that the point-of-view and emotional centre of the story always remains with shy Todd. While he is predominantly a *passive* character, he still manages to internally transform, making him a Change Character with an Optimistic Arc.

Los Silencios (2018)

Passive characters have a tendency to be 'watchers' who stand back and witness the drama as it unfolds. This next case study is an excellent example of this quality. Selected for Directors' Fortnight at the 2018 Cannes Film Festival, the film, written and directed by Beatriz Seigner, is a rare gem that confidently maintains an immersive atmosphere of quiet drama as it slowly reveals its intentions. The result packs a profound emotional punch. SPOILER WARNING: If you haven't seen the film, I'd suggest enjoying the experience of a first viewing before reading on. It will be worth it.

The story opens at night as a boat approaches a river island on the borders of Brazil, Colombia and Peru. On the boat is pre-teenager Nuria, her mother, Amparo, and younger brother, Fabio. They arrive on the dark, quiet banks of the island where they are greeted by Amparo's elderly aunt who is both surprised and relieved to see them. As they settle into the village, it becomes clear the family are refugees from the decades long (and real life) conflict between the Colombian government and the rebel group FARC. As Amparo makes beds for the family in a vacant house, Nuria is withdrawn and quiet, presumably a result of the trauma she has experienced (her *internal/external* worlds).

The next day, after dropping Fabio off at the local school, Nuria and Amparo go to a church that supports refugees. Nuria watches on as Amparo shows video footage of the fighting to prove the threat to their lives. She explains her husband, who was involved with the rebels, and daughter are missing following an accident at an oil refinery caused by government militia. Unfortunately, to claim reparations from the oil refinery for their loss, Amparo must employ an attorney to find the bodies of her loved ones back in Colombia. With no money or food vouchers available Amparo struggles to feed her family let alone pay for the attorney. By her side through all of this, Nuria holds her mother's hand, or comforts her, never speaking, simply watching, helpless to help.

Effectively, Nuria's position as a young child in a very difficult adult situation renders her largely passive. What can she do besides comfort her mother? She has no control or agency in this unfamiliar place. She's a kid.

One day, Nuria returns home and is shocked to see a man in the family's house. From his earlier description, it is clear this is her father, Adam, but Nuria seems unnerved to see him. Without saying a word, Adam signals to Nuria to stay quiet as he slips upstairs and hides. She does as she's told and doesn't mention his presence when Amparo and Fabio return.

Over the next little while, Amparo finds a job as a labourer in a fish market and, bit by bit, makes a meagre home for her family. An attorney contacts her and offers to take her reparations case if she will accept a smaller upfront payout. At the same time, Fabio starts to hang around some troublesome youths while Nuria attends school and, despite being ignored by the other children, makes a friend with a girl called Maria. Kind and attentive, Maria warns Nuria to be careful of the ghosts that haunt the island and make the people do bad things. When she is not hanging with Maria, Nuria helps prepare the family meals and is treated to the occasional long warm bath by Amparo. Even Adam, her father, comes out of hiding with little fanfare and joins the family at the dinner table. Despite their struggles, Nuria and her family seem to be finding their feet.

All the while, Nuria has not said a word. Not a single sentence. It is not immediately obvious given the gentle observational nature of the storytelling and Nuria's seemingly passive nature. And no one seems concerned by her silence either; not Maria, or Amparo, or Fabio, or Adam who is similarly quiet. Yet at a certain point the clues to this puzzle start to drop and the true nature of the drama reveals itself.

When a ceasefire is called between the Colombian government and the FARC rebels, Maria invites Nuria to a community meeting. She explains that the community want to know what the *ghosts* think of the peace deal.

At the meeting, led by Amparo's aunt, speakers one by one recount their experience of the long conflict, the pain they suffered, and the loved ones they lost. With each painful story it becomes clear that the speakers are *ghosts from the war*. In fact, their clothes subtly glow with an otherworldly quality. Listening on are the living residents of the island, including Amparo and Fabio. Nuria and Adam are there too but they are glowing like the other ghosts. Finally, Nuria speaks. Held by Maria, and with tears in her eyes, Nuria says she wants her mother to know that they are OK and that none of this is her fault.

In the final sequence of the film, the community come together with the ghosts in a river ceremony. The living and the dead sing as the bodies of the ghosts, including Nuria and Adam's, glow in colourful patterns drawn from Colombian custom and culture. The singing comes to an end. All is quiet. Nuria closes her eyes.

Like Chance in *Being There* and Todd in *Dead Poet's Society*, Nuria's passivity is central to the story and themes of *Los Silencios*. The narrative cleverly hides the true nature of her passivity behind the fact that she is a child who lacks agency in an adult situation. Eventually, however, the story reveals that Nuria and her father are both ghosts who are lingering in the lives of their family.

But what about the moments when Amparo interacted with Nuria or spoke with Adam? Set against the backdrop of her grief, these exchanges are reframed as Amparo's emotional struggle as she works through her loss and uncertain future. More widely, Nuria's interactions with her great aunt and Maria reveal a community that is aware of the ghosts in their midst. The ghosts live on in the pain of those left behind, waiting to be released. The (real life) ceasefire towards the end of the story provides the impetus for Nuria, and the others, to finally find a sort of peace, making her a Change Character with an Ambivalent Arc.

Summary: Detached, observant, impotent

Passive characters are the quiet heroes of storytelling. They're not in the thick of the action, looking the problem in the eye and deciding what must be done. Instead, they generally try and stay out of the way or, if they lack the power to get involved, are pushed aside by the brave ones.

Despite this, passive characters, when handled carefully, can become a reservoir of powerful, pent-up emotion as the drama grows and the audience wonders what will be done to resolve the tension. The feelings that surge up as Chance stumbles his way towards the presidency, as Todd defies authority and steps onto his desk, or as Nuria speaks for the first time, are utterly unforgettable. As lovers of film and storytelling in general we would be remiss to ignore the emotions these stories provoke and wonder how these quiet, retiring characters made us feel this way.

There is no doubt, passive characters are rarer birds in film and television where the ability to convene drama through visual action is an imperative of the medium. But I wonder about other mediums like theatre or novels. Isn't *Waiting for Godot* famously a play where nothing happens, twice? Its characters Pozzo and Estragon certainly do a lot of passive waiting around. And isn't Nick Carraway, the narrator and point-of-view in *The Great Gatsby* largely a witness to the exploits of Jay Gatsby? He certainly doesn't seem to do anything to shape the events of the narrative. And the eponymous hero of *Candide* by Voltaire stumbles hilariously from disaster to disaster, never intervening, never changing. I haven't done a wide survey of other storytelling forms or cultures but I suspect passive characters are not as rare as cinematic traditions might suggest.

Despite this concession, I think it's worth stressing that, in my experience, passive characters are incredibly tricky to write. Their value, I suspect, is specific to particular themes and ideas, ones of power, control or agency, as we've seen in the above case studies. I've witnessed many young writers embrace passive characters in an attempt to capture the randomness and meaningless they feel like they're experiencing in life – only for the resulting stories to be dead on arrival from a lack of energy and direction. What does seem to bring a story featuring a passive protagonist to life is an ensemble of surrounding characters who are surging with motivation – Neil and the other boys in *Dead Poet's Society*, Ben in *Being There*, Amparo in *Los Silencios*. It seems it is often a matter of balance as the passivity of the main character is offset by those around them.

Nevertheless, despite their challenges, passive characters have a place in our storytelling. Perhaps we avoid them because their lack of drive is too close to the bone, a reminder of the times when we watched when we could have acted. But we should take the time to listen and learn from passive characters, because they have much to teach us.

For more examples of films featuring a passive main character check out; *Boyhood, Forrest Gump, Remains of the Day, Black Robe, The Graduate* and *Good Will Hunting.*

CHAPTER 12

Character arcs in television

So far, we've explored a range of different character arcs using feature films as examples. We've looked at how *external* change can shape a character's circumstances, the *conflict* this introduces to their *internal* and *external* worlds, and the *choices* they make to resolve the conflict. Sometimes these choices are *new or unfamiliar* for the character, indicating they have been *emotionally changed* by the events of the story. Other times, the character holds fast to their usual choices, for better or worse, indicating they have remained *emotionally constant* throughout the story. All of this comes together to give a character an arc that is *optimistic, ambivalent or pessimistic.*

As we've seen, the range of stories that is possible within these broad character arcs is extremely wide. The films we've examined are not comprehensive – storytelling is too various for that – but they certainly capture a broader range of storytelling possibilities than the narrow paradigm of the Three-Act Hero's Journey. But feature films are only one form of storytelling. We also have theatre, novels, short stories, radio plays, fiction podcasts and, of course, television – arguably the most dominant storytelling form of the last two decades. So, can this approach to character arcs be used for other storytelling forms?

I've never written a novel or a radio play or a piece of theatre, so I'll let others comment on those art forms. But with my background in television, I can say with absolute confidence that television writers employ the principle of character arcs all the time.

A character arc to a television writer is like a wrench to a plumber. It's always in their toolbox. This is not to suggest that all television writers approach story in the same way. Every writer is different, just as every story is different. Some want to start by discussing a character in detail. Who are they? Where do they come from? What drives them? What do they believe in? What are they afraid of? What do they want?

It's an 'inside-out' approach to story development where the writer wants to get inside the head of the character (I've heard so many television writers describe it this way) and imagine the world from their particular point of view. They want to discuss the *internal world* of the character.

Other writers, however, want to know what's happening in the external world of the story. How does the story start? What happens? Where is the conflict coming from? How does this put pressure on the character? What obstacles are in their way? How does the conflict escalate? These writers are more plot-driven and enjoy imagining surprising and exciting events that can put pressure on the character. They want to discuss the *external* world of the character and shape their personality traits around it.

Then, more rarely, there are writers who want to talk about the big picture. They're happy to discuss characters as well as plot, but what they're really interested in is what the story adds up to, what it says about the world, what its point of view is, how it captures a 'universal truth' or tells us something we don't already know. For these writers, character and plot are a way to explore big ideas about people, the world and life. They want to discuss the *themes* of the narrative.

All of these approaches are both utterly vital and complementary. They need each other. But at some point, the writing team, no matter which approach they take, will bring their discussions about character, plot and theme together and connect them to the character's arc. Because a show's characters and themes are already well developed by the time most television writers join a production, they will be thinking about character arcs from day one. The writer will ask questions like 'What happens to this character in this episode? Where do they start and where do they end? Are things better, worse or somewhere in between? What's their arc in this episode?' But why do television writers inevitably gravitate towards arcs?

It's a long story...

Television stories are very, very long. A typical season of television drama can last between six and twenty episodes. Depending on where in the world you're filming, if it's a drama, those episodes generally last between 45 and 60 minutes. If it's a comedy, the episodes are between 20 and 30 minutes (or shorter if it's a web series).

If you compare a season of television drama to a film you might watch at the cinema, the shortest is about two hours long (the length of an average movie) and the longer ones can go for upwards of twenty hours (a mega-sized movie requiring a lot of popcorn and numerous bathroom breaks). But television seasons weren't always this long. They used to be longer!

Before the internet fragmented television's mass audience (more on that later), dramas would often have seasons of 30 or 40 episodes a year. Even today, soap operas around the world screen every weeknight during ratings seasons, creating upwards of 100 hours a season! That's a lot of story!

Unless a writer is superhuman, like Aaron Sorkin (*The West Wing*) or Noah Hawley (*Fargo*) or Michelle and Robert King (*The Good Wife*), it is extremely rare for one writer to have the creative and physical endurance needed to write every episode in the required timeframe. So other writers are recruited to help.

With a room full of writers, the head writer needs a strategy to both *generate* enough story to fill a season of television, and a means for everyone, including the audience, to *follow* everything that is happening. The way they do it is with arcs. Remember, an arc is, literally, a *shape*. It describes a particular trajectory, a movement through space. But in storytelling, that shape is also a movement through *time* as the story evolves through changing events, escalating conflict and the character's choices. So, an arc is the *shape of a story*.

Because television is so very long, its stories are not made up of just one arc – they're made up of lots of arcs. To understand this, let's take a look at the different sorts of arcs a television writer uses to shape the story. Firstly, each show has a unique balance of *episodic* and *serial* arcs. Some shows favour episodic (also called series or 'procedural') arcs where every episode has a discrete story that has a beginning, middle and end. They often take on a 'case of the week' structure, which explains why shows about lawyers, doctors and cops are often procedural. This effectively allows an audience to watch any episode of the show, in any order, and still know what is going on. Examples of this sort of television show are *Law and Order*, *House*, *The Mentalist*, *Rick and Morty*, *Castle*, *Elementary* and *CSI*.

Meanwhile, other shows favour serial arcs where the story

extends across numerous episodes and even across whole seasons of a show. This makes it harder to casually drop in and out of the show, but it also allows for a deeper exploration of the characters and their evolving relationships. Examples of this sort of television show are *The Sopranos*, *Succession*, *Fleabag*, *The Walking Dead*, *Mr Robot*, *LOST*, *Stranger Things*, *The Americans*, *Mad Men*, *Game of Thrones*, *The Wire* and *Friday Night Lights*.

It's extremely common these days for most shows to employ both episodic and serial arcs. It's a best-of-both-worlds approach that allows for deep character and relationship exploration while still delivering a self-contained story in each episode for the more casual viewer. Examples of this sort of television show are *The Good Wife*, *Parenthood*, *Silicon Valley*, *Better Call Saul*, *The Good Place*, *This Is Us*, *The Thick of It*, *The Crown* and *Breaking Bad*.

Each episode can have a little mini-arc that fits inside the bigger season arc, which also fits within the overall story arc of the entire show. To be able to write an effective episode, a television writer not only needs to understand the arc of the episode they're writing, they also need to be aware of the season arc before and after their episode. But that's not all!

It's a long story with many parts...

Think about your favourite television drama. How many characters does it follow? If it was made in the last thirty years, it likely features at least three or as many as twenty recurring characters, all of whom have a unique character arc. In contrast to feature films, where stories about a single protagonist dominate, television likes a big cast of characters.

In *Breaking Bad*, there's Walter as well as Jesse, Skyler, Hank, Marie, Gus, Saul, etc. In *Line of Duty*, there's Steve as well as

Ted, Kate, Lindsay, Tony, etc. In *Girls*, there's Hannah as well as Jessa, Marnie, Shoshanna, Adam, Charlie, Ray, etc. In *Game of Thrones,* there's Jon Snow, Daenerys, Arya, Khal, Tyrion, etc.

Even when there's a lead character who defines a show, they are rarely left to carry the story. In *Seinfeld*, Jerry is joined by Elaine, Kramer and George. In *Grey's Anatomy*, Meredith Grey is supported by Derek, Christina, Alex, Mark, etc. In *The Sopranos*, Tony is shadowed by Christopher, Carmela, Adriana, Paulie, Junior and many more.

In television, we are rarely locked into one central point of view. We will often follow a range of unique character arcs at regular intervals. In fact, it's not uncommon for audiences of a television drama to follow upwards of a dozen story arcs at once, each of them featuring different combinations of characters. The longer a show is on air, the more story arcs and new characters are needed to keep it evolving.

When you think about how we watch a movie – with one central character and only a handful of storylines – it's actually amazing how many stories and characters we can follow over years or even decades! It's also a testament to the creative skill and endurance of many television writers. When a complex and long-running television series can successfully balance all its character arcs for years without losing an audience's attention, it's a marvel. But when the writers conclude that show with an emotionally satisfying finale, it's the Olympic equivalent of winning the marathon only to top it off with a perfect ten in the floor routine.

So when a television writer is preparing to write an episode, they will break it down into a number of character arcs. Sometimes they'll describe it as the 'story strands' of the episode or the 'A, B and C' stories or the 'beats' for each character, but they all mean the same thing.

It's a long story with many parts and ups and downs

Because television shows are so long, with so many different characters to track, arcs are used to break down episodes and seasons into manageable sizes, both for the writers and audiences. For some characters, things might be looking optimistic at the end of an episode, only for everything to fall into a pit of pessimism a few episodes later. Maybe they'll be able to rebuild just in time for the season finale. Or it might take them another seven seasons of ups and downs to put their life back together.

Writers will track these specific highs and lows, but they will also track the wider ensemble to make sure all the serial arcs aren't doing the same thing. In other words, it's important that all the arcs aren't too high (optimistic) or too low (pessimistic). There should be a range of tones.

Another thing the writers will keep a close eye on is how much the characters *emotionally change*. This is very important. Like feature film characters, television characters can be understood through an examination of their internal and external worlds. They have fears and desires and beliefs just as they have friends, family, social standing, a career, etc. But television characters are different to feature film characters in one very crucial way: they don't change much. Remember, television drama is very long, which means that television character arcs are also very long.

So if a television character is going to emotionally change, it's going to take some time. There are going to be a lot of ups and downs along the way. And despite all the struggles, the character will only emotionally change in increments. They might learn something new in an episode, see things from a different perspective, try something new or unfamiliar, only to fall back to their old ways in the next episode. Two steps forward, one step back.

If *Breaking Bad* was a movie, Walter White would transform from a high school teacher into a psychopathic drug lord within the space of three hours maximum. But as a television show, it happens gradually over five seasons, totalling sixty-two hours! Because it's television, there's time to go deep into Walter's character as well as the relationships around him. We don't just understand Walter in detail, we come to understand the people and circumstances around him that led to his transformation.

I think this is one of the reasons television has, in recent years, emerged as a storytelling powerhouse capable of creating complex and endlessly fascinating characters. There is time to go deep into a character and explore their inner world by placing them under an endless variety of pressures to see how they emotionally change – or not!

As we've seen, fictional characters don't have to experience an emotional transformation, and television is no different. In fact, television comedy was traditionally built around the promise that you would be able to come back each week and see the characters make the same hilarious mistakes all over again. Some shows have catchphrases (e.g. 'Doh!') that underline how incapable the characters are of emotional change. Comedies have started to incorporate more nuanced character arcs in recent times, like *Parks and Recreation*, *Community*, *The Good Place* and *Big Bang Theory*, but even if the characters do change, it is extremely gradual – glacial even!

My favourite example of a television character incapable of change is Tony Soprano. In one of the last episodes, after years of psychiatric treatment, Tony's long-suffering therapist, Dr Melfi, realises her sessions with the mob boss have simply helped him sharpen his anti-social behaviour. She realises he will never be cured. He can never change.

Arcs or acts?

As you can see, arcs are very important to television writers and audiences. It's what makes these long, complex, multifaceted stories comprehensible. But what about acts?

There is a perception, particularly among advocates of the Three-Act Hero's Journey, that all stories break down into three discrete acts – a beginning, a middle and an end. How you define what an act is and where it starts and ends is highly contested, even among people who insist that there should be three acts in a story.

Acts are definitely employed in television, but not in the way advocates of the Three-Act Hero's Journey use them. Traditionally, most television dramas came from networks who relied on advertising to fund their programmes. In this model, the storytelling would abruptly stop every ten or so minutes and networks would force audiences to watch a series of loud and completely unrelated advertisements in the hope that some of them would buy what was being presented. Network executives, not writers, would determine how many commercial breaks they would sell to advertisers, depending on the time of day and the popularity of a show. There could be four, five, six, sometimes seven commercial breaks in an hour.

This strategy worked and still works at a commercial level because lots of television and web content is made this way. But it was, and still is, very disruptive. So writers had to find a way to draw audiences back to the storytelling after watching a noisy piece of visual pollution.

Their solution was to create 'act' breaks in the story where, just like feature films, a dramatic development would happen in the story (e.g. a clue was found, an affair uncovered, a secret exposed, etc.) or a character makes a big decision (e.g. confronts an enemy, declares a love, takes on a new case, etc.).

Television writers became experts in shaping their stories into a number of 'acts' or segments. Each act was separated by a dramatic turn in the story that would hook the audience so strongly that they would happily endure the commercials to see what happened next.

In recent decades, subscription cable and streaming services, like HBO, AMC and Netflix, who are less reliant on advertising, have gained prominence with high-quality television shows that do not rely on commercial breaks. And, of course, public broadcasters around the world have rarely had advertising.

Shows like *The Sopranos*, *Mad Men* and *Deadwood* boldly embraced highly serialised stories that deliberately rejected the rigid structure of the network shows they were trying to differentiate themselves from. Without act breaks, the shape of these television stories became more expansive and less formulaic, with storylines that took on demanding novelistic proportions. David Simon, the creator of the acclaimed HBO drama *The Wire*, was asked how he took account of the 'casual viewer' for his complex and multi-layered crime show about power and corruption on the streets of Baltimore. His reply was characteristically to the point: 'Fuck the casual viewer. Who wants a viewer who is casual?'

Nevertheless, even without designated commercial breaks to provide an overt structure, cable and subscription television shows still give shape to their stories by employing character arcs, instead of acts. In fact, with their embrace of highly serialised storylines in cable and streaming shows, character arcs have become even more important than they were before.

I suspect the term 'character arc' is now so culturally pervasive that it is no longer industry jargon – it is routinely used by fans and viewers (yes, even casual ones) to talk about their favourite characters and television shows. Just look at the reactions to the series finale for *Game of Thrones.* Most of the complaints around the finale swirled around the unsatisfying arcs of several major characters whose stories viewers had been following for years. Let's just say the fans were *not* happy.

Whether it's an arc or an act, television shows have a similar but different way of shaping their stories. Like feature films, they use character arcs, but there are many arcs, not one. They use acts as well, but these are determined by network executives, not a mythic script formula.

We can be antiheroes

The Three-Act Hero's Journey doesn't just struggle with the long story arcs, large ensembles and commercially driven act breaks of television. It also struggles with the sorts of characters television produces – particularly in the last couple of decades.

Let me give some context. For many decades, television was seen as a cheap and inferior form of storytelling compared to novels, theatre or even cinema. Production values were low, the sets were (literally) made of cardboard, the actors were movie-star wannabes, the stories were mass-produced, factory line, cookie-cutter templates that were roughly the same week after week.

But sometime in the '90s or '00s (there's a lot of debate about exactly when), television changed. It got good. Really good. Shows like *The Sopranos, The Wire, Six Feet Under, Breaking Bad, Mad Men, The Leftovers, Fleabag, Bojack Horseman* and *Atlanta* demonstrated the incredible range and depth of television storytelling. Its sophistication and ambition not only rivalled cinema but, in many ways, surpassed it. Suddenly, a movie started to feel like a short story, while a television drama felt like a multivolume series of complex novels.

So what happened? What transformed television from the cheap runt of the storytelling formats to the most bingeworthy artform of the last two decades? There are many reasons for this dramatic (pun intended) transformation, the explanation of which would fill many books (and blogs and podcasts). Here's my summary of the phenomenon. Historically, television drama was exclusively for mass entertainment, until the internet and cable television fragmented its audiences by creating much smaller markets of viewers who wanted to watch niche, challenging and buzz-worthy content whenever and wherever they wanted.

This explains how *Fleabag*, a show about a potty-mouthed, psychologically traumatised sex addict, has become the most celebrated show of the last few years. This doesn't mean that all shows are as niche or challenging as *Fleabag*. Networks all around the world still survive on mass-appeal shows like *Big Bang Theory*, *Modern Family*, *The Good Doctor* and *This Is Us*, all of which have their own strengths. But there has been an undeniable shift in the types of shows that are *possible* on television now, especially with the rise of global streaming formats like Netflix and Amazon, whose very business model seems to be about creating niche, must-see shows that will clog your newsfeed with chatter for months.

What's interesting about this current 'golden age' of television is that the very shows that have defined the era – *The Sopranos*, *Breaking Bad*, *Six Feet Under*, *Mad Men*, *The Leftovers*, *Fleabag* – are more often than not about *antiheroes*.

Tony Soprano from *The Sopranos* is a psychopathic mob boss; Walter White from *Breaking Bad* transforms from a well-meaning chemistry teacher into a ruthless drug lord; Don Draper from *Mad Men* is a narcissistic and emotionally distant adulterer; the Fishers of *Six Feet Under* are a highly dysfunctional family of undertakers; Kevin and Nora from *The Leftovers* are recovering from emotional trauma and frequently suicidal; the eponymous Fleabag is, well, a mess. These characters are not 'heroic' in the Hero's Journey sense of the word, and neither are their arcs. Things do not end well for Tony Soprano (whether you believe he's dead or not), Walter White, or Don Draper (personally, I see his arc as the most tragic and pessimistic). The Fisher family has a deeply moving but incredibly Ambivalent Arc, as do Kevin and Nora in *The Leftovers*. Only *Fleabag* has anything approaching optimism at the end, but it's mixed with lashings of sadness and regret.

Like movies, television dramas are not always about a protagonist who experiences an emotional change where things look super rosy at the end. Sometimes things look terrible (e.g. *Breaking Bad*), ambivalent (e.g. *The Leftovers*) or sort of optimistic (e.g. *Fleabag*). Sometimes they have a dramatic transformation (e.g. Walter White); other times they don't (e.g. Tony Soprano). In other words, they don't follow a traditional Hero's Journey.

Mind you, if you think of *Fleabag* as a 'flawed' character rather than an antihero (which, let's face it, is probably fairer), you could argue that her story is a single point of view where she overcomes her hang-ups and grows on an emotional level. So maybe she does go on a Hero's Journey of sorts, assuming there isn't another season coming. Originally, *Fleabag*'s creator, Phoebe Waller-Bridge, insisted that the show would only have one season. But if that were the case, *Fleabag* would have had a very Pessimistic Arc after Season One. Thankfully, Waller-Bridge had an idea and delivered a second season that was even better than the first. And it was much more optimistic! Maybe there's another season percolating in her head. Maybe there's another act to Fleabag's journey...

That's the thing about television. Unlike the formulaic Three-Act Hero's Journey, television drama is often structured like a never-ending story with a never-ending cast list. Multiple storylines come and go, just as characters can come and go, year after year.

No wonder it's a struggle to bring so many stories, characters and arcs to a final season that lives up to the years of dedication fans invest in a show. For every triumphant finale (*Breaking Bad*, *Mad Men*, *Six Feet Under*, *The Sopranos*), there's an audience-dividing disaster (*Game of Thrones*, *Dexter*, *LOST*, *How I Met Your Mother*). Now, if someone could come up with a formula for that little problem, they'd be onto a winner!

PART V
WRITING

CHAPTER 13

Writing with character arcs

The time has come. You've done the work. You've read through the previous chapters. You've seen in detail how character arcs have a powerful influence over the shape and feel of a story. You've read about stories of uplifting optimism (*Star Wars, Erin Brockovich, Moana*), troubled ambivalence (*The Social Network, Amour, Winter's Bone*) and dire pessimism (*Mulholland Drive, The Godfather, Under the Skin*).

You've learnt how the shapes of these arcs are influenced by the main character's capacity to *change* or remain *constant* to their internal values and beliefs. Luke Skywalker destroys the Death Star because he is able to *emotionally change*. Erin Brockovich is able to win the legal case because she remains *emotionally constant* and, instead, changes the attitudes of the people around her.

Using the common sense principles of *character, change, conflict* and *choice*, you've gained a sense of how stories build drama in distinct stages, or acts, as the main character struggles to resolve the central conflict tearing their life apart. Sometimes the story breaks up into three acts (*Moonlight, Sweet Country*). But it can also break up into four (*Lady Bird, The Godfather, Under the Skin, Moana, Mulholland Drive, Winter's Bone, The Nightingale*), five (*Burning, Amour, Erin Brockovich, The Terminator, The Social*

Network) or more (*The Hurt Locker*). Other times, the story takes a minimalist approach, where the story is less shaped by dramatic act breaks than by the character's quiet internal choices (*Lost in Translation, Paterson, Call Me By Your Name*).

You've also seen how some stories are shaped by multiple character arcs (*Hidden Figures, Shoplifters, Thelma and Louise*), including television drama, which uses multiple characters to play out arcs that will take many seasons to resolve. Yep, you've covered a lot of ground. Now you want to know how to write your own story. How do you turn a vague idea into a coherent and compelling story? What's the process you need to guide you through? What's the secret? Well, you already know it. Think of the last film you saw. Think of the main character. Are they a Change Character or a Constant Character? What is their arc?

I'll play along too. The most recent film I saw before writing this chapter was an Icelandic film called *A White, White Day*. It's about a husband grieving the death of his wife. And, without giving away too many spoilers, I have no hesitation in saying that the husband is a Change Character. Most definitely. What about the type of arc? How do things play out for the main character? Too easy. *A White, White Day* has an Optimistic Arc. It's heartbreaking and cathartic, yes, but things definitely look up for the grieving husband at the end of that movie.

How about the last movie you saw? Take a second to think about its story. Did the main character change or remain constant? Was it an Optimistic, Pessimistic or Ambivalent Arc? If you can answer, then you already understand a lot about how the film's fundamental story is shaped, the emotional journey of the main character, and the nature of its themes.

What about the number of acts? That's a bit harder. With *A White, White Day*, I'd guess four or five acts, but I'd have to watch it again to know for sure. It wouldn't be hard to work it out. I'd look for a significant *external change* followed by a clear *internal choice* by the main character to mark the transition between one act and the next. Once you get the hang of it, you'll start seeing the act breaks in every film you watch. A lot of the time you can just *feel* the change in the character as they decide what to do about their dramatic new circumstances.

So you already know a lot about what shapes a story. In fact, getting comfortable with these dramatic building blocks can help you build your own story. Not sure? Okay, here's what I want you to do.

Five films

List five films that inspired you to write your own stories. Now hit the couch and watch them – or even better, read the screenplays. What can you say about the main character's internal and external worlds? What sort of character is the protagonist? Change or Constant? What sort of arc do they experience? How many act breaks do you see in the story? Where are they? How far apart are they? What are the external changes and internal choices that separate each act?

If you want to be *really* nerdy, you can map out the acts and the character arc in a diagram like the ones in this book, but it's not essential. It's easier to bed these ideas down when you're dealing with films you love, especially if you haven't taken the time to think about why they work and how their drama is shaped. By the time you finish those five films, you'll see them in a whole new light. In fact, finding patterns in the stories you like will give you clues about the sorts of stories you want to tell.

You might also start to see a pattern in the types of character arcs you gravitate towards. Personally, I find myself most fascinated by Change Characters with Ambivalent Arcs. Not that I don't like other types of stories. I try to see the broadest range of films I can. It's just that I find that the messiness and complexity of an Ambivalent Arc suit my worldview. To me, it really feels like the world is an incredibly complex and chaotic place, so a film that captures that feeling makes a lot of sense to me. What about you? Are there certain types of characters and story arcs you're drawn too?

Take those lessons and start looking at your own story ideas. What do your instincts tell you about the type of character and story arc that might be relevant to each one? Is there a pattern to the types of stories you want to tell? Are their arcs optimistic, pessimistic, ambivalent? Do you prefer Change Characters or Constant Characters? As you decide on what story idea you'd like to tackle, here's something else you can do. Watch more films and read their screenplays, not to copy them, but to see how they work (or don't) and learn from their success (or failure).

Learning any new art form involves immersion in the breadth and depth of techniques used by more established artists so you can find your own way of doing things. Gaining a sense of the large-scale shape of stories relevant to your current project is a great way to get you thinking about the shape of your own story and character arc.

Working with scenes

You can also take the same approach to a great scene. The principles of *character*, *change*, *conflict* and *choice* don't just work at the large-scale level of acts or overall story. They also work for small-scale scenes or sequences. Once again, think of your favourite scenes from your favourite movies. How do they work? Why do they work? It's hard to tell sometimes because you're so swept up in the character and what's happening. But take a step back and break it down. Every scene or sequence should be about

a *character*...
who experiences a *change*...
which creates *conflict*...
that forces them to make a *choice*.

In *Star Wars*, when Ben suggests that Luke Skywalker should join him to help the rebels, Luke feels conflicted and chooses to return home to help his uncle on the farm. In *Moonlight*, when Kevin leans in for a kiss on the beach, Chiron initially hesitates. He's conflicted until he chooses to take a risk and accept the intimacy. In *Winter's Bone*, when Teardrop urges Ree to sell the family's forest crop before the bondman takes it, the teenager is torn and turns to her mother for help. In *Thelma and Louise*, Thelma is about to escape on her weekend away and chooses not to tell her husband where she is going. In *Hidden Figures*, Katherine initially chooses to say nothing when confronted with a 'blacks only' coffee pot.

In *every* scene, in *every* sequence, the *character* is faced with *change*, *conflict* and *choice*. This is what makes it a scene. This is what makes it *dramatic*. Have a look at your favourite scenes. Watch the character as they face a *change*, experience *conflict* and make a *choice*. Sometimes the character's choice is relatively small, such as the coffee pot in *Hidden Figures* or Thelma leaving without a note in *Thelma and Louise*.

Other times, the choice is big enough to create a new act

in the story as the character tries a new course of action to resolve the conflict. For example, Chiron's attack on Tyrell in *Moonlight* signals a newfound embrace of violence and Moana's decision to restore Te Fiti's heart in *Moana* sees her choose a destiny she always instinctively knew was hers to fulfil. The choices the character makes ripple through every scene, as well as every sequence and act, in a cascade of cause and effect. These choices can lead to a dramatic emotional change for the character (*Moonlight*) or leave the character emotionally constant (*Moana*). Being aware of this will help you connect every scene and every choice your character makes, no matter how small, to the overall story arc in a meaningful way.

Secondary characters and subplots

The same principles can be applied to secondary characters. We've already seen how some stories are a combination of parallel character arcs (*Hidden Figures*, *Thelma and Louise*, *Shoplifters*). Each character has a distinct, but inter-related, character arc that reflects and supports the journey of the other characters. They all experience, in every scene, in every act, a *change*, that creates *conflict*, which forces them to make a *choice*. You can apply these principles to the secondary characters in your story. Each character has an arc. Their choices may not be as big as the main character's, and they may not face as much conflict or undergo as much emotional change, but they still have an arc.

Think of Han Solo in *Star Wars*. He goes from a self-interested rogue to fully-fledged rebel fighting the Empire (in many ways, he has a better arc than Luke!) What about Lady Bird's mother Marion in *Lady Bird*? She struggles with her own demons and thwarted dreams as her daughter prepares to abandon her (or at least that's how Marion sees it). She's probably a fairly Constant Character, but there is optimism in her arc as Lady Bird finally appreciates her sacrifice.

How about a minor character like Katherine's supervisor, Paul Stafford, in *Hidden Figures*? He's a major antagonist in the story, but, by the end, he's serving a coffee to Katherine, rather than insisting she use the 'Blacks Only' pot. He's certainly a Change Character, and we get the sense that his life is richer now because of Katherine, giving him an Optimistic Arc. Each of these secondary characters has a story of their own. Even the baddies. Especially the baddies.

If you want to write authentic, believable, three-dimensional secondary characters that are more than a plot device, hackneyed archetype or cardboard-cutout baddie, you've got to give them an internal life of their own. What are their internal beliefs and values? What are their fears, desires, hopes and dreams?

One way to think about it is this: if your story was about one of the secondary characters, what would their story be? Are they a Change or Constant Character? Is their arc optimistic, pessimistic or ambivalent? It doesn't have to be much. You don't want their story to be more interesting or more complex than your main protagonist. But you do want to give your secondary characters enough dimensions that they feel authentic, real and alive. It's easy to forget about secondary characters and turn them into well-worn cliches. But they play a vital role in your main character's story arc and the *subplots* of your story.

As we've seen, a story is rarely a single story. Sure, there is the main plotline (also known as the 'A' plot), but there are various subplots the protagonist moves through as well, populated by important secondary characters. The 'A' plot in *Lady Bird* is her desire to be accepted into a good college. But her subplots revolve around a cast of multidimensional secondary characters – Marion, Danny, Kyle, Jenna – all with stories of their own that reflect and build on Lady Bird's emotional struggles. Without them, Lady Bird herself would be less interesting and less accessible.

Similarly, in *Moonlight,* Chiron's struggle with his sexuality is reflected in and built on the storylines with Juan, Kevin, his mother Paula and his nemesis Tyrell. The stories of these secondary characters provide the emotional backdrop for Chiron's journey, giving it extra weight and complexity. Secondary characters are not just plot devices or a way to deliver clunky exposition. Think of them as characters in their own right, with an inner life and story of their own.

Working with themes

Finally, let's talk about themes and how they relate to character arcs. A theme is a notoriously tricky concept to grasp when discussing stories. It's often described as the moral of the story, such as 'be kind to strangers', 'the greedy will be punished' and 'respect your parents'. But I think this is too reductive and simplistic. Stories don't always have a clear moral that adds up to a lesson in life. What's the moral of *Under the Skin*? Don't be an alien or kill humans? What about *Mulholland Drive*? Don't be jealous and kill your ex? *The Hurt Locker*? Feelings don't help you defuse bombs?

The way I like to think about themes is to treat them as the unique and personal worldview of the storyteller. Looking at how the storyteller shapes the characters and their arcs tells you a lot about how they might see the world. As we've seen, *Under the Skin* features a Change Character with a Pessimistic Arc. What does that tell you immediately? Things do not always work out okay in this storyteller's worldview. It's a brutal and bleak outlook, and despite undergoing a dramatic emotional change, the character's story still ends in violence and death. There is no easy redemption here. If you are not the hunter in this world, then you are the hunted. And there is no escape. The story emits a pervasive sense of doom and dread against the recognisable backdrop of modern Glasgow. As a result, the story evokes powerful themes of gendered violence in a contemporary world. Its pessimistic character arc only reinforces the ongoing danger present in a seemingly intractable cycle of violence.

Apart from looking at the character's arc, the principle of *choice* can also be a useful way to understand the storyteller's worldview and the story's thematic intentions. When we think of choice, we usually think of something intentional. I make a choice, so the choice must be mine, right? But, as we've seen, a choice can be heavily influenced by a range of external factors the character faces. For example, a killer robot from the future in *The Terminator*, or the threat to Michael Corleone's family legacy in *The Godfather*.

In a way, a choice is not always a choice. Could Sarah Connor make any other choice than to go with crazy Reese? Probably not. Could Michael Corleone have chosen to stay out of his family's illegal business? Possibly, but he would have turned his back on everything his beloved father fought for. His family's history and values doomed him to 'get involved'. Did he really have a choice?

The choices a character makes are not taken in isolation. They are influenced by the world around them. Even their values and beliefs are shaped by cultural traditions, rituals and habits that they cannot control. How a story frames a character's choices can provide a key insight into the writer's worldview and the thematic intentions of the film. For example, in *Erin Brockovich,*

Erin's bold choices change the world around her, suggesting that writer Susannah Grant wanted to explore people's prejudices and assumptions about working-class single mothers and what they are capable of. In *The Nightingale,* the protagonist Clare is profoundly changed and humbled when she recognises the parallels between Billy's motivations and her own choices, suggesting writer, Jennifer Kent, wanted to explore the dynamics of power, injustice and empathy in a colonial setting. In *The Social Network*, the character of Mark Zuckerberg does emotionally change, but only after his choices have destroyed every relationship he ever had, suggesting that the writer, Aaron Sorkin, wanted to explore the caustic nature of status, and the drive to succeed at the expense of family and friendship.

The principle of choice is central to understanding the thematic worldview the writer hopes to explore with a story. Does the nature of the character's choices change over the course of the story? Do they emotionally change? What does that suggest about the world this story exists in? How does this reflect the world around us as we, the audience, understand it? Does it affirm the world we know, or does it challenge us to see things from a different angle? Understanding the concept of choice will not only help you understand the thematic intentions of a particular story, it will help you understand story in general.

Summary: Character, change, conflict, choice

Nice work. You're in a great place. Using the principles of *character, change, conflict* and *choice*, and the understanding you now have about character arcs, you've laid the groundwork for writing your own stories. I'm not going to say these principles will work for absolutely every story you conceive. In fact, I suspect this approach has a particularly Western conception of how a story works, especially when it comes to 'choice' (which is perhaps a topic for a different book). But I think I've demonstrated that these principles can be extremely useful in analysing, discussing and writing a wide variety of stories.

The step-by-step process you use to write your own stories will develop and refine over time. With each story, each success and failure, you will understand how *you* write and what *you* want to say. Like stories, the process of writing is so varied that there is no one-size-fits-all approach. Every writer is different, just like every story is different. They start from different places, they're inspired by different ideas, they need different things. In many ways, learning to write is a process of learning how *you* write, which is exactly what we will explore in the final chapter.

CHAPTER 14

Discovering your writing practice

It's often said that writing a story is a lot like building a house – you draw up some plans (write an outline), you lay the foundations (map out a Three-Act Structure) and, brick by brick (scene by scene), you build your mansion (story). It might not be exactly what you planned, the bathroom might be a bit pokey (i.e. the final act is shamelessly derivative), but it's a house (story).

It's not a bad analogy, but it misses two crucial differences. Firstly, when you build a house, you employ an architect who has ideas and employs people to draw up plans on how to build it, then you contract a builder who employs specialist labourers, electricians, plumbers, painters and others. Everyone works together to get your house as close to the plan as possible, making thousands of decisions to get to the desired result. That's what happens when you build a house. It's a team effort.

But when you write a story, it's mostly just *you*. The whole time. Making thousands of decisions about who the story is about, what the character's traits are, what colour the fabric of their favourite jacket is and what that says about them, how they speak, what happens to them, how things start out, how it all ends, what happens in the middle, and what it all means! Of course, you can call on your partner or best friend or trusted colleague or, if you're really lucky, your agent, to read what you're writing. But to do that, you have to write something first, which involves making a whole bunch of decisions that no one else can make but you. Sure, if someone eventually wants to turn your story into a film, there will be a director and a producer and hundreds of other people who will have ideas and opinions to help (or hinder) your story. But to get to that point, you have to write a screenplay for them to read first. A *really* good one. By yourself.

The second crucial difference between building a house and writing a story is that one is a linear process and the other is a non-linear process. When you build a house you have to start with the foundations, then build the walls, then put the roof on top. It's the Three-Act Structure of building a house. You don't really have much choice about the order of this process, so the decision-making around this is, well, not really a decision. It's a very linear process that is generally well understood by everyone involved. But writing is usually a non-linear process. Sure, your story can be linear in that it has a beginning, a middle and an end, but the process of writing an original story rarely moves forward in a methodical, step-by-step way.

You can start the process of writing a story at the beginning (the foundations), but then the middle sections (the walls) could be way too short and the end (the roof) may not fit at all. In fact, it may look like it belongs to a different story (house). There's stuff you like, but it's going to need another draft. Or seven. To do this, a writer will rarely progress in a linear way and will, instead, make regular detours to research, redraft, experiment, backtrack, refine, rethink and reject what they are doing. In other words, writers rarely 'know' the details of their story before they start writing, at least not in the way an architect 'knows' the plans for your house. Instead, writers 'discover' the details as they are writing.

This is something few people outside the creative arts understand. The process of making a new creative work, particularly one that starts with a blank piece of paper, is the process of *discovering* rather than *knowing*. That's because you're creating *something from nothing*. As a result, it is an *iterative process*, meaning it is circular and non-linear. Some writers, often novelists, start at page one with a vague idea of a character or an incident and work their way to the end by discovering the story from page to page or chapter to chapter. Others, more frequently screenwriters, have a broad plan that they follow, but there is still a great deal to discover along the way about their characters and the story.

Even in the highly formulaic genre of procedural television, a screenwriter will work with other writers (a rarity in itself) in a process of throwing ideas around, throwing ideas away, trying one thing, trying another, until a story starts to emerge. Only then does the writer attempt a broad outline of the story, which then gets revised before they attempt a first draft, a second draft and so on. Once each draft is finished, the writer starts the whole process again, making changes, learning from the previous draft, trying new ideas and refining old ones. Sometimes writers trash the lot and start again with a completely different approach. As Ernest Hemingway famously said, 'The only kind of writing is rewriting'.

If we asked builders to make a house this way, each 'draft' would involve knocking half of it down and starting again. So, writing a story and building a house are very different things. As a result, the whole thing can feel kind of *overwhelming* (because it's so non-linear) and, frankly, *lonely* (because you're on your own a lot of the time). Sometimes it's so hard you can't write, no matter how much you want to. This is where having a *writing practice* can help you. In fact, it won't just help you, it will save you from the feelings that can stop you writing.

Discovering how you write, what works for you, what motivates you and, most importantly, what sort of stories you want to write, will lead you to a way of working, or a practice, that will make you more creative, productive and original. A practice is a habit. It's something you do automatically, without thinking. It's the time and space you create to make writing possible. One way to think of it is this: it's your job. And like a job, you turn up and do it regularly. You work hard, you do your best and you do what needs to be done until it's finished. If you're super lucky, you'll enjoy doing it. The main difference with writing is it's a job where you have to be willing to turn up even if no one is paying you – or worse, even if no one reads what you've written.

I feel like I should pause here as a few of you gently put this book down or throw it across the room. But I want to be honest with you. Practice, and having a *practice* where you regularly practise your craft, is everything. Whether you're being paid or not or if someone is going to read your writing or not. It's true for all writers as well as musicians, actors, photographers, painters or any creative. No one pays artists to learn the foundations of their craft (that only happens after they've conquered the basics). It involves lots of time and unwavering love for what they do. No professional creative skips their practice. Practice separates the fakers from the makers.

If you want to learn to write stories, and write them well and/ or even professionally, then nurturing a writing practice needs to become a fundamental part of your life. Writing and thinking about stories needs to feel like a heartbeat in your daily routine – automatic, ever-present and endlessly stimulating. But what should your writing practice be? What does it look like? Well, it's different for every writer. It can take time to discover what works best for you. But it's vital that you take the time to find out (don't worry, this chapter will give you some handy pointers).

Developing a writing practice may not be a shortcut to writing a hit screenplay. But it's the only approach I can honestly say will increase your chance of one day *writing in your own voice*. Which is, ultimately, what every writer is trying to do.

Not only are we trying to figure out the story we're trying to tell, but we're also trying to tell it in a way that is *all our own*. It's a story no one has heard before, told in a way that captures our unique voice and perspective as a writer. And the way to discover the sound of your unique writing voice is to practise, practise, practise! Here a few things you can do:

Write regularly

Writing takes time. Huge swathes of it. It is not unusual for first-time screenwriters or novelists to take years, sometimes decades, to squeeze out their first masterpiece. But even when they've 'made it', it still takes time. An average contract for a feature-length screenplay can be between three and six months for the first draft, then a few months for the redrafts. By comparison, an average novel can take a year to write.

While taking long walks and talking to friends in cafes is no doubt a regular part of many writers' schedules, that walk is haunted by looming deadlines and friends who are bored with hearing about how terrible the draft is going. While the writer might not be smashing keys every minute, their mind is usually consumed with the project (or projects) they're currently wrestling with.

Apart from time, writing also requires concentration, focus and energy. Some people are lucky enough to have all of these things in abundance. They probably also have a supportive partner with a high-paying job, a quiet office with a fireplace, a trust fund, a lakeside holiday home in Italy and either a nanny or no children.

For the rest of us, finding the time and energy to write is a major logistical challenge. Life demands so much of us – friends, family, children, marriage, career. How do you jam something as consuming as writing into that timetable? The first thing you need is a breakdown (not a psychological one, but it's okay if you need to have one). I'm talking about breaking down the task of writing. Here's an example of what I mean. If you took one hour a day to write three hundred words (a bit over half a page) and did that five days a week (take the weekends off), by the end of the year you'd have a novel that was 80,000 words long. That's a good size! *Fight Club*, *We Have Always Lived in the Castle* and *The Hitchhiker's Guide to the Galaxy* are all less than 50,000 words. *Of Mice and Men* is 30,000 words!

Similarly, if you put aside one hour a day to write one page of a screenplay (which is much less than a novel), you'd have a chunky 120-page draft in six months. You can also tackle the problem by regularly setting aside a larger block of time where you can focus and concentrate. It might be two hours every second day, or even one day a week, or maybe one weekend a month when you can turn off the phone, log off social media, close your email and just write.

Producing pages regularly means you're writing. There are words on a page that you have arranged into a story, which makes it easier and less embarrassing to call yourself a writer. A writer writes regularly. It's part of the rhythm of their everyday existence, even when there's no deadline or pay cheque. Writing is the way writers make sense of the world. It's a part of their life. So, if you want to call yourself a writer, then write (like, actually *write*) regularly. Do it long enough and you'll eventually have a draft of your story. Of course, it's only a draft. There's still work to do. But it's *something*. And something is infinitely better than a whole lot of *nothing*.

Finish the draft

During your regular writing sessions, it will be very tempting to do anything *but* write. It will be a pull like you've never felt before. For example, just before I wrote the last sentence, I emptied the dishwasher. Did the dishwasher need to be emptied? Yes. Did it need to be emptied right now? No.

There will be an endless cascade of distractions pulling at your focus, dragging you away from the next word on the page. They will range from the trivial, such as emptying the dishwasher, arranging that messy bookshelf, checking your email/social media (again), adjusting the air conditioning until it's just right, to the substantial, such as paying the rent, feeding your children, nurturing your relationships, having a life.

Distraction comes in many forms. Sometimes it disguises itself as something that *sounds* really important and productive, like researching an important historical detail or upgrading your writing software or completely replotting the opening of your story (again) or bullet pointing your protagonist's back story (again) or driving to the shops to get those coloured index cards because you're sure they'll fix all the structural issues you're having with this draft. But you're wrong. The biggest problem with your draft is that it's not finished yet. There will be other problems after that, but you will get to those – after you finish this draft. I can't stress this enough. Only writing gets it written.

Something that will help you finish the draft is a deadline.

Ironically, the easiest deadline to hit is one that is out of your control, like a deadline from your producer or publisher or boss. For some, the fear of failing to meet other people's expectations is more than enough to crank out the pages and get that draft done.

It's much harder to hit a deadline you've set for yourself. As we've discussed, doing something other than write is really easy. The only person you have to disappoint is yourself. But the more you write, the more you'll come to respect deadlines. I wouldn't go so far as to say you'll come to like deadlines – I doubt any professional writer would say that – but you'll come to appreciate their purpose. Deadlines focus the mind and strip away the distractions that threaten to derail the draft you're trying to finish.

Be careful when setting deadlines for yourself. It's important to be realistic. Think about the other personal and professional demands you may have. How many pages can you reasonably write each day, week or month? Okay, now halve that figure because, you know, life gets in the way! Use this figure to work out your deadline and how much you need to do in each writing session.

For example, when I had a day job, I would get up at 5:00 am and write one page of a screenplay in one hour. That's all I could manage. In the last year of working my day job, I wrote three television pilots, two of which were optioned by production companies. That's one hour and one page per day – and it worked for me. Each time you hit your daily, weekly or monthly word quota, be nice to yourself. You're on track. You've done well. This is hard. If you get behind, don't freak out. Nail your quota tomorrow. Or the day after. Get the words on the page. If you let distraction and procrastination whittle away at your productivity, then you are not writing. You're loading the dishwasher.

Nurture your idea (but don't smother it)

Every story idea is an impulse to write. It motivates you because you want to see if your idea works. Will this make a good story? How does the story work? How does it end? Will people like this story as much as I do? At the beginning you think, 'Yes, absolutely, people are going to love it', so it's easy and fun to write. But the further you go, the more your idea will be challenged. The story is a bit slow. The characters feel kind of generic. You're not sure how it ends. Maybe it was a bad idea. Maybe you're not up to it. Maybe there are other things you should be doing. Your idea starts to wither and your impulse to write wanes. Pretty soon, you've stopped writing.

It's very normal for your confidence to ebb and flow throughout the process. You'll catch a wave and ride it for a while, only to find yourself stranded not long after. This is where you need to find ways to *nurture your idea* so that you can build up the impulse to write again, to catch the next wave and ride it as long as you can. Nurturing your idea involves figuring out what your idea needs in order to realise its potential.

Some ideas need a lot of planning and plotting. If you're writing something like a thriller or mystery story, then you're going to need to do at least some pre-plotting so you can stay one step ahead of the audience and maintain the suspense. You might even want to nerd out and map the acts and character arcs in a fancy diagram.

If you're writing a carefully observed character piece, or a nuanced 'slice of life' story, then you might find yourself spending a fair bit of time thinking about the characters – their unique voices, their backstories, their complex motivations and the cultural forces shaping the important decisions in their lives (like what they have for breakfast). Or, if you're writing a narrative that has a very particular setting or historical/cultural backdrop, then you might need to hit the books or consult experts to soak up the atmosphere and authenticity of the world you're writing about.

All of these are worthwhile exercises that can help nurture your idea and realise its potential. Of course, it's inevitable that you'll need to address plot, character, setting, structure, theme, genre and tone as well. But, as we've discussed, writing a story is an iterative, non-linear process. You already know this is going to take a few drafts and you're going to discover a lot along the way. In fact, it will not be unusual to discover the most important elements of your story as you're writing it. In essence, you don't need all the answers at the beginning.

Knowing and accepting this is an extremely important part of nurturing your idea. Being prepared to discover at least some of the answers along the way will maintain your impulse to write. It will also open you up to a level of surprise and excitement that will ensure your writing is alive, vibrant and motivated, instead of a plodding, colour-by-numbers exercise.

You only need enough to start writing with confidence. You've nurtured your idea, you've done some pre-plotting, you've thought about the characters and dived into a bit of research about your subject or setting where needed. Good work. You're feeling a strong impulse to start writing. Do it. Don't wait. I repeat, you don't need all the answers at the beginning. Trust that the answers can and will come as you're writing. As they do, you'll be tempted to go back and start again. Don't. Ride your excitement to the end of the draft. Finish the draft. It'll be a mess, but that's okay. In fact, it's recommended. With the new ideas you've collected along the way, you'll have all the energy, drive and impulse you need to turn around and dive into the next, and even better, draft.

By nurturing your idea and giving it just enough to spark your impulse to write, you'll maintain your energy and excitement for the draft, which will come out on the page. Your writing will be alive and vibrant with passion for the idea you've nurtured and will continue to nurture across every subsequent draft.

It is very common for writers, particularly newcomers, to spend months or even years planning their masterpiece. But they never write it. The process of preparation, or overpreparation, kills their impulse to write. Instead of nurturing their idea with just enough planning and reflection to get going, they suffocate it with a million details they can't possibly keep in their head while writing.

This sort of overpreparation often comes from fear. A timid writer will use it to delay the act of writing for as long as possible because they're scared it won't be good. Let me help you, *it won't be*. Not at first. It never is. And that's okay. Because every draft is a chance to nurture your idea a little bit more, to look at it, feed it with thoughts and reflections, and strive to make it even better. Nurture your idea. Trust it. Trust yourself. And start writing.

Think small (yes, small)

Writers who start writing for pleasure early in life usually begin with short stories. They might be for a school assignment, to entertain a younger sibling or friend or just to immerse themselves in their own secret world for an afternoon or summer holiday. Drawing on the stories they've seen and heard as well as observing the world around them, these young writers create stories for their own pleasure or the pleasure of others.

But when an aspiring writer starts writing later in life as an adult, it's not unusual for them to tackle something much bigger than a short story, perhaps a feature-length screenplay, a television series, a book or a series of books! After all, they're an adult. Adults do big, important things. They know about the world. They have stuff to say. Short stories are not ambitious enough. You can't pay the rent with short stories!

But the beauty of writing short stories (or scripts) when you're starting out is that you can write lots of them. This will help you build a writing practice, establish a repertoire of ideas and genres you're good at and, importantly, enjoy writing. In other words, you'll fast-track the process of figuring out what sorts of stories you want to tell. As you write more stories, you'll start to hear *your voice*.

So, while it's fine and admirable to be ambitious in your selection of projects – a trilogy of feature films, a seven-season television show, a ten-part book series – I would strongly suggest nurturing a range of ideas of different lengths, including a number of short stories you can draft up in a week or two. Having a range of shorter stories on your writing slate means you will enjoy the heavenly satisfaction of not only completing a draft but actually completing a story.

It's an intoxicating buzz that you'll never get tired of, no matter what anyone thinks of your story afterwards. It's a chance to hold a tale in your hands and know it exists because you created it out of thin air. You will also learn a great deal about your craft – what's working, what needs more work. The more you experience the joy of a completed story, the more confident, competent and capable you will be of finishing those bigger, more ambitious projects.

Apart from 'thinking small' regarding the size of your stories, it's also worth tackling a range of storytelling forms that are both more affordable and achievable (e.g. a web series, a blog, a short play, a podcast, a collection of poems). This is because film and television, even the low-budget stuff, usually costs more than the house you live in and sometimes burns more cash than the GDP of a small nation.

In fact, in these turbulent times, where the old ways of telling stories are giving way to new voices and new perspectives, it is much more common for screenwriters to establish their voice in another art form before making the leap to the heady world of screenwriting. Just look at Phoebe Waller-Bridge (*Fleabag, Killing Eve*) and Michaela Coel (*Chewing Gum, I May Destroy You*), who both wrote short plays for years before their first screenwriting gig. Ilana Glazer and Abbi Jacobson's *Broad City* was a no-budget web series first. Diablo Cody (*Juno, United States of Tara, Tully*) was a blogger, columnist and a published author before her big screenwriting break. David Simon (*The Wire, Treme, The Deuce*) started in journalism. Aaron Sorkin (*The West Wing, The Social Network, The Trial of the Chicago 7*) was originally a playwright. Each of these successful screenwriters nurtured their voice in other art forms first, so when they finally 'arrived', their work stood out.

Nurturing a range of stories both small and big will also give you an insight into what sorts of ideas you're attracted to, which ones you struggle to complete, which ones are a breeze, and which ones you excel at. Every time you finish a story, it tells you something about what sort of writer you are now, as well as what sort of writer you want to be.

Each writer will have a different way of tracking their various ideas – a notebook of synopses, a folder of scribbled notes, a spreadsheet of one-line pitches, a pile of index cards. There's no one way to do it. The main thing is, don't lose track of your ideas. Remember to nurture them. You wrote them down for a reason, so there was something in those ideas.

Revisit your notebook/folder/spreadsheet regularly and actively think about what story you should be tackling next. Is there some research you could do to get your mind ticking over? Is there a selection of films or books you can dive into to see how others have tackled similar ideas? Is there an art exhibition you can see that might spark ideas or a particular musician that feels relevant? Open your mind to any influence – artistic, historical, philosophical – that will nurture your idea and build your impulse to write.

Of course, don't fall into the trap of abandoning your existing story to work on something else. That's procrastination, not writing. Finish the draft you're working on. Only writing gets it written. Nurturing a slate of ideas will not only provide a solid foundation for building a writing practice, you'll also be able to move between smaller, achievable ideas and more ambitious projects. It will even give you an insight into the sorts of stories you want to tell as you nurture your unique voice as a writer.

Find your people

As discussed earlier, writing can be a lonely exercise. It's often just you and your idea, with a blank screen or piece of paper in between. Some people revel in the opportunity to be alone with their thoughts and ideas for long periods of time. I don't have any specific scientific study to back this up, but my hunch, from decades of hanging out with professional writers, is that a lot of them become writers because they are totally cool with spending huge amounts of time alone. They're introverts. I'm an introvert too. It doesn't mean these writers don't like people – people are mostly what we write about. But the fact that their professional life involves spending 90 per cent of it alone is an appealing quality rather than a drawback.

Of course, not all writers are introverts. In my experience, screenwriters are broadly more outgoing than novelists, partly because film and television are highly collaborative mediums. If you write feature films, the first iteration of your story is usually a verbal pitch given to a room of potential investors or producers. If you write television shows, you likely work as part of a team of writers, sitting around a table for weeks at a time 'breaking story' (as we say in the industry) for upcoming episodes.

In these environments, the ability to be outgoing and a good collaborator is an essential asset as each writer (respectfully) competes to pitch their angle on the story or come up with the line of dialogue that gets the biggest reaction. Mind you, these rooms can still be filled with natural introverts (people who enjoy the alone part of writing), but they've learnt to work productively with other writers.

Whether you're outgoing or shy, at some point you're going to have to show your work-in-progress to someone. You're going to have to involve other people. That's what all this is about. My suggestion is this: don't just show it to anyone, especially at an early stage.

A lot of people will happily hear your pitch or read your work and offer an opinion, even if they've never written anything in their lives and have no interest in whether your story is the one you hoped it would be. Most people figure, 'I've seen movies. I've read books. I know story'. And they do to an extent, but do they know the story you want to tell? Probably not. Not in the way you do. Instead, try and find 'your people' – the ones who have an appreciation for the sorts of stories you want to tell. Surround yourself with both professional and personal contacts who will be thoughtful and constructive with your work-in-progress, who will try to understand what *you* are trying to do.

This doesn't mean they have to be writers as well. They can be friends, family, partners or colleagues who have spent enough time with you to have an appreciation of your passion for writing and telling stories. Ideally, they've seen enough movies with you or know the sorts of books you love to read and subjects you like to discuss at a dinner party. In short, they have an appreciation of *you* and are looking for that person in the story you're trying to tell.

Of course, it would be great to also have a collection of fellow writers or creatives, people who understand the intricacies of your craft and the creative struggles you're wrestling with, and who can offer informed insights into your work. You might find these people in the writing class you're taking, a script reading, an industry meet-up or a book club. This sort of networking can be hard for introverts but push on through. It will be worth it. Finding your people will not only make writing less lonely, it will also strengthen your work and your voice as you hear honest and constructive feedback that you can trust.

The trust part is important. You have to believe what your readers are saying. They're trying to help, even when they offer feedback you might not agree with. Trusting your reader's intentions allows you to hear their insights with an open mind and judge later.

Personally, I have a handful of friends and colleagues – 'my people' – whose tastes I know and trust and whose opinions I respect. For a bottle of nice wine or a home-cooked dinner, they're happy to read my work-in-progress or hear my pitch and offer their thoughts. And I do the same for them. With their wisdom on hand, it's easier to return to my work and make it even better, knowing that they have my back and want to see me succeed.

Listen for your voice

This is what we're here for. Your voice. The concept of a writer's voice is one of the most overlooked and misunderstood aspects of storytelling, particularly in highly collaborative art forms like screenwriting. But it is vital to understand that, as audiences, we aren't just looking for an original story to entertain us. We also crave original voices that can tell a story in a different way.

Audiences don't just love the story of *Fleabag*, they love the way Phoebe Waller-Bridge tells the story using a mix of comedy, profanity and vulnerability. One of the most enjoyable things about *The Social Network* is its rapid-fire dialogue that Aaron Sorkin has spent his whole career perfecting. The sparse poetic storytelling of *Moonlight* brought into focus an approach that writer/director Barry Jenkins had been working on over numerous short films and features. It didn't just happen. It's something he worked on. For years. Think about it. What is *your* voice? How do *you* tell a story? How are *your* stories original and unique?

A writer's voice can emerge from the sorts of characters they often write and the particular internal and external traits that shape their lives. How do they talk? How do they think? Where do they come from? What's the world around them like?

A writer's voice might be present in the types of conflicts their characters have to overcome – a difficult family history (*Winter's Bone*), an against-the-odds battle for survival (*The Terminator*), a failing career (*Inside Llewyn Davis*). It can come from the dramatic external changes that shape a writer's stories – trapped on a planet-destroying space station (*Star Wars*), an impulsive act of repressed anger (*Thelma and Louise*), the discovery of a mythical cave (*Moana*). Or maybe it's the surprising and authentic choices the characters make to try and fix their problems – accepting an invitation from a long lost friend (*Moonlight*); lashing out in violent revenge (*The Nightingale*); betraying a friend to win (*The Social Network*). Or perhaps a writer's voice is captured in the recurring themes or the world view their stories explore; the simple poetry in everyday life (*Paterson*); the blurry lines that separate dreams, nightmares and reality (*Mulholland Drive*); the struggle for women to find their place in the world (*Lady Bird*).

There are myriad other factors, such as tone, genre, pace, setting, etc. But all these come together, over time, over numerous stories, to shape a writer's voice. It's their unique way of telling a story. If, at this point in your writing career, you can't definitively say what you think your voice is, don't freak out. Many professional writers spend years writing before they discover what they've been trying to say their whole career. Over years, they've been refining their writing practice, honing their voice. With each new story, they've tried different things, different approaches, even different genres, as they've tried to harness their singular way of spinning a tale no one has heard before.

Like a story that has to be discovered along the way, a writer's voice is not something you can just 'know' right from the first story you write. You have to discover it. As you write, listen out for your voice. If you write enough, you'll start to hear it. Eventually, other people will start to hear it too and they'll recognise it as your voice, your way of telling a story. And they'll want to hear more.

Conclusion: Shadows on the wall

As I write this conclusion, I have just watched a stunning Icelandic film called *Echo* by writer/director Rúnar Rúnarsson. The film comprises fifty-six scenes, each captured with a single shot, depicting Iceland during Christmas and New Year. Each isolated scene is a sort of cinematic tableau: a woman nurses a child while watching the snow fall, butchers in an abattoir dance to Christmas tunes, a grandmother tries a virtual reality headset for the first time. The scenes are predominantly performed by non-professional actors who do not appear in the film again. So, how might an analysis of character arcs help us appreciate a film like *Echo*?

We don't know much about the characters' circumstances (or even their names) beyond the scenes they appear in. And the scenes are so brief that there's not much time for character development or an arc. They are also isolated from each other and have no impact on other scenes. Sometimes we witness a moment of 'external change' between two characters (e.g. a woman apologises to another for bullying her as a teenager), but there are many other scenes where almost nothing happens (e.g. a car drives slowly through an automatic car wash). Is this even a story? If it is, does it feature Change Characters or Constant Characters? Are their arcs optimistic, pessimistic or ambivalent? There's no way of telling – and it doesn't matter.

To dwell on these questions in order to fit *Echo*'s story into a character arc or a Three-Act Hero's Journey is to miss an opportunity to see the film for what it is – a quiet and hypnotic meditation on community, ritual, landscape and time. Sure, there are fascinating characters and stories in there, but the power of *Echo* is not simply about wondering what happens next in a narrative sense. It is about letting go, being still and observing a place and its people during private moments, between one year and the next.

I mention *Echo* because a film that takes a different approach to storytelling can capture the world from a new angle, one we might not normally expect to see. Despite how short and disconnected its scenes are, *Echo* is rich in character and story. Many of these characters and stories are worthy of a feature film in their own right. But the 'story' Rúnarsson is interested in telling is not about the personal triumphs and struggles of a specific individual, as we would normally expect to see. Instead, the character in this movie is a *community*, a collection of people, each one different from the last, yet with so much in common. The storyteller has presented a story through a different narrative lens, one that is wide enough to capture a whole *community of experiences*.

It's easy to forget that our stories are always presented through a narrative lens of some sort, whether it's *Echo*'s 'community as character', the Three-Act Structure, the Hero's Journey or Arc Analysis. Just as a character's internal and external life shapes the story they experience, so too does our lived experience shape the stories we imagine.

Becoming aware of how our lived experience shapes the stories we tell is an important step in becoming a writer with an original voice. How else can we strive for something original if we're not aware of the creative and cultural conventions we unconsciously adopt from the world around us? I think all professional writers instinctively find their own way to write. Over the years, they've tried (and failed at) enough stories to know there is no one way to do it – there is only *their* way.

Find yours, whatever it is. If the ideas I've presented in this book help you get there, that's great. If they don't, then at least you know what doesn't work for you. Make no mistake, the techniques we've explored in this book are just another lens through which to see the world of storytelling. I've argued that character arcs take in a wider range of stories than conventional approaches like the Three-Act Hero's Journey. But even this approach is not wide enough to capture the full depth and breadth of storytelling traditions from around the world and throughout history.

Stories might be ancient, but storytelling techniques are always a work-in-progress as new generations reimagine the human experience through their own eyes. In a way, our stories are the mesmerising shadows on the wall of Plato's cave. This is because our stories are not the real world. They are imagined. We make them out of thin air in an attempt to describe the real world as we experience it. And that's okay. Because that's the only way it could be.

The moment we believe there is only one way to tell our stories is the moment those stories start to die. Even though they're not real, we still can't take our eyes off the shadows on the wall. As humans, we need the shadows and the stories they tell. We always have and always will. Stories reveal who we are, what we love, what we fear, what we dream of and what we'll fight for. They might not be real, but that doesn't mean that they can't be true. That is the purpose of art, science and religion. They all strive for truth. As writers, the noblest thing we can do is strive to make our stories the truest, most compelling, most fascinating and most entertaining shadows of reality they can be.

List of films

A Fantastic Woman (2017)
Amour (2012)
Being There (1979)
Burning (2018)
Call Me By Your Name (2017)
Dead Poet's Society (1989)
Erin Brockovich (2000)
Hidden Figures (2016)
Inside Llewyn Davis (2014)
Lady Bird (2017)
Los Silencios (2018)
Lost in Translation (2003)
Midsommar (2019)
Moana (2016)
Moonlight (2016)
Mulholland Drive (2001)
Paterson (2016)
Shoplifters (2018)
Star Wars: A New Hope (1977)
Sweet Country (2017)
The Big Lebowski (1998)
The Father (2020)
The Godfather (1972)
The Hurt Locker (2008)

WRITING

The Nightingale (2018)
The Social Network (2010)
The Terminator (1984)
Thelma and Louise (1991)
Under the Skin (2013)
Winter's Bone (2010)

Acknowledgements

A book like this is the result of countless conversations with a lot of very smart people over many years about a lifetime worth of screen stories. Through them, my views have been challenged, dissected, affirmed, decimated, changed, rebuilt, rearticulated and changed again until this book came out the other end. The following people are a select but important sample of those who have helped along the way.

My early readers, Krissy Kneen, Lucas Taylor, Cass Moriarty, Sally Piper, Stephen Vagg, Jackie Turnure and Simon Kennedy. Thank you for your intelligence and patience as I gathered my thoughts. In particular Ashley Hay who, despite not having read a draft, was able to offer an insight that cracked open the ending of the book for me – that's how good she is.

My agents, Jane Novak and Dayne Kelly, for the time and effort you put into my projects and the enduring faith you have that good things will continue to come out of my head.

NewSouth Publishing, particularly my publisher Harriet McInerney, project manager Sophia Oravecz, copy editor Gabriella Sterio, designer Josephine Pajor-Markus and cover designer Josh Durham. The enthusiasm and passion you all brought to the project was incredibly energising at just the right time.

From Creative Essentials, series editor Hannah Patterson, publisher Ion Mills, designer Elsa Mathern, production director

Claire Watts, publishing controller Ellie Lavender, and proof reader Steven Mair.

Mirandi Rewoe, Cass Moriarty, Laura Elvery and Sally Piper of the (unofficial) 'Brisbane Literary Mafia' who suggested this book after attending one of my screenwriting workshops. I am eternally grateful for your encouragement.

My doctoral supervisors Trish Fitzsimons, Margaret McVeigh, Charlie Strachan and Penny Bundy, and my master's supervisors Gerard Lee and Stuart Glover. Many of the ideas in this book are a direct result of conversations with you.

Anyone who's ever rolled the dice on me as a storyteller, particularly Debbie Lee, Penny Chapman, Tony Ayres, Nathan Mayfield, Tracey Robertson, Jackie Turnure, Noel Manzano, Ian Collie, Jo Dillon, Nadine Bates, Kristen Souvlis, Veronica Fury, Melissa Fox, Mark Chapman and Gabrielle Jones. And to the fellow screenwriters who taught me everything I know, especially Lucas Taylor, Warren Clarke, Paddy Macrae, Tim Hobart, Belinda Chayko, Matt Cameron, Benjamin Law, Marieke Hardy, Niki Aken, Hannah Caroll Chapman, Michael Lucas, Christine Bartlett, Kristen Dunphy, Alice Addison, David Hannam, Michelle Law, Joan Sauers, Sarah Lambert, Blake Ayshford, Daley Pearson, Shayne Armstrong, Leigh McGrath, Stephen Irwin, Stephen Vagg, Simon Kennedy, Phil Enchelmaier, David Megarrity and Kier Shorey.

Thanks to the filmmakers whose films I've used as case studies throughout the book. There are too many to name here but, suffice to say, uncovering a substantial and well-realised film remains one of the enduring joys of my life.

I'd also like to thank the screenwriting teachers whose books I have read over the years in an effort to understand my craft, particularly (the late) Syd Field, Christopher Vogler, Jeff Rush,

ACKNOWLEDGEMENTS

Ken Dancynger, Kristin Thompson, Linda Seger, Robert McKee, (the late) Blake Snyder, John Truby, Linda Aronson and KM Weiland. Your insights are always appreciated and respected, even when I disagree. Screenwriting is a mysterious and misunderstood art form. As William Goldman said, 'Nobody knows anything', and that includes me.

Finally, I'd like to thank my parents, Helen and Peter, who watched on with faith and mild bemusement as I tried to figure out what I was doing with my life. Still working on that.

And Krissy Kneen, my best friend and partner of thirty years (so far). Without your belief I may never have written or created anything, ever. You've been there for every step. I owe you everything.

●LDCASTLE BOOKS

POSSIBLY THE UK'S SMALLEST INDEPENDENT PUBLISHING GROUP

Oldcastle Books is an independent publishing company formed in 1985 dedicated to providing an eclectic range of titles with a nod to the popular culture of the day.

Imprints vary from the award winning crime fiction list, NO EXIT PRESS, to lists about the film industry, KAMERA BOOKS & CREATIVE ESSENTIALS. We have dabbled in the classics, with PULP! THE CLASSICS, taken a punt on gambling books with HIGH STAKES, provided in-depth overviews with POCKET ESSENTIALS and covered a wide range in the eponymous OLDCASTLE BOOKS list. Most recently we have welcomed two new digital first sister imprints with THE CRIME & MYSTERY CLUB and VERVE, home to great, original, page-turning fiction.

oldcastlebooks.com

| OLDCASTLE BOOKS | KAMERA BOOKS | HIGHSTAKES PUBLISHING
| POCKET ESSENTIALS | CREATIVE ESSENTIALS | THE CRIME & MYSTERY CLUB
| NO EXIT PRESS | PULP! THE CLASSICS | VERVE BOOKS